Teaching Academic Literacy

❦❀❧

The Uses of Teacher-Research in Developing a Writing Program

Teaching Academic Literacy

❧❀❧

The Uses of Teacher-Research in Developing a Writing Program

Edited by

Katherine L. Weese
Hampden-Sydney College

Stephen L. Fox
Indiana University-Purdue University Indianapolis

Stuart Greene
University of Notre Dame

LAWRENCE ERLBAUM ASSOCIATES, PUBLISHERS

1999   Mahwah, New Jersey   London

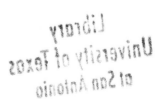

Lawrence Erlbaum Associates, Inc., Publishers
10 Industrial Avenue
Mahwah, NJ 07430

Cover design by Kathryn Houghtaling Lacey

Library of Congress Cataloging-in-Publication Data

Teaching academic literacy : the uses of teacher-research in
developing a writing program / edited by Katherine L. Weese,
Stephen L. Fox, Stuart Greene.
    p. cm.
    Includes bibliographical references and indexes.
    ISBN 0-8058-2802-8 (cloth : alk. paper) — ISBN
0-8058-2803-6 (pbk. : alk. paper).
    1. English Language—Rhetoric—Study and teach-
ing—Case studies. 2. English language—Rhetoric—Study and teaching—Wisconson-Madison. 3.
Academic writing—Study and teaching—Wisconsn-
Madison. 4. Academic writing—Study and teaching—Case studies.
    I. Weese, Katherine L. II. Fox, Stephen L. III. Greene,
Stuart.
    PE1404.T368   1999
    808'.042'070775—dc21   98-37046
                                      CIP

Printed in the United States of America
10 9 8 7 6 5 4 3 2 1

To Jeanine, Dan, and our students

Contents

How do teachers of writing learn how to teach?

I adopt ~~A multi-dimensional~~ → research-based/writing,
A student-centered approach to literacy instruction.

Foreword

Barbara Walvoord
University of Notre Dame

How do teachers of writing learn how to teach? What support and stimulus do they need? The oft-lamented gap between published theories about writing and actual classroom practice suggests that teachers do not learn by reading theory—either because they do not care to read it or because, reading it, they cannot integrate theoretical principles with their own practice, cannot envision how to pour the rich wine of classroom experience into someone else's wineskin. And, too, one needs somehow to construct oneself as a teacher of writing, much as students need to construct themselves as writers. The wellsprings of authority are problematic in both cases. How is a TA, an adjunct, a new assistant professor, or a veteran teacher trained in criticism of literary work, to assume the authority of a writing teacher? For that matter, how is someone who had read all of Bakhtin, Bleich, Freire, and Flower to walk into a classroom and connect in some meaningful way with the real people there who are struggling to be writers?

This volume is a wonderful resource for that need—the need to connect practice to theory, the need to connect one's own life to one's classroom, the need to connect both in a human but also in a scholarly way to the human beings for whom one is teacher. *Teaching Academic Literacy* has the power to change a teaching life. It receives its authority from the voices of real teachers, TAs, adjuncts, students of rhetoric—and from the voices of their students. By their own example, the writers show how to observe writers and classrooms, how to collect and interpret systematic data about student

ix

learning, and how to theorize one's own classroom, rather than merely reading theory and somehow applying it.

But not only do readers of this volume see teacher–researchers in action, readers also see the curriculum and the pedagogy that emerge from careful thought and investigation into writing and writers. Even if a reader of this volume cannot adopt, or does not wish to adopt, the curriculum of Wisconsin's literacy course, the writers demonstrate something that will be useful to every teacher–reader: the way a curriculum is built from an understanding of, and respect for, students as thinkers and writers; the way a classroom research agenda connects theory to practice and teachers to students; the way authority as a writing teacher may be constructed from listening, from observation in one's own classroom.

Preface

Linda Flower
Carnegie Mellon University

Teaching Academic Literacy is a freshly stimulating picture of educational research in action. Stuart Greene, his colleagues, TAs, and students have turned the camera on themselves. As these underprepared students write literacy autobiographies, study each other, and entertain academic arguments around literacy, they are also collecting real data on discourse in action around their city. These students are turning a freshman argument class into a self-directed inquiry into literacy.

Meanwhile, the TAs have asked the class to tape and reflect on what happens in their small group sessions. As students analyze their own talk, the TAs are reading theory, reading students, and reflecting on the issues of learning and teaching this cross-talk raises.

This entire, integrated, interactive process of observation-based theory building is leading to the kind of revisable, grounded curriculum John Dewey would have admired. Out of teacher research, teacher talk, and teacher reflection (based on student research, student talk, and student reflection) Greene and his colleagues began to develop a body of strategic knowledge for, as they put it, what to teach, strategies for doing so, and the conditions such learning would require.

This book is the story of a deeply rooted, highly situated body of local practice. At the same time, it illuminates a highly transferrable process for creating a collaborative, strategic, reflective curriculum elsewhere. If there is a lesson from this successful program, it is how to make everyone into teachers and learners.

Introduction: The Value of the University of Wisconsin-Madison's First-Year Writing Curriculum

Katherine L. Weese
Hampden-Sydney College

Stuart Greene
University of Notre Dame

Stephen L. Fox
Indiana University-Purdue University Indianapolis

Teaching Academic Literacy explores how concepts about composing operate in student writing and how a writing program can evolve as administrators and writing teachers gain, from close analysis of their students' work, a greater understanding of student writers' needs. The first three chapters in this volume present an overview of a first-year writing course by explaining its inception and development, the rationale behind the choices for the content of the course, the collaborative classroom practices employed, and the course's design. The second group of chapters analyzes the findings of classroom research studies that inform the way the course is taught. As instructors in the program identified problems that arose in teaching beginning writers, data was collected to increase our understanding of how students responded to our assignments. These studies have produced valuable, localized kinds of knowledge about student composing processes that help us understand what real students do in real writing situations. Unlike decontextualized studies, our data provide a cognitively, socially, and

How Can we let them write with a sense of authority

culturally contextualized basis for understanding students' choices and strategies. As we observed students' difficulty with writing about sources while still maintaining their own voices, we asked ourselves how we could best encourage students to become authors of their own ideas or to write with a sense of authority over the subject matter of their essays. Through a unique interplay of composition theory, classroom research, and practical application, we explored the ways in which we can encourage this goal (unpacked in detail in chapter 1) through increased understanding of what factors in students' backgrounds influence the ways they approach writing tasks at various points in the composing process. In turn, this volume captures the ways in which the UW writing program has evolved through the 1990s: The process of learning that we have observed and our increased ability to account for student learning inform the changes in the way the program as a whole is run and individual classes are taught.

HOW THE UW ACADEMIC LITERACY COURSE IS ORGANIZED

The writing program described in this volume was developed at the University of Wisconsin-Madison for first-year writers identified as needing further composition instruction beyond what they received in high school.[1] The course itself is divided into three units, each of which explores ideas about literacy and what it means to read and write in different contexts. The first unit of the course, The Personal Dimension of Literacy, asks students to focus on their previous experience within the different contexts where they have been readers and writers: in their homes, in their schools, in their religious and social affiliations, in their jobs, in their social interactions with peers. During this part of the course, students produce a literacy autobiography that draws together their previous experience with reading and writing, and makes some hypotheses about why they hold the views of writing that they hold and how they came to develop these views. The students' literacy autobiographies are published and distributed to the whole class, at which point they become a text that students study in conjunction with professional writers' texts about literacy (cf. Bartholomae and Petrosky's approach to their students' autobiographical writings on adolescent growth and development as described in *Facts, Artifacts, and Counterfacts*; cf. also David Bleich's "Ethnography and the Study of Literacy" 186). The literacy theme has proven itself valuable in providing a context in which students' existing expertise is privileged. Whether they realize it or not, incoming first-year students are already quite knowledgeable about what does and does not work in education. In arguments based on personal experience for Unit I, first-year students in one class at the University of Wisconsin helped one another understand the conditions that foster literacy

---

[1] Chapter 3 in this volume describes the sequence of assignment for the course in greater detail. The exact assignments themselves are provided in an appendix.

How can we bring WAC theory into practice.

and the conditions that impede its development in school, particularly the way that students are often silenced in their classes.

In the second unit of the course, students reexamine their own hypotheses about literacy in light of texts by professional writers who consider the current crisis in literacy in American schools and who discuss issues of power and culture as they relate to literacy. In this unit, A Conversation About Literacy, students learn what it means to argue a position about the role literacy plays within the American education system. Here they must negotiate their own ideas and the ideas of the professional source texts with the goal that they will evaluate, reorganize, hierarchize, and challenge the assumptions of their sources. By reading widely in Unit II about what others have written on issues in education, they gain a more solid base for making their arguments about tracking, the importance of recognizing alternative intelligence in assessing what students know, the presence of gender bias in the classroom, and the importance of providing differently abled learners with a sound education.   (WAC)

Finally, in the third unit of the course, Reading and Writing in a Discourse Community, students engage in field work to further investigate literacy at the university or in another academic setting, this time in a specific field or discourse community that interests them. Students are challenged to develop a research question and answer it with original research. In conducting this research, several students observed classroom discourse in high school to see who is called on and how teachers interact with both male and female students; one student visited three day-care centers to examine the presence of gender bias, observing the activities that girls and boys engaged in and interviewing day-care workers. Others have interviewed professors or other professionals within a field about the writing conventions that inform the field, analyzed a sample of writing in the field, and produced a paper assessing their findings. Other field project possibilities exist: Students might volunteer as literacy tutors and write about their experiences or take on the role of an ethnographer by studying what goes on in others' tutoring sessions. By thus making academic discourse conventions themselves the subject of a beginning writing course, we enable students who have been repeatedly labeled outsiders to those conventions to enter into them in a self-conscious manner.[2]

As readers see in the pages that follow, the primary focus of the writing course we describe is helping students learn how to craft an argument based on (a) their experiences in different contexts, (b) the reading they do in the course and (c) original research, which includes conducting surveys and interviews. Although college students are expected to write argumentative

---

[2]Cf. Rose ("Remedial Writing Courses"): "another meaningful context for student writing is the very academic environment in which students find themselves" (123). Cf. also approaches described by Bleich ("Ethnography and the Study of Literacy: Prospects for Socially Generous Research"), by Kutz, Groden, and Zamel (*The Discovery of Competence*), and by Heath (*Ways With Words*).

Reading people's experiences dealing with writing as a craft.

The starting point of instruction is students' ideas about a set of issues.

essays based on different sources of information, students often come to us with little experience negotiating the demands that writing an argument places on them.

This course was conceived with the conviction that the starting point for instruction is students' ideas about a given set of issues—ideas that grow out of their reading, writing, discussion, and research—rather than instructions about how to write an argument. If students are to write well about a given topic or problem, they need time to develop their thinking, so that they come to terms with what they feel and believe (see also Bartholomae & Petrosky). Thus it makes sense to let them write arguments based on personal experience at the beginning of the course, so that they can define a problem for further inquiry and then develop an argument based on their reading and original research that is meaningful to them. We can and should give them some reading to get them started, but then they must have the opportunity to select their own sources of information. This step is especially important if we expect students to advance an argument that foregrounds what they think rather than merely summarizing others' points of view.

HOW TEACHER RESEARCH DRIVES THE UW PROGRAM

This curriculum we describe evolved over time. Perhaps most importantly, the teachers writing in this volume have observed how different students approach the tasks of writing arguments based on multiple sources of information. Through taking field notes, audio taping classroom discourse, collecting think-aloud protocols, interviewing students, and studying students' drafts, we have provided data that have helped us think through and revise our understanding of how to teach writing. These data are vital to the development of a writing program as the staff interprets the information we gather; staff members test these data against their own experiences in weekly staff meetings, raising questions that we continue to pursue: How can we go about integrating reading in a writing course? How can we help students formulate effective research questions that can guide research? How can we teach students to foreground their own thinking in writing about the ideas of different authorities? What are the conditions that enable writing groups to work most productively?

Asking such questions is a significant part of doing teacher research because these questions represent the kind of reflective teaching that can help instructors to develop strategic knowledge (cf. Flower et al., *Making Thinking Visible*): (a) knowing what to teach, (b) knowing how to teach certain strategies for writing, and (c) understanding the conditions under which students might be able to acquire knowledge about how to use certain strategies. Based on the teacher research conducted by Greene and Smith (chapter 8, this volume) to understand how writing groups can support student learning, methods for using writing groups were modified, and instructors in the program at the University of Wisconsin now regularly tape record group talk.

Reading writing discussion — *Research.*

Specifically, instructors ask workshop groups to record, transcribe, and analyze the talk that goes on in their group—and have found the exercise very rewarding. In studying the transcripts, students focus on some of the following questions: What topics are being discussed? Are most questions and comments about student writing directed at the idea level, structural level, sentence level, or word level? How are topics brought up—with a question or a comment? Who more frequently initiates talk—the writer or the reader–supporters? What roles do different group members play? Did the author open the session with specific questions or concerns? Did the reader–supporters begin by giving specific positive feedback? In turn, members of each group identify at least two things that are working well in the groups and at least two things that they could improve. They are then asked to consider how the group might go about making those improvements. Finally, each group develops a brief presentation (3–5 minutes) for the class. The point of the presentation is to share their findings with other groups, who may be able to relate and share ideas. It also forces students to come to consensus about what their group's goals for future talk are.

The findings students share not only provide the basis for class discussion, but build on and extend what we learn from the kind of study that Greene and Smith conducted in a first-year writing class. Similarly, by conducting systematic studies of their own classrooms, teachers can discuss their findings in the context of orientation meetings and monthly staff meetings. When such findings are shared, the data teachers collect in their own classrooms call attention to the ways that different purposes for writing, different cultural backgrounds, and different knowledge about writing conventions can override even the most explicit and well intentioned instruction. Thus teacher research of this sort can complicate our understanding of what to teach, how to teach something, and the conditions under which learning can occur.

Our approach to understanding and teaching argument is based not only on what others have observed (e.g., Kaufer, Geisler, & Neuwirth), but also on close observation of students over time. In particular, our approach to argument is based on a theory that has sought to account for the ways both readers and writers construct multisource arguments in comprehension and composing. Such an approach recognizes that readers and writers identify main paths of arguments, faulty paths or arguments that should be avoided, and return paths that shift emphasis away from faulty paths back to the main path of argument. Other theories have neither accounted for the ways readers construct meaning in reading arguments based on multiple sources nor for the ways writers argue as they interweave what they know (i.e., not limited to but including reading and experience) in advancing their own points of view. Our approach also helps students identify problems and frame questions by teaching them to recognize that arguments grow out of problems. With this knowledge, students learn to differentiate among topics, issues, and problems. Finally, in teaching argument, we try to guide students through the process of asking questions that can help students meet the expectations of readers in a given field: What is at stake in the issue the writer has identified; that is, why should we care about the issue that you have chosen to write about? What happens if things change? What happens if things stay the same? Who would disagree?

Through close observation, we have also begun to understand both the complexity of writing assignments and the implications our studies might have for teaching writing. Research (e.g., Flower, Greene, chapter 5, this volume) and teaching tell us that many students are energetic and thought-ful in their attempts to fulfill their own goals and purposes as writers on the one hand, and to meet our expectations on the other. The problem is that our students do not always know what these expectations are, even in our efforts to design seemingly clear and cogent assignments. Unfortunately, our expectations are often merely tacit, even when we think we have articulated them.

We have learned two important things from Greene's study of how students interpret the task of writing an argument. First, when we design our writing assignments, we need to consider the nature of the writing task itself, reflecting on the language of the assignment and the kind of learning we want to foster. What are our objectives? Are we asking students to summarize, analyze, or synthesize information, and are they aware of our learning goals? As well, it is worth considering whether the task is well-de-fined, giving students relatively clear direction about what is required or if it is open-ended, allowing students to choose their own topics or issues. It is important to reflect on the costs and benefits of giving students either an open-ended or well-structured task. Focusing on these concerns about task interpretation has forced those of us at Wisconsin to make our objectives explicit, both for ourselves and our students, in the syllabi we distribute and the criteria we use to evaluate the effectiveness of written argument. Second, we also learned that we need to focus on what students bring to the tasks we design, including their prior knowledge, goals, and skills. For example, are they familiar with the ideas presented in class and in the reading? Are they aware of different rhetorical strategies, such as how to use a comparison to establish an argument? By exploring students' assumptions about writing, we can begin to develop practices that build on their knowledge and extend their emerging abilities to use language in different contexts.

As a result of these observations of students over time, we are able to more effectively train new writing instructors and make adaptations in our courses to best meet the students' needs. The chapters in this book are written by professors and teaching assistants who have taught beginning writing multiple times at the University of Wisconsin-Madison, most using the literacy materials, and some using other materials that are informed by the same practices and goals as the literacy course. The instructors in the program participate each term that they teach the course in a 3-day, start-of-semester orientation session and in a weekly colloquium throughout the semester, where many of them have the opportunity to present to the whole group of teachers and administrators some aspect of their teaching practice as it is informed by what they have observed in their students' work in the class. The chapters here have evolved from these presentations and are collected each year into an expanding volume used to orient new instructors to the goals and methods of the literacy course. Written by teachers who have completed graduate courses in or who are experts in the field of composition studies, the chapters are informed by the recent developments in composition theory that have shaped the field over the past two decades. Many of the authors have also participated in systematic classroom research projects, studies that are often points of discussion at the colloquia. In a less formal approach to research, most of the authors draw liberally on the evidence of student work, written and verbal, to form their conclusions about beginning writers' literate practices. Finally, several of the contributors, as they gained seniority in the program, became Assistant Directors of Freshman Composition at UW, and hence have participated in the program's administration. The writing teachers and administrators are thus also the writers and researchers whose work makes up this volume, a unique aspect of the UW program and the book that evolved from it.

A strong reciprocal relationship has emerged between, on the one hand, the theory and research that lie at the heart of these chapters, and, on the other hand, the teaching practices of the instructors and the design of the UW composition program as a whole. The process of student learning observed in the classroom, presented at the staff colloquia, and formally written about here in turn finds its way back into the composition classroom because it serves as the basis for training both new and experienced teachers.

HOW THE UW COMPOSITION CURRICULUM AND WRITING PROGRAM CAN BE APPLIED ELSEWHERE

The specific curriculum that was introduced and developed at UW-Madison and the principle of teacher research employed in that program are widely applicable to other writing programs at other institutions. We compiled this volume with the conviction that our classroom-based research studies and the curriculum that has evolved from them can shape writing instruction and program administration at any institution in several ways.

First, instructors can, on an individual basis, adopt/adapt the curriculum proposed in Part I of this volume to construct a course that is thoroughly planned from beginning to end and well-grounded in theories about how students gain knowledge. Second, writing instructors can gain insight from the classroom research studies presented in part II of this volume. They can use these studies to better understand their own beginning writers' practices and can plan new strategies for more effective instruction to meet the students' needs. Instructors can also draw on the model studies provided here to learn about constructing and carrying out classroom research projects at their own institutions and can design their own studies to better understand the writing practices of their own students. Finally, classroom research studies point to the broadest way in which the Wisconsin program can be adopted at other institutions: in administration and program development. The way the program itself has developed as a whole—the mechanics of training new instructors, the policy of having instructors present their studies to the staff, and the process of having a curriculum evolve as teachers learn from their students' practices—are all aspects of the UW composition model that could help other programs evolve.

Several contributors to this volume have applied curriculum and principles from the UW program at other institutions where they became members of the faculty. For example, with minor adaptations, Fox and Weese have successfully taught Forms of Academic Literacy at places as diverse as Indiana University Purdue University-Indianapolis (an urban commuter campus with nearly 50% returning adult students) and Hampden-Sydney College (a very traditional, all-male, rural, southern, small liberal arts college). For teachers anywhere, the primary advantage of the Wisconsin literacy program in composition classroom work is that they are able to discuss and examine students' histories of academic literacy. Students at any university or college are ready and willing to talk about and to examine their secondary school literacies and to consider the writing expectations they face in college. They see this endeavor directly relating to their current situations, as something that will help them meet the challenges they face in their first year of college. The composition class can begin with a shared critical analysis of literacy practices and the legacy of high school training; then the class is able to move on more easily to other analyses.

The Wisconsin program provides for teachers the opportunity to move students toward critical writing and reading. It enables teachers to increase students' understanding of the expectations and conventions of the university in a context meaningful to them. It encourages writing for real purposes instead of school exercises. It highlights the students' stakes in education. And it provides them an entrance into cultural analysis. Members of such a composition course appreciate the student-centered approach to writing instruction. They sense that the curriculum, although demanding, is aimed at their real needs and concerns. They understand that it is designed to increase their power over the academic text and the institutional system of which they have become a part. And they are eager to obtain this knowledge and skill. The student-centered approach practiced at Wisconsin changes the character of classrooms considerably, allowing teachers to adopt the role of ally, coach, or mentor, someone who enables students to develop new literacy skills. This role has been very satisfying for teachers and students alike at the various institutions where the UW curriculum has been adopted.[3]

---

[3]The editors are indebted to Nicholas Preus for these observations.

Beyond the individual classroom, the UW literacy course can influence the shape and administration of a writing program, just as the UW program itself has evolved over the years to keep pace with the findings of research studies performed there. For example, Stephen Fox, at IUPUI, has helped create a slightly different version of the UW curriculum, but one nonetheless based on similar principles and administrative practices. The program at IUPUI is administered by a Writing Coordinating Committee. As this committee met to revise the curriculum for the first-semester writing course required of all students, Fox, citing the success of the UW course on literacy and of Bartholomae and Petrosky's Pittsburgh course on adolescence (*Facts, Artifacts, and Counterfacts*), suggested that the writing class be designed as an academic seminar focusing on the topic of work. Given the many returning adult students at IUPUI, work seemed a widely applicable topic, one that students of diverse areas and backgrounds could write about with some sense of personal authority. As with the Wisconsin literacy curriculum, students in the IUPUI composition class analyze their personal experiences as an entry into academic analyses of topics that are also treated in readings. A pilot group of instructors developed this curriculum, and writing faculty plan to engage in more program-based research, research that will inform IUPUI's already strong tradition of providing extensive professional development for adjunct faculty in composition. There is thus quite a bit of continuity between the UW program and both existing practices and new developments at IUPUI.

At Hampden-Sydney College, Katherine Weese has not only adopted the syllabus from the Wisconsin literacy course in Hampden-Sydney's beginning writing course, but she has also used the information about student authority central to the research efforts at Wisconsin to understand the writing practices of Hampden-Sydney students engaged in research projects in the second-semester Rhetoric course. Weese highlighted an approach to research that she believed would enable students to "enter into conversations" (Rose, *Lives* 58): Students wrote a proposal for their research papers, the results of which are examined in more detail in chapter 1. As Weese learned from their proposals that students struggled with the idea of generating an original argument, she devised assignments for subsequent sections of the course to help students see how to incorporate source material without simply bowing to the authority of already published writers. Weese also presented this information at a day-long Rhetoric staff retreat to familiarize the rest of the staff with the issues surrounding student authority and strategies for teaching research writing in Hampden-Sydney's Rhetoric Program.

Currently, Weese is planning a classroom-based study of Hampden-Sydney's focus on editing as a component of the Rhetoric program. Each semester, at the end of their Rhetoric course, students take an editing test that consists of 50 sentences, each containing a single grammatical error that students must correct. The grammar component of Hampden-Sydney's program is not designed to overshadow emphasis on argument and writing as process; in fact the process movement thoroughly informs the Hampden-Sydney program. Yet teachers often find that students—even when they have been explicitly instructed otherwise—perceive grammar as the most important aspect of writing. This fact, in many ways consistent with Greene's findings about task interpretation and student assumptions, is cause for concern, and more research needs to be done in classrooms throughout the program to determine if this is indeed a dominant perception. Drawing on knowledge gained from teaching in the UW program and using student protocols and observation of students' responses to their work in Rhetoric, Weese will study students' responses to grammar instruction.

To assist in administrators' attempts to understand student responses to the editing component of Rhetoric, some experimental sections of Rhetoric will be taught in which grammar instruction will be based on Martha Kolln's *Rhetorical Grammar: Grammatical Choices, Rhetorical Effects* rather than solely on a traditional handbook. Kolln, who conducted a workshop on Rhetorical Grammar for our staff in the Spring 1997 term, stressed the possibilities that the English language provides for expression and the expectations readers have when they encounter prose. Her approach thus differed markedly from the emphasis on error avoidance that handbooks often embrace. In order to determine if a more positive, less punitive, rhetorical approach to teaching grammar is effective, writing samples from students in these experimental sections that use Kolln's book will be compared to writing samples from other sections to assess how students use complex structures in writing; scores on the final editing tests will be compared; and most important, think-aloud protocols from students taking the experimental sections of the course and other traditional sections will be employed and compared.

We hypothesize that students taught from Kolln's book, in conjunction with other course materials, will see grammar less as error avoidance and will be less inclined than students in other sections to perceive our program's primary emphasis as sentence-level correctness. If our hypothesis is borne out, members of the staff hope to devise new ways to teach editing and to test students' abilities to write clear sentences so that students do not see correctness as being more important than other qualities that determine good writing. Summer workshops, monthly staff meetings on pedagogy, and biannual day-long retreats are already a part of Hampden-Sydney's well-established Rhetoric Program; these venues provide ideal opportunities to present to the whole staff information gleaned from the kind of classroom research studies used in the UW-Madison composition program, and to discuss the impact that such data could have on curriculum development and approaches to teaching.

In closing this introduction, we do so with the conviction that the chapters that follow describe approaches to teaching and studying writing that can be applied to writing programs anywhere and to students at

How can we empower the student?
Providing him with — Collaborative experiences
— reflecting upon his own private experiences
— respecting his voice —

any level, in any context. In short, we offer approaches to using close observation of students' writing practices to understand how we can teach more reflectively, questioning what we can easily leave unquestioned in the teaching of writing.

THE CHAPTERS IN THIS COLLECTION

All of the chapters that follow analyze, from various perspectives, the problems involved in helping beginning writers to develop their own thinking and to approach writing tasks with a clear sense of their authority as writers. The three chapters following this Introduction establish the rationale and context for the course by describing the materials and methods in some detail. In chapter 1, Katherine Weese makes a case for composition instructors using their own classes in teacher-research projects and describes the interplay of theory, research, and practice as all three inform the Wisconsin program. Using some case studies from students at her current institution, she defines the problem of authority that beginning writers encounter, then goes on to ground her observations of that problem in the theoretical literature on composition in anticipation of the teacher research essays that comprise the second part of this collection.

In chapter 2, Fox examines the rationale for using literacy materials with first-year student writers and enunciates five principles that have guided the design and teaching of the academic literacy course. He argues that the principles of process and collaboration can be revitalized within a first-year college writing course designed to foster academic literacy. When literacy becomes both the goal and the topic of an interactive classroom, Fox posits, students can explore connections among diverse forms of literacy and situate academic writing conventions in larger social contexts. A collaborative pedagogy that respects student language can equip students to act through academic literacy on behalf of themselves and their communities.

In chapter 3, Weese postulates that a carefully sequenced set of assignments helps students learn to speak from a position of authority. She argues that principles of narrative theory offer a model for developing a plotted beginning writing course in order to help students transcend the often fragmented nature of their educational experience. Exploring the interconnectedness of the three major units of Forms of Academic Literacy, Weese offers a general model that encourages instructors and students to see the purpose of each assignment and how it is linked to other assignments within the course, stressing the ways in which the first autobiographical assignment encourages students to read professional texts as writers and to adopt a critical stance toward others' ideas.

In the second section of the collection, the authors analyze the results of their classroom research studies, each one examining the data through a different lens. The findings of these studies complicate the goals established in the first part of the book, exploring the various factors that influence student writing practices and examining the implications for teaching.

How can WAC shortens the Gap between expectations high school & college of writing ch. 4

Nicholas Preus, author of the fourth chapter, has been a high school teacher and has taught college English majors about to begin student-teaching practicums in high schools. He has firsthand experience with the kinds of tasks students encounter in secondary education, tasks that contribute to a considerable gap between high school and college expectations for writing. In his chapter, Preus explores how entry-level college writers are heavily conditioned by vocabularies about writing they have developed and how they struggle to replace the old vocabulary with a more relational discourse about writing. Through a fine-grained analysis of student talk and student writing from a section of the Forms of Academic Literacy Course, Preus characterizes the powerful secondary school discourse, its contexts, and the way it shapes college writing. The chapter traces a shifting relationship in the data between the students' well-learned set of terms (which are often quantifications or gestures to authority), and their newly emerging acceptance of a more contingent authorial situation. Preus finds in the students' efforts to enter the discourse of the college writing classroom tentative contextual and cognitive moves toward authorship.

In the fifth chapter, Greene builds on what Preus finds about how high school writing tasks interfere with college writing expectations. Greene focuses on task interpretation for the synthesis assignment in the UW academic literacy course, with particular interest in "the decision-making points that can enable us to understand the hidden logic that motivates what a writer does." He explores these decision-points as students negotiate the task of synthesizing conflicting points of view on literacy and evaluating these views through the lens of their own experiences. With attention to the cognitive and social factors that condition a student's response to assignments, instructors will be in a better position to understand "why some students assume the role of authors and others do not." Greene examines the protocols and texts produced by two students who adopt different stances to the synthesis assignment, stances that he theorizes are rooted in students' cultural backgrounds and prior training.

Marie Paretti, in chapter 6, examines task interpretation in another light by performing a Bakhtinian analysis of the different genres in which students write in the course—journals, e-mail discussion lists, and formal papers. By combining analysis of student texts with retrospective interviews, Paretti explores whether or not students are able to use multiple formats productively to enhance their writing. She finds that students often view all these genres, even when they see distinctions among them, as belonging to the larger genre of school writing, with teacher as audience and grade as goal. She also finds that students do not easily perceive informal writing exercises as building blocks for formal essays. Paretti explores the implications for teaching that her research suggests and proposes ways teachers can help students use multiple genres more effectively.

Jana French, in the seventh chapter, examines the data collected from student conferences to provide another kind of insight into the student's experience in the UW literacy course. French analyzes taped conferences between instructors and student writers in various stages of the composing process, including prewriting, drafting, and revising. In each of these stages, her analysis suggests, students benefit from a dialogic approach to their evolving texts and a low ratio of instructor-to-student talk. Such strategies allow the instructor to ascertain the type and extent of prior assumptions students bring with them to the beginning college writing classroom and hence to gain some insight into the otherwise hidden logic that motivates their task interpretation. French also argues that student-centered conferencing, which displaces authority from instructor to writers and their peer groups, combats beginning writers' legacy of self-doubt, allowing them to develop a new relationship to published sources and to feel more confident taking on the role of author.

Next, Greene and Erin Smith (chapter 8) examine through the lens of constructivist theory, how the choices students make in writing unfold in the collaborative process. In contrast to many previous studies of collaborative peer groups that focus on consensus (e.g., Bruffee 28—51), Greene and Smith's chapter stresses instead the important role that conflict plays in the writing process. The authors note first a conflict within the individual writer as his/her talk about writing reveals discrepancies between the student's old and new ways of talking about writing, or old and new discourses of authorship. Second, they explore how conflicts between individuals who interact in collaborative groups can help students acquire a new discourse; Smith and Greene focus especially here on how a writer's social and cultural concerns motivate the ways students approach new discourses of authorship. Ultimately, the authors note that students were able to transform their ideas of what it means to be an author and to develop more deliberate and strategic approaches to writing tasks. Yet they caution that new discourses often challenge students' sense of cultural identity that may be fundamental to their writing strategies; instructors need to see the logic that motivates students' choices in order that they may know when and how to intervene.

To close this section of the text, we reprint David Bartholomae's "The Study of Error," a publication that captures the spirit and methods by which grammar is taught in the Wisconsin program. Bartholomae argued that if instructors study patterns of error in basic writers' texts, they can then "plan instruction to assist a writer's internal syllabus". Bartholomae proposed ways instructors can study their students' errors and how they can use what they learn to help students grow as writers; he demonstrates his methods with a close reading of one of his own students' texts. Ultimately, Bartholomae claims:

> by having students share in the process of investigating and inter-
> preting the patterns of error in their writing, we can help them
> begin to see those errors as evidence of hypotheses or strategies

they have formed and, as a consequence, put them in a position to change, experiment, imagine other strategies. (chapter 9, this volume)

Finally, in an afterword, Deborah Brandt draws the entire collection together and discusses the work as a whole from a writing teacher's perspective. She highlights both the UW literacy course's advocacy for students to use writing to produce ideas (rather than simply to produce writing about ideas), and the course's focus on teacher research for finding answers to teaching problems by looking within one's own classrooms and within one's own students. Brandt argues that these moves represent a valuable shift in thinking about how basic writers learn to write and a shift in where teachers typically look for answers and guidance.

WORKS CITED

Bartholomae, David, and Anthony Petrosky. *Facts, Artifacts, and Counterfacts*. Upper Montclair, NJ: Boynton/Cook, 1986.

Bleich, David. "Ethnography and the Study of Literacy: Prospects for Socially Generous Research." *Into the Field: Sites of Composition Studies*. Ed. Anne Ruggles Gere. New York: Modern Language Association, 1993. 176–192.

Bruffee, Kenneth. *Collaborative Learning: Higher Education, Interdependence, and the Authority of Knowledge*. Baltimore: Johns Hopkins UP, 1993.

Flower, Linda. *The Constuction of Negotiated Meaning*. Carbondale: Southern Illinois University Press, 1994.

Flower, Linda, et al., eds. *Making Thinking Visible*. Urbana, IL: National Council of Teachers of English, 1993.

Greene, Stuart. "'Making Sense of My Own Ideas': Problems of Authorship in a Beginning Writing Classroom." *Written Communication* 12 (1995): 186–218.

—. "Students as Authors in the Study of History." *Teaching and Learning in History*. Ed. G. Leinhardt, I. Beck, and K. Stainton. Hillsdale, NJ: Lawrence Erlbaum Associates, 1994. 133–168.

Heath, Shirley Brice. *Ways With Words: Language, Life and Work in Communities and Classrooms*. Cambridge, England: Cambridge UP, 1983.

Kaufer, David, Cheryl Geisler, and Christine Neuwirth. *Arguing from Sources: Exploring Issues through Reading and Writing*. NY: Harcourt Brace Jovanovich, 1989.

Kolln, Martha. *Rhetorical Grammar: Grammatical Choices, Rhetorical Effects*. 2nd ed. Boston: Allyn and Bacon, 1996.

Kutz, Eleanor, Suzy Q. Groden, and Vivian Zamel. *The Discovery of Competence: Teaching and Learning with Diverse Student Writers*. Portsmouth, N.H.: Boynton/Cook, 1983.

Rose, Mike. *Lives on the Boundary*. New York: Free Press, 1989.

Rose, Mike. "Remedial Writing Courses: A Critique and a Proposal." *College English* 45 (1983): 109–128.

THE WISCONSIN PROGRAM

Chapter 1

Learning From Students: An Approach to Teaching Beginning College Writers

Katherine L. Weese
Hampden-Sydney College

THE INTERPLAY OF RESEARCH, THEORY, AND PRACTICE IN THE DEVELOPMENT OF THE WRITING PROGRAM

Too often one reads of the theory–practice split in composition studies, where texts that emphasize one aspect of composition or the other fail to wed the two. Indeed, David Bleich, drawing on Stephen North's *The Making of Knowledge in Composition*, noted that the split North identified between researchers–scholars and practitioners poses the problem of "how we as members of the composition discipline/profession can integrate all kinds of knowledge in our profession—those emerging from the variety of theoretical 'methods' along with the local knowledge of working teachers" (Bleich 176). This local knowledge is what North termed lore: the "accumulated body of traditions, practices, and beliefs in terms of which Practitioners understand how writing is done, learned, and taught" (North 22). Bleich proposed ethnographic studies of the classroom conducted by interested parties rather than by outside observers as a way to "loosen the boundary between theorists and teachers" (177). Similarly, in our experience, classroom research, the kind increasingly undertaken by writing instructors and increasingly represented in the body of literature of composition studies, provides a key means of bridging the theory–practice gap. Although theory provides a vocabulary through which to discuss writing and has a certain predictive value, allowing us to think systematically about and hypothesize what will happen in a given writing situation, classroom research helps us test and refine theories and to develop a greater understanding of what students actually do in the composing process. Through systematic research studies that formalize lore, several contributors to this volume refine or extend theoretical speculations about the writing process.[1] Such classroom research projects, conducted through close observation, videotaping, and audio recording of students at work in collaborative groups, of whole-class discussions, of conferences, of protocols of students' thoughts as they compose outside of class, and of cued question sessions provide valuable information for the instructor seeking to understand features of student writing left unaccounted for in theories of the composing process. Precisely because they are unaccounted for, these features become important in our research. In turn, this research provides us with practical ways of defining and redefining our roles in the classroom and our assignments in order to best facilitate our students' learning.

Although all students need to appreciate the complexity of writing, the values and contexts that shape it and their responses to it, perhaps beginning writers most urgently need to be immersed in classroom situations that foster such appreciation. The research-based classroom provides the opportunity first to unveil and debunk the myths of writing (see Frank Smith), myths from which most beginning writers' experiences probably stem. What better way than through exploring their own writing practices can students be convinced that the rules and conventions that have often paralyzed them as writers do not adequately define good writing? What better way than through the systematic examination of their strategies and procedures can students recognize the logic of what they do, understand the reasons for that logic, and learn how to transform their approaches into a series of self-conscious processes for writing tasks?

Second, beginning writers often come from various ethnic backgrounds, bringing with them their own forms of literacy. Kutz, Groden, and Zamel pointed out the limitations of decontextualized studies of cognitive and intellectual development, noting that "to better understand [students'] learning, we needed theories of development that would be contextually based and culturally sensitive" (49).[2] Just as theorists have often derived theories in a vacuum, so too have researchers produced studies that, as James Berlin noted, "often suffer from a conception of composing as an exclusively private, psychologically determined act, a stance that distorts

---

[1]See also Patricia Harkin's "The Postdisciplinary Politics of Lore."

[2]See *The Discovery of Competence*, pages 49–51, where the authors describe how the theories of Lev Vygotsky and Mikhail Bakhtin are useful for studying the effect of social context on writing. Likewise, Greene and Smith (chapter 8, this volume) draw on these theorists as they conduct their classroom research.

because it neglects the larger social contexts of composing."[3] Berlin went on to mention ethnographic study as a remedy to this problem, pointing to the work of Shirley Brice Heath (*Ways With Words*), Dixie Goswami and Peter R. Stillman (*Reclaiming the Classroom*), and Donald A. Daiker and Max Morenberg (*The Writing Teacher as Researcher*), whose work situates "instruction in text production and interpretation within the lived cultures of students, within class, race, gender, and ethnic determinations" (113). Context-based theories and classroom research projects are crucial for gaining an understanding of the complex internet of influence and intention that underpins beginning writers' activities. And, just as teachers need such information to understand their students' processes and choices, beginning writers need to see how the language practices and values of different cultures circumscribe choices that writers make. A research-based writing classroom provides an entry into studying issues of ethnicity, gender, class, and language that will help students consciously situate themselves in relation to (within or against) the language practices of the dominant culture.

Such an approach is student-centered in several ways. First, the data obtained from classroom research studies that are designed to provide more information about specific teaching problems we encounter comes from the students' own reading and composing processes so that the evolution of our teaching and our program begins with what we learn about our students' process of learning. Second, the course's theme—literacy— encourages a problem-posing approach; that is, the materials we use pose the problem of what it means to be literate, but there is no right answer to this question that instructors expect their students to find. Rather, the course's theme encourages an exploratory approach so that the definitions of literacy that emerge through the semester derive from a process of investigation into the students' own literacy histories and their experiences in and observations about the university setting.[4] In no two sections of the course, whether they are taught by the same instructor or different ones, will emerge quite the same understanding of literacy or its uses. Students and instructors alike work collaboratively to probe a problem and create new knowledge in the process of investigating its many facets.[5] Such a course clearly cannot work in a traditional transmission pedagogy, where

---

[3]James A. Berlin, "Composition Studies and Cultural Studies," 113. Berlin refers to the limitations of some of the protocol analyses conducted by Linda Flower and John R. Hayes in "A Cognitive Process Theory of Writing."

[4]See also Henry A. Giroux, "Reading Texts, Literacy, and Textual Authority."

[5]Cf. Kutz, Groden, and Zamel, who argued that a writing course should be designed so that it "casts the teacher as a co-searcher rather than a guide, a leader, or a lecturer, as one member of a collegial group all of whom share the responsibility for constructing whatever insights and understandings eventually derive from the work" (93).

students are passive recipients of knowledge handed down by teachers. Our work offers a process-oriented model for teaching beginning writing that challenges traditional notions of remediation. In spite of the important work on basic writing published in the mid- and late 1980s by authors such as Mike Rose (*Lives on the Boundary*) and David Bartholomae (*Facts, Artifacts and Counterfacts*), many traditional and outmoded models still prevail, models that depict writing as a set of skills rather than as meaningful engagement with ideas. There is a clear need for more works that provide contemporary models. In order to help beginning writers understand and participate in the kinds of projects that engage real writers, we have developed a course that hinges on students' own experiences. Ultimately, our challenging beginning writers with real writing situations and heightening their awareness of what it means to read and write in the college setting enables a crucial goal of our work: preparing students to write with a sense of their own authorship or authority over the meanings they make. This is a key problem we have noted in teaching beginning writers, one that has formed a central point of exploration in our classroom research. Our book addresses how we can effectively teach students to value their insights and experiences as evidence about what it means to be literate, and how we can teach them to write college papers that incorporate source material without losing that authority, without simply deferring to what they frequently see as the authoritative voices of the experts.

THE PROBLEM OF AUTHORITY IN BEGINNING WRITERS' WORK: CASE STUDIES

In keeping with Greene's research, we use the construct of authorship as a means for understanding beginning writers'

> attempts to contribute to a scholarly conversation knowledge that is not necessarily found in source texts, but that is carefully linked to texts students read. These sources can provide the basis for students' essays in the form of support and elaboration, particularly as students begin to assimilate the ideas of other writers and find a way to say something new (Kaufer and Geisler).[6] ("Students as Authors" 138)

Moreover, as Greene suggests elsewhere,

> writing an essay that contributes a unique perspective requires students to adapt information from sources and prior knowledge to meet their goals within the bounds of "acceptable" academic discourse. This type of writing also requires them to restructure the information from sources. Restructur-

---

[6]Greene's reference is to David Kaufer and Cheryl Geisler, "Novelty in Academic Writing." *Written Communication* 6 (July 1989): 286–311.

ing may entail supplying new organizational patterns not found in sources, appropriating information as evidence to support an argument, and making connective inferences between prior knowledge and source content. The source of an author's authority derives from an ability to create and support his or her vision, one that recognizes that more traditionally accepted sources may fail to function as adequate models or fall short of providing adequate solutions to problems. ("Making Sense" 187)

Although authorship is often associated with romantic conceptions of individual writers who act freely of any sort of institutional or social practice, authorship is a relational term that calls attention to the fact that writers are always situated within a broad socio-cultural landscape. Thus, the story of authorship is very much about the social, historical, and cultural contexts that influence the development of certain rhetorical behaviors and writers' willingness or ability to contribute something new in order to move an intellectual conversation along. Authoring a text depends not only on writers' abilities to establish an intellectual project of their own, but upon certain authorizing principles that exist outside of themselves as writers. These authorizing principles can be seen in the texts that define the work of a discipline, in a field's conventions, or within certain cultural and social imperatives, each of which gives legitimacy to the form and substance of one's writing (Greene, "Making Sense" 188).

Authorship is a difficult stance for beginning writers to adopt. We all frequently encounter the student who relies solely on the authority of professionally authored texts, viewing research as an opportunity to restate what others have said rather than to create knowledge. When I taught freshman composition last year, for example, I encountered a couple of students whose struggles with research papers exemplify some of the struggles that the essays in this volume address. Despite my emphasis on research writing as a site to add knowledge to an ongoing conversation, my students exhibited difficulty in integrating their visions with source material when asked to write research papers about some aspect of twentieth-century American popular culture (the theme of the course).

Christopher,[7] for example, wanted to write about the role of the automobile in rising teen pregnancies, a topic suggested to him by a Hollywood

---

[7]Students' names are pseudonyms. The examples of the students Christopher and James help define the principle of authorship and illustrate the difficulties students encounter when asked to adopt this stance. The writing course in which the students were enrolled, however, did not use the literacy materials; I set up the first part of a year-long sequence with the Forms of Academic Literacy materials, and these students were enrolled in the second half of their Rhetoric requirement. I should also note that I teach at a men's college, so my references are necessarily all to male students. Finally, the college's students are largely White, upper-middle class individuals; hence my discussion does not focus on factors of difference in their backgrounds. Many of the subsequent chapters in the volume take up these complex issues of students' sociocultural background.

film he had seen recently and by the fact that his mother worked for Planned Parenthood and had mentioned to him the car's role in increasing teens' opportunities for sexual encounters. Christopher was interested in adding other films to his discussion—I suggested *American Graffiti*—but as he researched the project, he nearly changed his mind because, as he said, "I've never written about a movie before and I don't know how to do it." He struggled throughout the process of writing the paper with the idea of using the films to support his ideas because none of his sources talked specifically about films' role in the culture. He came to me repeatedly to ask me where in the paper he should incorporate his discussions of the films. In early drafts, he left them out altogether. His final paper shows an extreme reluctance to make any judgment about how films depict the automobile and teen sex. Here is the way he frames his argument (the ellipses indicate the discussion of specific scenes in the film; the first part of the quotation is where Christopher begins the argument, and the second part is his conclusion to the discussion; the entire discussion of the films comprises about two pages of the paper):

> By portraying dating in this way, *American Graffiti* glamorizes sex in the car and also implies that even if the girl does not say she wants to go "parking," she really does. The portrayal of dating in this way is unfavorable, but it was not seen as bad because of its closeness to reality. . . .
>
> On the whole *American Graffiti* portrays dating in a way that may be bad, but it portrays dating in an accurate way. The film was not "bad" because it was made in a classy and tasteful way. By making the film classy and tasteful, George Lucas makes an accurate portrayal of dating at this time.

Christopher's final commentary on the way *American Graffiti* uses the automobile to glamorize teen sex thus revolves around his sense that he cannot judge the film "bad" for perpetuating or participating in this mythology; nor is he able to look at the film as itself being critical of its own subject matter, as offering a critique of the way American culture makes it possible for "a beautiful car [to] enhance the fascination of a beautiful woman" (Christopher's paper). Instead of producing either one of these possible readings, he retreats into what is likely more familiar ground for him: the issue of realism or accuracy, and also George Lucas's reputation as a talented Hollywood director. These features render the film good, as Christopher shies away from the interesting implications of his own argument, opting to end instead with a thumbs up/thumbs down judgment of the film.

Yet he comes quite close to a more sophisticated reading of the film's relation to our culture's fascination with the glamour of the automobile: His use of the passive voice early in the excerpt ("it was not seen as bad because of its closeness to reality") distances him as author from this statement—he attributes this judgment to some nonspecific agent. He is not drawing on a review here; his bibliography included no such source. The passive construction, which contradicts his prior statement that "the portrayal of dating in this way is unfavorable," appears rather to be a sign of an unrealized urge on Christopher's part to say something else. Moreover, Christopher's own use of quotation marks around the term bad toward the end of the excerpt suggests that he is, in a latent manner, questioning his own terms of assessment and reaching for another vocabulary with which to talk about the film. He implicitly calls into question his reading but ultimately is unable to find other terms.

It is likely that with more coaching in how critics can use films as texts in ways other than pronouncing them aesthetically good or bad, Christopher would have been able to take his observations in a more complex direction, rather than ending as he does. A close reading of his paper now allows me to think of how I could have encouraged him to develop this more complex relationship to his material; I believe by showing him how to find a review of a film and how to find a scholarly journal article on the same film, and then asking him to explain the differences between the two, I could have provided him with a model for producing a different kind of reading of *American Graffiti*. He is unfamiliar with film criticism as a field of study and therefore unfamiliar with what its conventions are and how they can be used to illuminate films as cultural artifacts. By creating sequenced assignments that lead up to the research paper itself, I could have helped Christopher along in the process through smaller tasks that familiarized him with the conventions of film studies and thereby changed his notion of authorship as he approached the paper. Such a move would provide him with an expanded set of authorizing principles (Greene's term, "Making Sense" 188) that would encourage a different kind of authorship on Christopher's part, one that would not only allow him to access new conventions for writing about film but one that would allow him to use those conventions for his own purposes in the research paper. The only set of conventions to which he had access at the time of composition—aesthetic evaluation, director's reputation—does not allow him to use the films as sources to fit the project of his essay and hence prevents him from adopting a more complex kind of authorship.

Another student in the same course illustrates a very similar difficulty that students face in adopting a position of authority when dealing with an unfamiliar writing task. James initially approached me with the idea of writing about dude ranches and the American Dream; he wanted to show that the image of the American west that is appealing to Eastern city slickers who want to relive that part of the American dream is a false one, distorting the role of the cowboy in American culture. I was pleased that James was using the research paper assignment to investigate something that had real life application for him because he would spend the summer employed on a dude ranch. James struggled with a contradiction he saw in the contemporary vacation dude ranch and the real lives of cowboys, a contradiction that I viewed as crucial to the paper, indeed, the source of the paper, or his reason for writing the paper. Yet for James, this contradiction became a stuck point that nearly caused him to drop the topic. As he reported to me, he had a set of source material that dealt with what cowboys did in real life, and a set of sources that described, without evaluating or judging, the contemporary dude ranch experience. Although James in fact began the research process intending to develop a paper about the contradiction between these two sets of sources, he soon lamented that he could not take that direction in the paper because, as he put it, "I didn't find that information . . . none of my sources said that." It never occurred to James that he could use the split between his two sets of information to develop his own argument, to apply his own analysis of the dude ranch in contemporary American culture. Instead, James was restricted by notions of writing from sources that only validate what authoritative texts have already said. His case illustrates perfectly what composition theorist Don Bialostosky noted of his students. Drawing on Mikhail Bakhtin, Bialostosky lamented that "the voice under the influence of the authoritative word repeats it thoughtlessly or imitates it confusedly or cites it passively or complies with it formally or defers to it silently" (16).

In order to help students avoid these pitfalls, to help them transform source texts (Higgins' term, "Reading to Argue: Helping Students Transform Source Texts"), I could have the class study a professional writer's argument that transforms its sources; with a concrete model for constructing an argument that questions the authoritative word, which shows how a researcher works with previous authorities and transforms their texts to produce a new authoritative voice, perhaps students would be able more easily to produce and support original ideas. Of course using models is something most instructors do, yet frequently they draw on such models to illustrate the mechanics of research writing (how to integrate quotations, paraphrase legitimately, cite properly) rather than to point out precisely how authors reorganize, hierarchize, synthesize, and, especially, in Greene's terms, "make connective inferences between prior knowledge and source content" ("Making Sense" 187). Asking students to write a paper analyzing how one of their own sources restructures information from its sources would thus prove a valuable research assignment that might enable students to engage more critically with their own sources as they put together their research projects.

Part of my class's research paper assignment asked students to submit a brief proposal that fulfilled four criteria: to introduce the question the student intended to investigate, to explain why the topic was worthy of extended investigation, to preview some of the ideas that the student felt he could contribute to the body of knowledge surrounding the topic, and to describe the kinds of source material the student would use as he explored the topic. James struggled painfully to satisfy the third of these criteria, but instead of discussing what his voice could add, he repeatedly found himself beginning to detail what his other sources said. (I noticed this trend among the entire class, in fact. Students variously read and interpreted the question, having little sense of what I was asking them to do.) James' proposal went through several revisions, yet as many times as I asked him to include that information, I saw new drafts that failed to do so. Like his classmate Christopher, James was a conscientious student, one who brought creativity, insight, and energy to his research project, a hard worker who frequently wanted to discuss his ideas. If he was not lazy or inattentive to my concerns or an unwilling reviser, perhaps he simply could not provide his own analysis because he had never been asked before to consider research the way I was asking him to consider it.

As we talked in class and in conferences, I encouraged James to return to the ideas that led him to want to write the paper to begin with. He produced drafts initially that still did not incorporate his own critique of the dude ranch but merely described it. His final draft did include such an analysis, but that information about how the dude ranch continued to glorify and falsify the image of the cowboy was shunted off to the end of the essay rather than informing the overall structure of the essay. James' experience, like Christopher's, showed that he had difficulty forming an argument about a text when he could not find the kind of argument he wanted to make already embedded in one of his source texts.

In "Reading to Argue: Helping Students Transform Source Texts," Lorraine Higgins noted a similar phenomenon; she cited numerous studies that describe the strategies students use for incorporating source material, concluding that weaker college writers often rely on familiar structures and patterns for their essays, failing to construct original arguments that would require them "to adapt and organize source information for more complex purposes" rather than simply requiring them to report it (72). As Higgins pointed out, "when students are asked to argue from sources, they need to do more than invoke a familiar text structure or fill in information that is already 'known' to them or can be directly transcribed from their reading" (72–73).

Here is where classroom research becomes so valuable to our teaching practices. For James and Christopher, I have only a few scattered memories and their products (papers) through which to reconstruct their difficulties with the assignment and with adopting a full-fledged stance as an author. I wish that I had think-aloud protocols from my students as they approached the research paper proposal just discussed. I wonder what processes led them to interpret my assignment as they did—in a way different from how I expected them to interpret it—when they encountered my instruction to write a proposal that showed how they would contribute something to the body of knowledge surrounding their topics. Access to such information would better allow me to understand how preconceptions about writing research papers influence their choices; it would also allow me access to other factors, like sociocultural background, that might otherwise remain as invisible (and therefore poorly understood) influences on their writing. Such information would help me the next time I make a similar assignment—what I learn from my students would alert me as to how I can clarify the task for them. Of course, students themselves would benefit ultimately, not only because I could better see the logic of their choices, but equally because such research would heighten their own self-consciousness about their composing strategies. As Ann Penrose and Barbara Sitko pointed out in *Hearing Ourselves Think*, "teachers can create environments where active learning about writing, reading, and thinking can take place. The research-based classroom provides students and teachers the opportunity to collaborate in the inquiry process" (7). The chapters that follow highlight ways we can understand students' processes of learning by going beyond studying their finished products and studying as well as the various stages in their writing.

THE PROBLEM OF AUTHORITY IN BEGINNING WRITERS' WORK: STUDENT AGENCY VERSUS IMITATIVE AUTHORITY

These scenarios and student strategies for writing from sources probably sound familiar to most writing instructors who teach beginning writers; the question "how do we encourage our students to become active contributors to a body of knowledge rather than passive recipients of knowledge?" is the starting point from which those of us who contributed to this volume began. The challenge is perhaps made greater by the fact that we teach beginning writers: writers who lack confidence, who lack a repertoire of strategies or options with which to approach writing tasks or cling to strategies that do not work, writers whose texts are often painfully error-ridden. Yet as Greene pointed out, "though the writing basic writers produce may be filled with miscues, they come to us as [students capable] of thinking, comprehending, and solving problems. Basic writers can achieve beyond anyone's expectations if we set up situations that reflect what writers do" ("Teaching Basic Writing as Writing" 3). In the effort to reach the population of college students labeled "basic writers," we have put together this collection for other instructors who are, like us, concerned about designing programs and courses and providing guidance in real writing for such students, with the ultimate aim of enabling students to guide themselves through the writing tasks they encounter in the university.

Since the 1970s, numerous scholars in composition at various programs across the country have developed whole-language models for teaching basic writing (see Hairston, "Winds of Change"). Of particular relevance is David Bartholomae's work; Bartholomae began teaching a course at the University of Pittsburgh in the late 1970s that inspired his article "Teaching Basic Writing: An Alternative to Basic Skills" and his later book, co-authored with Anthony Petrosky, *Facts, Artifacts, and Counterfacts: Theory and Method for a Reading and Writing Course.* These arguments for teaching basic writing advocate making challenging demands on students by instructing them in critical thinking as an intimate part of the writing process rather than as something separate from it, something to be delved into after they have mastered the basics of composing sentences. Like Bartholomae's, Glynda Hull and Rose's recent writings about the status of remedial instruction in the American education system pose a very different model for teaching "remedial" students ("Rethinking Remediation"). Elsewhere, Rose argued that in traditional writing instruction, "writing is defined by abilities one can quantify and connect as opposed to the dynamism and organic vitality one associates with thought" ("The Language of Exclusion" 347). As Rose further pointed out, "many of our attempts to help college remedial writers, attempts that are often well-intentioned and seemingly common-sensical, may, in fact, be ineffective, even counterproductive, for these attempts reduce, fragment, and possibly misrepresent the composing process" ("Remedial Writing Courses" 109). Although Rose named several central problems with basic writing instruction, one is of key interest to the authors of this volume—that "remedial courses are self-contained; that is, they have little conceptual or practical connection to the larger academic writing environment in which our students find themselves" (109). Rose's and Bartholomae's concerns intersect in their advocacy for a course that initiates students into the discourses of the university at large.

Behind Bartholomae and Petrosky's Pittsburgh course lies the philosophy that a student must gain an entry into academic discourses; they have developed an elaborate course designed to place the student in a "position that would authorize her as a reader and a writer" ("Facts, Artifacts and Counterfacts" 7). To meet this goal, Bartholomae and Petrosky argued,

> a course in reading and writing whose goal is to empower students must begin with silence, a silence students must fill. It cannot begin by telling students what to say. And it must provide a method to enable students to see what they have said. . . . It fails if it assumes that it need only provide the preliminary skills, some groundwork that will enable students to begin later, perhaps after the basic writing course or the freshmen English course

or the introductory course—when, for the first time, they will sit down with the responsibility of having something to say. ("Facts, Artifacts and Counterfacts" 7)

The course encourages students to develop their own expertise on adolescent growth and development, and then to test their ideas and the set of terms they develop against those of professionals (31), thus encouraging students to see that they can create knowledge. By forming their own ideas first,

> students are prepared to see how someone else's ideas fit into a project they themselves have begun. They are not, now, left with nothing to write about but what they can pull out of books in the library. . . . Having come from a project that they took to be their own, they are also prepared to be more critically aggressive in reading the work of others. . . . They don't, that is, see these more official texts as speaking with an oracular authority—speaking a truth that forces a student to be silent. (Bartholomae and Petrosky 37–38)[8]

Like the students in the Pittsburgh course, students in the UW-Madison course engage with challenging academic material; they are considered as authors, and their work is read as one might read any other author's text. By fully respecting their ideas and the rhetorical situations they construct to express those ideas, we not only gain a greater understanding of their rhetorical strategies but we also help them overcome the notion that experts speak with an authority that excludes them; their discourses enter into the realm of knowledge surrounding the field they study. Beginning writers become writers in the richest sense of the word.

But the UW-Madison course builds on the foundation of the Pittsburgh course in two important ways. It does so first by emphasizing what we learn from students' processes of learning in addition to what we learn from the products they create. The Pittsburgh course teaches students to begin negotiating the task of "having something to say" ("Facts, Artifacts and Counterfacts" 7) by realizing that "certainty and authority are postures, features of a performance that is achieved through an act of writing, not qualities of vision that preceded such a performance" (Bartholomae and Petrosky 21; see also Bartholomae's discussion of commonplaces in "Inventing the University"). But other factors (cognitive and social, economic, and cultural factors) do precede and influence a student's ability to adopt a posture of certainty and authority. In the Forms of Academic Literacy course, by asking the students to engage with the discipline of writing itself through an investigation of their own literate practices, instructors gain

---

[8]Cf. Kutz, Groden, and Zamel: "It is not a specific set of truths, attitudes, or set forms of discourse that our students must acquire; it's the sense of their own right to be thinkers, challengers, askers, and arguers in a community that values these activities" (81).

insight into students' writing *processes*. Such insight allows instructors to see the various influences that govern a student's ability to try on or dress up in an academician's clothes. Although *Facts, Artifacts and Counterfacts* describes a course that encourages students to adopt an authorial stance in relation to the subject matter, or our work *Teaching Academic Literacy* problematizes this goal, unveils the difficulties students face as they attempt to meet this goal, and probes their difficulties in order to locate the various sources of those difficulties. It answers the question, "What is going on with students' writing practices when we give them complex assignments that encourage them to adopt a stance of authority?" By making the students' writing itself the subject matter of the course, we can begin to answer these questions about authorship and authority.

The UW-Madison course also builds further on the Pittsburgh course's paradigm of what constitutes authority for a student writer. When scholars focus on students' abilities to develop an imitative authority whose goal it is to approximate academic discourses already in existence (Bartholomae and Petrosky 40), they stress the authority of the academy at the expense of students' prior discourses, perhaps underestimating the influence of these prior communities—be they legacies of sociocultural background or what Nicholas Preus, following Linda Flower, called "legacies of schooling" (ch. 4, this volume)—and thereby minimizing the effects of these legacies on the processes by which students can adopt a stance of authority in the university's discourse community. In addition, the notion of a purely imitative authority perhaps undervalues students' potential to contribute to and reshape the knowledge of the academy.

Often, then, such approaches can have the effect of simply initiating or indoctrinating students to the authority that their teacher represents, thereby undermining the value of the students' experiences as potential sources of meaning. For example, Kenneth Bruffee's recent book on collaborative learning reveals such a notion of authority. As he described the activity that goes on in student "consensus groups" (28),[9] he noted that:

> collaborative learning tasks are nonfoundational, constructive, tool-making tasks . . . [T]hese tasks draw students into an untidy, conversational, constructive process in which, because they do not yet know "the old vocabularies," they create new ones by adapting the languages they already know. The result is not an undistorted view of a reality presumed to lie behind appearances. The result is a social construct that students have arrived at by their own devices and according to their own insights. (36)

The aim is that students will enter the discourse communities of their teachers (38). Yet entry into this community hinges on an interaction

---

[9]For a challenge to Bruffee's conception of the nature of collaboration, see Greene and Smith's "Teaching Talk About Writing," chapter 8, this volume.

between the students' ability to develop the tools for investigating issues on their own and an acceptance of the authoritative voices of professionals in the field. Bruffee wrote that:

> the final step in constructing knowledge and increasing its authority occurs when the class as a whole compares its consensus . . . with the consensus on that issue of the immeasurably larger and more complex disciplinary or linguistic community . . . that the teacher represents. If the two match, the authority of the knowledge that the students have constructed increases once again. (49)

Although students create their own ways of understanding, the understanding they produce is supposed to be in consensus with what the experts say. In this schema, students are allowed to assume the authority of contributors to the field only so long as they reaffirm the field as it stands; their authority, presumably, is reduced by ideas not "currently regarded as correct or acceptable by the teacher's disciplinary community" (46), regardless of the potential of those ideas to reshape the discipline in meaningful ways. Bruffee does acknowledge that a dissenting opinion might "move the teacher's own and the discipline's current view of what is acceptable in the direction of the dissenter's position" (46), but he regards such instances as rare.

In the literacy course, students draw on the material of their own literacy autobiographies not only to approximate professionals' discourse on the nature of writing but to contribute to the body of knowledge the evidence of their experiences as a way of reshaping professionals' understanding about writing and how it is learned. Several scholars wonder if it is such a beneficial goal to indoctrinate students to the languages valorized in the institutional setting in a way that implicitly elides any value attached to the knowledge students construct. Don Bialostosky, for example, argued that:

> while a disciplinary course encourages students to appropriate its languages and conventions accurately and completely, a writing course can put students in a position to answer those languages by minimizing their authority and finality. We should authorize our students to reaccent, not just reproduce, the disciplinary languages we and our colleagues impose on them. (17–18)

Similarly, Derek Owens argued that the writing classroom must "reflect the need for polycentric composition instruction" (172):

> students have to learn that the effects (and affects) of discourse, written and oral, merely reflect different communities and that the aims of the classroom are twofold: to teach students how to interact effectively with the discourse(s) of the academy, while simultaneously instilling a greater understanding of opposing means of making knowledge through writing that is prevalent in communities often ignored within the academy. (172)

Owens noted that writing instructors have a responsibility for teaching students to enter into the discourse community of the academy, but said that "if teachers stress only academic means of communication in the classroom, they do a gross disservice by rendering interdisciplinary, culturally diverse discourses invisible and thus nonexistent" (172).[10]

One goal of the Wisconsin course, as Stephen Fox discusses in ch. 2, is to keep visible culturally diverse discourses; the literacy autobiography assignment encourages students to explore these other discourses, and when students read each other's autobiographical essays, as they are required to do, their sense of the range of possible literacies is reinforced. Many beginning writing courses, especially at large universities, have a multicultural student body; precisely because they have been members of silenced communities or communities whose language practices are devalued, these beginning students need to see the value of their literate practices but also to see where such practices come into conflict with the literacies the university demands.

Beyond simply recognizing the validity of these other discourses, instructors can understand these discourses and learn from their students about how writing works. The conflict between these discourses, communal and official, creates an intersection of two kinds of subject positions for students, an intersection that itself becomes a source of study, the material of the course. When one positionality comes up against another with which it is fundamentally incompatible, the collision itself opens a space for change in one or another or both of the positions. In the beginning writing classroom, such a space results from the collision among or between different discourse conventions themselves. Collisions, rendered conscious for students, allow students to assume an agency whereby they can actively adopt, challenge, or adapt old conventions and new.[11] Research in the

---

[10]Cf. Patricia Bizzell, "Marxist Ideas on Composition Studies," and John Clifford, "The Subject in Discourse."

[11]Numerous literary theorists are eager to escape the pessimistic Foucauldian perspective that says that a subject cannot find a place to resist hegemonic discourse and are also anxious not to return to a strictly Enlightenment notion of the individual as a socially unrestricted agent. They find renewed possibilities for social change in the differences that emerge from the numerous and contradictory ways that the individual finds him/herself situated. See, for example, Terry Eagleton's "Capitalism, Modernism, and Postmodernism" and Paul Smith's *Discerning the Subject.* Perhaps the dialogic theories of Mikhail Bakhtin, theories frequently drawn upon in composition studies, further illuminate this notion. Bakhtin, in his "Discourse in the Novel," discussed authoritative and internally persuasive discourses, writing that "the internally persuasive word . . . enters into an intense interaction, a *struggle* with other internally persuasive discourses. Our ideological development is just such an intense struggle within us for hegemony among various available verbal and ideological points of view, approaches, directions, and values. The semantic structure of an internally persuasive discourse is *not finite,* it is *open;* in each of the new contexts that dialogize it, this discourse is able to reveal ever newer *ways to mean*" (345–346).

composition classroom can affirm and/or refine theories of authority by studying ways students negotiate conflicts among positions.

The chapters in Part II of this volume further examine the ways students negotiate the different identities that emerge from the demands of different discourse conventions. The studies often find that new ways of making meaning emerge only with tremendous struggle, particularly for beginning writers, but even if new ways of making meaning do not emerge as fully as instructors would like, there is still much to be gained from an increased understanding of how students negotiate conflicts or collisions, an understanding that has vast implications for teaching writing.

WORKS CITED

Bakhtin, Mikhail. "Discourse in the Novel." *The Dialogic Imagination.* Ed. Michael Holquist. Trans. Caryl Emerson and Michael Holquist. Austin: University of Texas Press, 1981. 259–422.

Bartholomae, David, and Anthony Petrosky, eds. *Facts, Artifacts and Counterfacts: Theory and Method for A Reading and Writing Course.* Upper Montclair, NJ: Boynton/Cook, 1986.

———. "Facts, Artifacts and Counterfacts: A Basic Reading and Writing Course for the College Curriculum." Bartholomae and Petrosky, *Facts, Artifacts and Counterfacts* 3–43.

Bartholomae, David. "Inventing the University." *When A Writer Can't Write.* Ed. Mike Rose. New York: Guilford, 1985. 134–165.

———. "Teaching Basic Writing: An Alternative to Basic Skills." *Journal of Basic Writing* 2.2 (1979): 85–109.

Berlin, James A. "Composition Studies and Cultural Studies: Collapsing Boundaries." Gere 99–116.

Bialostosky, Don H. "Liberal Education, Writing, and the Dialogic Self." Harkin and Schilb, *Contending With Words* 11–22.

Bizzell, Patricia. "Marxist Ideas on Composition Studies." Harkin and Schilb, *Contending With Words* 52–68.

Bleich, David. "Ethnography and the Study of Literacy: Prospects for Socially Generous Research." Gere 176–192.

Bruffee, Kenneth. *Collaborative Learning: Higher Education, Interdependence, and the Authority of Knowledge.* Baltimore: Johns Hopkins UP, 1993.

Clifford, John. "The Subject in Discourse." Harkin and Schilb, *Contending With Words* 38–51.

Daiker, Donald A., and Max Morenberg, eds. *The Writing Teacher as Researcher.* Portsmouth, NH: Boynton/Cook, 1990.

Eagleton, Terry. "Capitalism, Modernism, and Postmodernism." *New Left Review* 152 (July/Aug. 1985): 60–72.

Flower, Linda, and John R. Hayes. "A Cognitive Process Theory of Writing." *College Composition and Communication* 32 (1981): 365–87.

Gere, Anne Ruggles, ed. *Into the Field: Sites of Composition Studies.* New York: MLA, 1993.

Giroux, Henry A. "Reading Texts, Literacy, and Textual Authority." *Journal of Education* 172.1 (1990): 84–94.

Goswami, Dixie, and Peter R. Stillman, eds. *Reclaiming the Classroom: Teacher Research as an Agency for Change.* Upper Montclair, NJ: Boynton/Cook, 1987.

Greene, Stuart. " 'Making Sense of My Own Ideas': Problems of Authorship in a Beginning Writing Classroom." *Written Communication* 12 (1995): 186–218.

———. "Students as Authors in the Study of History." *Teaching and Learning History*. Eds. G. Leinhardt, I. Beck, and K. Stainton. Hillsdale, NJ: Lawrence Erlbaum Associates, 1994. 133–168.

———. "Teaching Basic Writing as Writing." Ms. University of Wisconsin–Madison, 1992.

Hairston, Maxine. "The Winds of Change: Thomas Kuhn and the Revolution in the Teaching of Writing." *College Composition and Communication* 33.1 (Feb. 1982): 76–88.

Harkin, Patricia and John Schilb. *Contending With Words: Composition and Rhetoric in a Postmodern Age*. New York: MLA, 1991.

Harkin, Patricia. "The Postdisciplinary Politics of Lore." Harkin and Schilb, *Contending With Words* 124–138.

Heath, Shirley Brice. *Ways With Words: Language, Life and Work in Communities and Classrooms*. Cambridge, Eng: Cambridge UP, 1983.

Higgins, Lorraine. "Reading to Argue: Helping Students Transform Source Texts." Penrose and Sitko, *Hearing Ourselves Think* 70–101.

Hull, Glynda, and Mike Rose. "Rethinking Remediation: Toward a Social-Cognitive Understanding of Reading and Writing." *Written Communication* 6 (Apr. 1989): 139–154.

Kutz, Eleanor, Suzy Q. Groden, and Vivian Zamel. *The Discovery of Competence: Teaching and Learning with Diverse Student Writers*. Portsmouth, NH: Boynton/Cook, 1993.

North, Stephen. *The Making of Knowledge in Composition: Portrait of An Emerging Field*. Portsmouth, NH: Heinemann, 1987.

Owens, Derek. "Composition as the Voicing of Multiple Fictions." Gere 159–175.

Penrose, Ann M. and Barbara M. Sitko, eds. *Hearing Ourselves Think: Cognitive Research in the College Writing Classroom*. New York and Oxford: Oxford UP, 1993.

Penrose, Ann M. and Barbara M. Sitko. "Introduction: Studying Cognitive Processes in the Classroom." Penrose and Sitko, *Hearing Ourselves Think* 3–15.

Rose, Mike. *Lives on the Boundary*. New York: Free Press, 1989.

Rose, Mike. "Remedial Writing Courses: A Critique and a Proposal." *College English* 45 (1983): 109–128.

———. "The Language of Exclusion: Writing Instruction at the University." *College English* 47 (1985): 341–359.

Smith, Frank. "Myths of Writing." *Language Arts* 58.7 (October 1981): 792–798.

Smith, Paul. *Discerning the Subject*. Minneapolis: University of Minnesota Press, 1988.

Chapter 2

Inviting Students to Join the Literacy Conversation: Toward a Collaborative Pedagogy for Academic Literacy

Stephen L. Fox
Indiana University–Purdue University Indianapolis

What does it mean to talk about literacy in the title and content of a course for beginning college writers? Is an emphasis on academic literacy compatible with a belief in multicultural literacy? And how does such a course incorporate an established, although still not universally practiced, pedagogy of process and collaboration? These questions recur throughout this volume and are asked and answered in different ways by various writers. In this chapter, I raise these questions by explaining how certain basic principles of literacy learning and teaching inform the first-year composition course at the University of Wisconsin-Madison. How well these principles have been implemented and how valid they prove to be in the context of students' and teachers' work and lives remain open questions, explored collaboratively through the kind of classroom-based research and theoretical inquiry represented in this book.

The general purpose of many beginning college writing courses, particularly those designed for underprepared students, is enabling students to develop an effective writing process that will serve them in a variety of expressive and transactional situations. Courses that share a process approach differ in the rhetorical situations they ask students to enter. As Katherine Weese has shown in chapter 1, the Forms of Academic Literacy course we present in this volume emphasizes the approach to beginning composition that initiates students into the written discourse of academia. Weese also explains our determination to integrate this academic approach with the more explicitly sociopolitical approach of fostering students' awareness of multicultural literacies. We are willing to serve the university and our democratic society by taking on these two tasks.

That we serve the academic community and the larger society does not mean we have lost sight of our own agenda in composition studies, one we have worked so hard to theorize, legitimize, and even canonize. I am speaking here of two essential principles in the composition catechism: process and collaboration. For some like-minded composition faculty, these once-radical principles might have become clichés, taken for granted except when we justify them for uninformed audiences such as new graduate students or members of other departments—and our own!—who inquire into what we do. In a course like Forms of Academic Literacy, we revitalize the principles of process and collaboration by investigating their role in fostering students' development of academic and multicultural literacy. Our approach integrates seemingly incompatible goals of beginning writing courses by making literacy itself the focal point of our curriculum. We ask students to examine their own literacy histories and theorize about literacy on that basis; they then use their personal and group knowledge to analyze academic and public debates about literacy. Students develop a sense of authority as writers by drawing on their own experience. They are also asked to synthesize ideas drawn from published writing about literacy issues into an academic argument. The course offers students an opportunity to investigate the uses of literacy in a specific academic setting or in the larger community: Some students interview a professor about writing in a particular academic field; some students do ethnographic observation of language use in a nonacademic setting; other students tutor in a literacy center and write about their experiences. The topic of literacy unites these assignments, providing continuity for the course, while students develop fluency in academic discourse through examination of personal experience, academic argument, and public debate. The strengths of several rhetorical approaches are thus combined.

We ask students to write a literacy autobiography at the beginning of the course, when we are also having them practice heuristics, share first drafts with peers, and experience revision as reseeing, rethinking, and rewriting. As they write about acquiring and using literacy in the past, they make comparisons with the way they are learning literacy in this course. They begin to make connections between literacy as part of their personal histories and literacy as the subject of an academic course. And soon they are using literacy practices to understand public conversations about literacy. The view and practice of literacy as a self-consciously collaborative process can shape students' reading of the literacy debates in our society. Both teachers and students in this beginning college writing course are the subjects of those debates, and through their developing literacy, the students also become participants in such debates.

A focus on literacy in a writing course is akin to a focus on critical controversies in a literature class, an approach suggested by Gerald Graff as a way of making students aware of the larger issues in the field of literary studies. Graff argued that we could help students "gain access to academic discourse communities" by bringing "conflicts of principle" into the curriculum. In this way we might "help students become interested participants in the present cultural conversation instead of puzzled and alienated spectators" (822). Some writing teachers briefly introduce the literacy controversy to their students by explaining their philosophy of writing instruction, contrasting it with other approaches students might have encountered. Such explanations often respond to the perennial student observation, "Another English teacher told me . . ." Of course, most of our students are not English education majors and might not care about pedagogical differences among English teachers. But a systematic exploration of literacy issues during the semester teaches students about the nature of language and its socioeconomic and political contexts. By reading and writing about literacy, especially academic literacy, students learn to write academic prose while also learning why they are expected to write in such ways. David Bartholomae put it this way:

> If my students are going to write for me by knowing who I am—and if this means more than knowing my prejudices, psyching me out—it means knowing what I know; it means having the knowledge of a professor of English. They have, then, to know what I know and how I know what I know. (277)

The academic literacy course represents one writing program's attempt to help beginning college writers know what their instructors know and how they know it.

But literacy issues are not merely academic; they are debated constantly in public forums, ranging from editorial pages to school board meetings. George Will, for example, wrote of "the education system's subtraction from national literacy," arguing that it is "common for high school graduates to be functionally illiterate" and accusing writing teachers of "academic malpractice" (D2). Newspaper columnists critique whole language. State legislators and citizens' groups condemn essay questions on state proficiency tests as subjective, intrusive, and unreliable. The academic literacy course invites students to join such debates and offers to sharpen their debating skills. In this way, the course aligns topic and process, the individual and the community, academia and society.

Before elaborating on the principles supporting this approach to beginning college writing, it is important to examine terminology as a way of making explicit certain assumptions about the course. I speak of beginning college writers for two reasons. First, the principles undergirding the

academic literacy course can apply to a range of first-year college composition courses at various institutions. At Wisconsin, English 101 has been
required only for students scoring in the lowest 10% on the placement
exam, thus constituting the course as in some way basic writing; basic
writers at other universities, however, with different placement procedures
and different student populations might not resemble the basic writers at
UW-Madison. Also, the UW-Madison first-year composition requirement is
being reinstated (or its reach expanded) so the Introduction to Academic
Literacy course will be serving a wider range of students.

My second reason for using the phrase beginning college writers is to
avoid the often debilitating connotations of such terms as remedial, basic,
elementary, and developmental. English teachers should understand the
importance of using language carefully. Rather than helping students adjust to university life, placement in a remedial or basic course might make
adjustment more difficult if students experience it as another confirmation
of their status in school and society. Edward White—who used the term
remedial without apology—found laughable some colleges' attempt to "in-
flat[e] course descriptions and numbers," like the California institution
with a course called "English 1000, Advanced Writing Workshop" (154).
Students certainly cannot be fooled by such double-talk; they know what
it means to be placed in a course that is a prerequisite for first-year composition, or to be required to take a course from which most first-year
students are exempt. But Mike Rose demonstrated eloquently the political
and pedagogical implications of terms like remedial:

> The function of labelling certain material remedial in higher education is
> to keep in place the hard fought for, if historically and conceptually prob-
> lematic and highly fluid, distinction between college and secondary work.
> "Remedial" gains its meaning, then, in a political more than a pedagogical
> universe. ("The Language of Exclusion" 349)

Rose also argued that such terms deny the literacy already attained by
underprepared college students:

> We forget, then, that by most historical—and current—standards, the vast
> majority of a research university's underprepared students would be consid-
> ered competently literate. Though they fail to meet the demands made of
> them in their classes, they fail from a literate base. They are literate people
> straining at the boundaries of their ability. (*Lives* 188)

Thus, it is not so much that we are trying to spare students' feelings;
we are trying to educate ourselves, administrators and teachers, so that we
approach our students with the respect they deserve and offer them the
instruction they truly need to cross those boundaries. When we design a

writing course for beginning college writers, we focus not on where the students have been, but where they are headed. We remember that this is a college writing course, not an eighth-grade grammar class or a unit in paragraph development (cf. Bartholomae 283). Perhaps we will remember our own beginnings: beginning the English major, beginning graduate work, beginning our doctoral dissertation, beginning our career as a full-time faculty member.

Another important term I use is literacy. I define *literacy* as the ability to make meaning with written language in a particular group or community that prizes that ability. Thus, one cannot label most people as either literate or illiterate; many actual and potential literacies exist for any particular person. Teaching first-year college composition means initiating literate persons into a new literacy.

In my definition of literacy, "to make meaning with written language" replaces "to read and write" in order to emphasize the commonality between reading and writing. Recent reading theories insist that readers make meaning rather than passively receive it; as some theorists would have it, readers actually write their own text, constructing meaning out of the words on the page. Writers also make meaning with words; they do not simply translate mental ideas into a written code. Perhaps people sometimes read words, silently or aloud, without making any meaning out of those words: For example, a novice student of French might be able to read a page of Sartre aloud without attending to the meaning, yet certainly such reading would not qualify such a person as literate in French. Rose described a more advanced stage of such illiterate literacy when he talked about reading a philosophical text as a college sophomore:

> because Burtt's discussion is built on a rich intellectual history that I didn't know, I was reading words but not understanding text. I was the human incarnation of language-recognition computer programs: able to record the dictionary meanings of individual words but unable to generate any meaning out of them. (*Lives* 50)

Rose's example makes clear that academic literacy involves more than processing written text: initiating students into academic literacy means helping them connect text and context. How can they learn to write texts that fit the academic context? How can they learn to spot the conventions of academic texts when reading so that they can imitate those conventions in their own writing? When we define our objectives in "basic" composition this way, we realize that they are only basic in the sense of fundamental or foundational. And we realize that our course belongs with introductory psychology, philosophy, sociology, and history.

Because the context or rhetorical situation of student writing matters so much, my definition of literacy emphasizes making meaning with written language in a community that prizes that activity. Becoming literate involves a process of initiation into the ways with words of a particular community. Not recognizing this fact leads to our impatience with students, our attributing their academic illiteracy to low motivation or low intelligence rather than to their not having been successfully initiated into the academic discourse community. Rose recalled struggling with words as a novice writer in senior high and college English: "I was encountering a new language—the language of the academy—and was trying to find my way around in it" (*Lives* 54).

I have already introduced several principles in discussing key terms, and the ensuing discussion demonstrates how thoroughly these principles overlap. I separate them only for the sake of identification and analysis; in the actual teaching of beginning college writing, they are intimately connected. The principles are as follows: (a) If we agree that the previous language experiences of beginning college writers serve as workable starting points for our mutual efforts to improve their facility with academic language, then students and teachers can recognize, celebrate, and build on the literacies they already bring to the course. (b) When students and teachers develop an understanding of how language works in our society, teachers can help students improve their ability to use conventional forms of written English without students feeling that they must devalue or discard their spoken or written idiolects, dialects, or native languages. (c) If we agree that one purpose of introductory college courses is to orient students to the ways of the university, teachers of the beginning writing course can help initiate students into the academic discourse community. (d) Because we continue to value the distinction in our field between process and product, teachers can help students develop a sense of writing as a process, an awareness of their own writing processes, and some strategies for making those processes work better for them in academic and other public settings. (e) If we see learning and writing as essentially (although not exclusively) social, then teachers and students can learn to work collaboratively, to see academic and public discourse as sites for communal activity.

If we agree that the previous language experiences of beginning college writers serve as workable starting points for our mutual efforts to improve their facility with academic language (the first principle), then students and teachers can recognize, celebrate, and build on the literacies they already bring to the course. Many writing teachers have learned that students, especially in beginning writing courses, work well when we help them recognize that they are already highly literate and build on their strengths. As teachers, we can invite our students to take inventory of their literacy abilities and experiences. Shirley Brice Heath in *Ways with Words* and Denny Taylor and Catherine Dorsey-Gaines in *Growing Up Literate* take inventories of the multiple ways people use writing and reading in their daily lives. Such an inventory serves as a valuable early activity in the composition classroom and leads naturally into presentation of the literacy autobiography assignment. Students will not necessarily value the reading and writing they record on such an inventory. One perceptive student, knowing what English teachers typically mean by reading, wrote on one of my questionnaires, "For pleasure I usually read books that you would probably consider trashy." Students are even less likely to see their out-of-school writing as significant. Small-group and whole-class discussion of the inventories can help students and teacher alike unpack the significance of nonacademic literacy events, such as this writing experience reported by one male student: "I got back together with my girlfriend after I wrote her a couple page letter. I don't know if I could have said the things to her face so I had to write them down."

Taking stock of one's literacy and language experiences is an explicit goal of the first major paper in the academic literacy course, the student's literacy autobiography. A literacy autobiography is an account of significant factors and events that have contributed to one's development as a reader and writer. In writing their autobiographies, students are asked to explore the origins of some of their attitudes and theories about reading and writing, as well as their reading and writing practices. They are urged to consider a wide range of information, including education and literacy levels of family members; memories of writing at home and at school; people and institutions important to their literacy development; barriers to that development; and the role of spoken and written language in their family, peer groups, and larger social groups. Students are invited to show how their experiences help illuminate the meaning of literacy. The course does not begin by giving students a definition of literacy; rather, it engages students in the process of defining and understanding literacy from their personal perspective. Students broaden that personal perspective on literacy by reading and sometimes writing about each other's autobiographies. Gradually, students are introduced to the perspectives of various published authorities.

The first semester I taught this course, my 18 students wrote about a wide range of literacy and language experiences. They remembered being read to as small children; going to the public library, usually with their mothers; receiving praise for reading from adults and even winning awards and contests; being in the highest reading group in elementary school; and reading a range of genres, including pop-up picture books, adolescent fiction, mystery and horror novels, and classic literature. They also remembered many different writing experiences although these were clearly fewer in number than the reading experiences: writing on walls, writing a diary, writing stories, writing notes to friends, writing a travel journal, writing letters to the editor, writing letters to relatives, and writing in school. One student clearly understood, as her title put it, "The Importance of Influence" in literacy development; she warmly recalled intimate experiences of reading with her mother, father, and sister, and also teachers who encouraged creativity in writing. Many students who were not motivated to improve their writing and reading as high school students looked back to early childhood experiences with literacy that they could celebrate; coming to college represented a fresh start, a chance to reconnect with those earlier, more playful and positive literacy practices.

As a writing teacher, I especially noticed positive memories of school-based literacy that centered around practices I used in my classroom—for example, students remembered the pleasure and pride of having something they wrote read aloud or published in some way. Here is an example from third grade:

> Mrs. Brown gave us back our papers, and after telling us how she liked them, she asked me to read mine aloud. I did this and was proud of my work, and what made me excited was the intensity with which everyone listened. Everybody reacted just as I had planned with a great laugh at the funny parts and in suspense over what would happen next.

That student did not have other such memories; he wrote:

> Once it was over that great moment just became another school day as I grew out of being creative and imaginative and moved into other things, though I will never forget the day I was among the Dickens and Shakespeares.

Teachers who read such statements are reminded of how important it is to give beginning college writers at least one other great moment, a chance to recover creative and imaginative uses of written language. Celebration of past experiences can inspire the creation of new good memories.

Of course, autobiography does not mean celebration for all student writers any more than it does for published writers. When we give such an assignment, we had better be prepared to help some students build from honest recognition not accompanied by much celebration of the past. Despite my students' determined optimism about their futures, I could not help noticing the persistence of painful memory. One student never forgot people making fun of her misspellings; she attributed her present fear of writing and of reading her writing aloud to those earlier experiences of being teased. One young man began his paper this way: "When I was younger I hated reading with a passion. At times I would throw the worst temper tantrums one could imagine." Less dramatically, he wrote later in the paper that "Writing has always been a struggle for me." That had not yet changed for him, except when it came to writing letters home to family and friends, a new experience for him. And yet, despite the paucity of joyful literacy memories, this student benefited from recognition of the past: "Never before have I evaluated the impact of my past reading and writing experiences."

If we ask students to engage in this kind of reflection on their personal history, we really should be consistent and do it ourselves. In fact, writing their own literacy autobiography has spurred many teachers to assign a literacy autobiography to their students; that happened to me and has happened to several graduate students to whom I assigned the literacy autobiography. Writing such an autobiography can help us recognize our own varied experiences with literacy and the multiple literacies that we bring with us in our present positions as standard bearers for academic literacy. If we share our autobiographies with our students (but not before they have written theirs, lest ours become a constraining model or an intimidating example), they can see that we, too, had our struggles with language and that we, too, sometimes find extracurricular reading and writing more rewarding than the academic versions.

We can also help students value their extracurricular writing and reading by explaining some of the scholarly interest in such activities. Students may not realize that scholars study popular culture; we ourselves may not thoroughly know the research in this area and can call on colleagues for assistance. But drawing on our own field of composition and literacy studies, we can share with students the work of people like Ann Gere, who has written about community-based writing groups, ethnographers like Heath and Taylor who write about literacy events in families and neighborhoods, and specialists in business and technical writing, who study writing and reading on the job. Teachers and students can discuss the contemporary notion that the value attributed to certain texts and certain kinds of textual production is always socially determined, not an absolute. Thus, when we ask them to master academic writing, we do so only because such writing matters in a community which they have joined—if only temporarily—not because academic writing is inherently better than other kinds.[1]

We can extend this first principle to our teaching of writing as a recursive, collaborative process. Just as we recognize the validity of multiple literacies, we recognize the validity of multiple writing processes. Composition teachers can slip into talking about *the* writing process, as though all writers follow the same series of steps. We also forget that just as our students come to us already literate, they also come to us with writing processes that have sometimes been effective. Our students' literacy inven-

---

[1]In a variation of the literacy course, Erin Smith asked students to explore the connections between culture, including popular culture, and literacy, especially academic reading and writing. See chapter 8, coauthored by Smith and Stuart Greene, for a brief description of her syllabus. See also chapter 1 for Katherine Weese's discussion of student writing in a composition course focused on American popular culture.

tories and autobiographies can reveal to us and them a range of writing strategies that they can draw on for academic writing. This principle of building on prior experiences applies to collaborative learning as well. When student writing groups encounter difficulties, one of my colleagues asks them how they have solved similar problems in other groups they have been part of. To borrow Gere's language, the curriculum of collaboration can draw on the extracurriculum of collaboration.

The second principle states that when students and teachers develop an understanding of how language works in our society, teachers can help students improve their ability to use conventional forms of written English without feeling that they must devalue or discard their spoken or written idiolects, dialects, or native languages. This goal, closely related to the goal of recognizing and building on students' prior literacies, depends largely on the teacher's attitude toward students' use and misuse of language. Teachers can help students learn to write Standard American English without shaming them; by examining the way language functions in our society, such teachers give their students room in their lives for their own dialects and languages (see Christensen). Larry Edgerton, an instructor at UW-Madison, approached Standard English in a low-key, commonsensical fashion, encouraging students to see switching to a conventional form of English as tuning the radio to a different band or using a Mastercard to purchase desired products. He saw the various dialects of English not as steps on an evolutionary path but as informed options. Other teachers and researchers are more pessimistic about the possibility for students to be truly bidialectal.

As teachers of beginning college writers, we can engage our students in such reflections on language, in individual conferences, class discussion, or even writing assignments. UW composition instructor Joyce Melville had students create their own handbooks; she asked them to start by learning the rule that led to a mistake, telling them that sometimes their " 'mistakes' will show a wonderful ingenuity, or they may not be 'mistakes' at all when you use them with friends or family members who say things the same way" ("Profiles"). Melville demonstrated that even editing can be taught as a process in a collaborative way.

As Min-Zhan Lu pointed out, English Departments are guilty of a double standard when it comes to multicultural literacy:

> Why is it that in spite of our developing ability to acknowledge the political need and right of "real" writers to experiment with "style," we continue to cling to the belief that such a need and right does not belong to "student writers"? (446)

Lu helped her students see that so-called errors in student writing can be seen as deviations from the rules of Standard American English—or as "efforts to negotiate and modify" academic discourse codes (448). Even though Lu knew that most of her students would choose to reproduce the official style, they would at least do so actively, aware that writers can struggle against that official style. Teachers with such attitudes toward language will not want a composition course that simply indoctrinates students into academic literacy. We are not asking for naive romanticism but pragmatic, informed decisions about language use.

Language issues arise in students' literacy autobiographies and in the published autobiographies read in the course. Students coming from bilingual (or even trilingual) households inevitably mention language, although not necessarily as an issue. One Laotian student wrote matter-of-factly, with humor at times, about English having been "my foreign language." His mother, fluent in French and well-educated (as was his father, a political prisoner), spoke broken English. Although this student wrote well and had a good experience in high school senior English, he continued to describe his use of English as a struggle. Playing on the title of Richard Rodriguez' autobiography, *Hunger of Memory*, this student concluded his paper this way: "If English is always going to be this difficult, I am full and not hungry for any more knowledge of it!" Here is a good example of what can happen in the academic literacy course as students use the published texts within their own writing. This student, at least, was able to implicitly challenge Rodriguez, making his own personal comment on the language issues Rodriguez addresses.

The published literacy autobiographies that have been used in the course usually show people becoming successful in mainstream society by using Standard American English, at least in their writing. But we can look with our students at how well such writers have been able to preserve their own cultural and linguistic heritage, considering the losses as well as the gains that accompany any degree of language assimilation. To enable more students—even those from mainstream families who might not at first glance seem to be bothered by questions of language diversity—to empathize with these issues, we can broaden such discussions beyond the usual focus on African-American and immigrant groups. Recently a student in my second-semester composition course wrote about code-switching among the gay and lesbian community: how people use terms in different ways depending on the group they are with. Her analysis drew heavily on studies of gender differences in language. Another student at Wisconsin wrote that he grew up speaking "barn talk" rather than the language needed to succeed in the business world. I have heard professors talk about reverting to family ways with language on trips home to a rural area or a different region. If we know our students—and the literacy autobiography offers much relevant knowledge—we can introduce sociolinguistics in any beginning writing course. A sociolinguistic perspective can help us improve our teaching of editing, and we can encourage our students to learn from each other that language differences can be a source of strength, not distress. Without this informed multicultural perspective, we are liable to discard collaboration when it comes to style and editing and revert to teacher-centered, product-oriented approaches.

If we agree, as the third principle asks us to, that one purpose of introductory college courses is to orient students to the ways of the university, teachers of the beginning writing course can help initiate students into the academic discourse community. In order for this goal to remain consistent with the first two, we need to recognize any and all discourse communities to which students aspire. Our students need to be intitiated into the academic club without being made to feel that it is the only or the best club in town. In fact, we know that many of our students are only seeking guest membership in the academic community; after 4 or more years, they will move into other communities. Perhaps we can convince them that the process of becoming fluent in the academic community's discourse can be adapted in the future as they move into other communities with different conventions. Perhaps they will convince us that their aspirations deserve equal recognition and in some cases might even override our focus on academia. One of my students, an English major in an intermediate writing course, was trying to reconcile his academic ambitions with his evangelical Christian background; he wanted to retain membership in both communities and find ways for their discourses to be mutually illuminating. But he recognized the inevitable strains. June Jordan related a dramatic narrative of helping her African-American students discover that they wanted to learn to read and write the Black English Vernacular (BEV) they spoke fluently. The literacy that they developed in BEV was not prized by the academic community or the mainstream media; letters they wrote when a classmate's unarmed brother was killed by police officers were not printed by *Newsday* or *The Village Voice*. In fact, some African Americans do not value BEV; Jordan's students at first reacted negatively to Alice Walker's use of it in *The Color Purple* (364). But under Jordan's guidance, their new-found literacy in BEV "mean more" to them than the literacy they had been schooled to attain in Standard American English.

More often, of course, our students want us to help them attain fluency in mainstream, academic literacy. They have every right to this goal and to our best-informed efforts on their behalf. Perhaps we can at least gently suggest that they might someday have other goals. If we read with them Rodriguez' account of his successful but costly journey into mainstream English and the academic community, we can remind them that years after publication of *Hunger of Memory*, he wrote of a different journey in *Days of Obligation: An Argument with My Mexican Father*, a search for his Mexican heritage. Bilingual students with a literary bent might enjoy Carlos Fuentes' essay, "How I Started to Write." Fuentes attained fluency in English at an early age, yet he still had to discover a discourse community that he wanted to join and that would give him identity:

> My passage from English to Spanish determined the concrete expression of what, before, in Washington, had been the revelation of an identity. I wanted to write and I wanted to write in order to show myself that my identity and my country were real. . . . I learned that I must in fact write in Spanish. (93)

The larger point Fuentes makes is that cultures retain their identity "in contact, in contrast, in breakthrough" (93). Although our major task is to help our students achieve a more secure identity in English academic literacy, we can also encourage contacts between different literacies. In that way, our emphasis on academic literacy need not undermine our belief in multicultural literacy.

We will not always know about our students' struggles with old and new identities, and many of our younger students will not even perceive the struggle yet—and I am not sure it is our place to force this maturing process. But we can remind ourselves of the psychic and social costs that membership in new discourse communities may exact.

Jordan's account of her unusual semester further complicates the question of which literacy we want our students to master. As she taught students to read and interpret contemporary poetry, she was initiating them into the academic discourse community. Yet she was also initiating them into the literate tradition of African-American writers, until recently not often recognized by the academy. And what kind of literacy were the students demonstrating when they wrote about that poetry in BEV?

Our situations in beginning writing courses may seldom be as radically decentering as Jordan's. But in any college classroom, we can find multiple literacies and aspirations to various literacies. Like Jordan, we can help students recognize the literacy choices available to them and the personal and social consequences of those choices. No literacy exists in a vacuum or has transcendence, but some literacies have more social and political power than others. Unless we continually remind ourselves and our students that what we do in college writing courses is a social and political activity with real consequences for our lives, even our most carefully theorized approaches to academic literacy and cultural studies may run aground. We can proceed confidently only by not being overly confident that we have any right to do what we are doing. We should in various ways seek our students' permission to initiate them into academic discourse, lest our initiation become indoctrination.

Having recognized the discourse communities that students come from, including a school discourse community whose ways they certainly negotiated well enough to earn admission to college, we can set about helping them enter this new community and learn its language conventions. As Rose pointed out, that means more than showing them how to write a term paper with documentation and bibliography or a critical book review; obviously, in one or two semesters, no writing teacher can teach and no composition student can learn all the academic genres and conventions. Rather, Rose emphasized that students need to learn the intellectual strategies of the university: summarizing, classifying, comparing, and analyzing are four he identified (*Lives* 138). He also noted ways of thinking that may be foreign to students: questioning all ideas and beliefs, for example, and using knowledge creatively (189–191).

In the Forms of Academic Literacy course, instructors guide students through a sequence of informal and formal assignments that require the very intellectual strategies Rose suggested. For example, my students summarized the main points Rodriguez made in one chapter of his autobiography. I also asked them to consider their own experiences in light of Rodriguez'; in the process, they analyzed his and their experiences and began comparing the two. Later, after summarizing points made by E. D. Hirsch and Bartholomae, they were asked to compare these writers' views on certain issues. Their second major assignment, after the literacy autobiography, required them to identify an issue related to literacy that had come up in the course and to write about that issue, synthesizing different points of view but also making their own contribution to the conversation. This important task of synthesizing is not mentioned by Rose but pulls together the four strategies he identified as crucial to academic writing.

As students move from the personal writing of a literacy autobiography to the academic synthesis paper on a literacy issue, we can show them strategies that work in academic discourse. When the reading material for the course includes such pieces as Bartholomae's "Inventing the University" and Rose's *Lives on the Boundary*, we can derive strategies from Bartholomae's notion of commonplaces (275–76) and Rose's discussion of the conventions and belief systems of the university. For my students, I adopted the machine suggested by one of Bartholomae's own teachers (cited by Rose 189); I asked them to fill in the blanks of statements like these:

Although many people think literacy is _____, a closer examination shows that it is _____.

Although many people emphasize the role of _____ in literacy, Rodriguez [or Hirsch or Bartholomae or Rose] emphasizes _____.

Rodriguez [or Hirsch or Bartholomae or Rose] rightly states _____ [something about literacy]; however, it is also true that _____.

[or, he neglects the role of _____. or, he doesn't sufficiently emphasize _____.]

Another prompt drew on Bartholomae's notion of commonplaces, which we had discussed in class:

> What are the commonplaces about literacy that you have heard or read? List them. Then decide in which discourse communities each commonplace might be valued and why. Find ways to challenge each commonplace; play the devil's advocate. For example, question the commonplace that "reading a lot of good books is the key to advanced literacy," or the one that "teachers who encourage students to read and write are the key to advanced literacy."

My students tended to confirm rather than question the commonplaces, but some were willing to argue with the published experts they read, especially Rodriguez. One student critiqued Hirsch's notion of cultural literacy by comparing it to the TV game show *Jeopardy.* But we cannot force students to see the world as we do; after all, how many of us challenged the commonplaces of our profession before the challenges themselves became commonplace? What we can teach them, as Bartholomae and Rose helped us see, are the reasons that academic scholars challenge commonly held beliefs, as well as the commonplaces that academic readers themselves recognize and use.

In writing about Rodriguez, my students moved into academic discourse without losing their own perspectives. One student grasped well Rodriguez' struggles:

> For the most part, Rodriguez expresses the complications involved in being a literate Mexican-American. . . . As he becomes more educated and literate, his private and public identity begin to clash. . . . The picture of Richard Rodriguez on the cover of the book shows a man with a private, bitter expression on his face. This expression fits the tone of the whole autobiography.

This student goes beyond summary to analysis, recognizing how a book's cover can be read in conjunction with the text; what I could have helped her recognize is that the book is a commercial product, not always consistent with the writer's intentions. I have pointed students to the book reviews excerpted by Rodriguez' publishers, suggesting that the publisher thereby frames Rodriguez' arguments in ways Rodriguez might not entirely endorse. Students can talk about the different audiences implied in pieces by Rodriguez, Bartholomae, and Hirsch, for example. In teaching students about academic discourse, then, we do not have to lose sight of the larger goal of analyzing discourse itself. We simultaneously accept and resist the service nature of first-year composition.

Not that designing and teaching a service course should be seen as an easy or humble occupation; such curricular design involves us in important academic inquiry. Discussions about writing with other faculty can help us and our students confirm, or modify, our belief in the central value of synthesis in the university curriculum. As we develop beginning writing courses that initiate students into academic literacy, we would be well advised to attend to writing-across-the-curriculum efforts on our campuses. Do we want to launch students into an approach to writing that is not used in other courses? Do we want other faculty (including the literature faculty in our own department) to assume that academic literacy is entirely our charge? This university-wide perspective informs one option for the final writing assignment in the Forms of Academic Literacy course. Students can study what it means to read and write in a specific academic field. Their interview with an expert in that field, usually a professor, provides material for their paper, but we also hope the interview will further the campus awareness of writing as a primary means of inquiry and of writing instruction as an interdisciplinary responsibility.

The fourth goal states that because we continue to value the distinction in our field between process and product, teachers can help students develop a sense of writing as a process, an awareness of their own writing processes, and some strategies for making those processes work better for them in academic and other public settings. A process approach to writing instruction can be highly individualistic and directed toward expressive rather than transactional writing. Students in such an individualistic, expressive classroom are urged to see writing as a recursive process of generating, organizing, drafting, revising, and editing. They are often asked to identify their already existing writing processes. Where these processes originate and what ends they serve, beyond the students' individual purposes as self-determining writers, are questions not always raised. Academic writing might be introduced—often only implicitly, and usually without examination of its purposes and conventions—as one purpose toward which a writing process can be directed. Students might be asked to write an argumentative essay, a literary analysis, or a research paper and, their teachers hope, they will write such pieces more effectively because they have developed a more efficient and self-conscious writing process. In other words, process can become a collection of strategies, thereby turning the writing course into a skills course, a prerequisite for the real intellectual work of content courses.

Another approach is to emphasize the desired products of academic writing; this product-oriented approach views process as merely the scaffolding that will eventually be taken down once the product is completed.

In this case, we might find ourselves working with students to achieve the type of academic essay assigned, congratulating them and ourselves when final portfolios contain "reasonable facsimiles thereof." Eliminating first-year writing as a separate course in favor of writing-intensive general education courses could lead to this product emphasis. In fact, even the most process-based courses often result in a similar emphasis on product because product is what receives the fullest and final evaluation.

Instead, we can allow notions of process and academic literacy to illuminate each other. We can remind ourselves and our students that academic discourses—the plural form matters here—involve many different processes and result in many different products. When we ask students to write an autobiographical essay, a summary, a critique, or a synthesis, we must ask them to consider the intellectual processes involved in writing and reading such texts. To realize that writing a critique requires a different process of reading and responding to a text than writing a summary—and to understand why certain rhetorical situations call for one and not the other—are more important achievements, perhaps, than producing a summary or critique that approximates professional versions of such texts. And students should see that different kinds of summaries and critiques are written, depending on the discipline, the situation, the audience, and the writer. These issues, which arise often in the Forms of Academic Literacy course, have as much to do with the writing process as freewriting, outlining, or revising. In fact, such academic issues provide a clear motivation for students to engage in recursive writing processes.

With literacy and literacy education serving as central issues in the Forms of Academic Literacy course, students can be prompted to reflect on the appropriate balance between process and product (or content) in education. If they read the preface to Hirsch's *Cultural Literacy*, for example, they will encounter his argument that the developmental theories of Rousseau and Dewey have strongly influenced modern American education, to its detriment. Hirsch argued that Dewey saw only half the truth; instead, Hirsch insisted, "Only by piling up specific, communally shared information can children learn to participate in complex cooperative activities with other members of their community" (xv). As students read Rodriguez' autobiography or Rose's autobiographical book on literacy education, they sometimes see these authors as basically in agreement with Hirsch about the importance of shared information but through discussion and writing, some of them realize that Hirsch himself only offers a partial answer. One of my students, after summarizing Hirsch's argument, went on to show how Bartholomae, Rodriguez, and Rose went "one step further," emphasizing that students need to learn how to comprehend and use the shared information. For a more provocative critique of process teaching, students could be shown Will's article alluded to earlier, in which he snidely summarized the profession's rejection of transmission models of learning composition and suggested that emphasizing process over content has been an academic fad resulting in less, not more, literacy. Will's critique must surely be persuasive to those outside the classroom; it would be interesting to see how persuasive our students would find his argument after a semester in a process-based, collaborative writing classroom that engages students with some very specific content, the public conversation about literacy.

If we see learning and writing as essentially (although not exclusively) social, the final principle states, then teachers and students should learn to work collaboratively to see academic and public discourse as sites for communal activity. Collaboration, like process, can be similarly disconnected from academic literacy; in fact, teachers and students sometimes see collaboration as a perhaps desirable but ultimately dispensable part of a writing process. Process and collaboration can be reduced to short-term techniques necessary for novice writers only. For example, we can continue to use peer response groups as a tried and sometimes true method that will help our students learn their academic literacy lessons more effectively than lectures and individual exercises. We suggest that once students master these lessons, they will be able to write alone, as expert writers do. We are also tempted to devalue collaboration by emphasizing academic literacy; after all, we reason, students need our expert knowledge of academic forms of writing. Facing an overwhelming array of instructional goals, we will be tempted to tell our students about academic conventions and writing processes. Certainly we need not abdicate the valuable role of mentor that Rose so eloquently described and advocated (*Lives* 39–65, 235–36). But lecturing about process will have less impact than inviting students to participate in process. In the same way, because language and literacy are social processes, lecturing about these complex human activities will have less impact than inviting students to engage in these activities together. Thus the importance of collaboration.

It is vital, therefore, that we not rest the case for collaboration on effective methodology alone. No one who has used collaborative peer groups in writing classrooms talks much about their efficiency; such groups can be difficult to set up, manage, maintain, and evaluate. Students themselves often complain about group work, at least on course evaluations, and want the instructor to show them how to do things. But this messy process pervades the academic community. Think about faculty committee meetings, conferences, and peer review of proposals and articles. The academic community is made up of people who stubbornly insist on their rights to be heard and to be involved in professional decision making. How can we claim to be initiating students into academic discourse—inviting them to act like members of such a community—if they remain dependent on our explicit instruction and evaluation? In courses with the ultimate goal of having students participate in some version of academic literacy, collaborative strategies might enable students to realize inductively the interactive nature of academic conversation.

The importance of collaborative learning is also reinforced by social constructionist views of knowledge; John Trimbur reviewed these developments in higher education and composition theory and pedagogy ("Collaborative Learning"). Instructors at UW-Madison have been influenced by Martin Nystrand's social interactive view of writing; Nystrand argued that writers and readers interact by "collaborat[ing] in their complementary and reciprocal tasks of composing and comprehending" (40). Face-to-face collaboration in writing groups can help students internalize the notion that even writers and readers who never meet collaborate in "an exchange of meaning or a transformation of shared knowledge" (Nystrand 40). Composition instructors who subscribe to some version of these social views of knowledge and writing will want the ways of learning in their classrooms to enact those views; as Trimbur summarized Henry Giroux and Kenneth Bruffee, "the form of learning is as much the content of a course as the subject matter is" ("Collaborative Learning" 94). Although Giroux and Bruffee are talking about the implicit curriculum constituted by our pedagogical values and practices, our rationale for employing collaborative learning can also become an explicit part of the course content, particulary in a course centered around literacy issues. In the UW-Madison course, students often begin the semester reading Frank Smith's essay, "The Myths of Writing"; one of those myths is that writing is a solitary activity. Smith explained that writing "often requires other people to stimulate discussion, to provide spellings, to listen to choice phrases, and even just for companionship" (796). After reading Smith's essay, students are asked to think about the extent to which their experience supports what Smith said; then, based on their experience and Smith's essay, they write their own essay suggesting some useful alternatives to the way writing is taught. As students write their literacy autobiographies and work through the educational theories of Hirsch, Bartholomae, Rose, and others, they are more likely to see the otherwise invisible curriculum of a collaborative classroom.

Without peer collaboration, initiating students into the academic community can become the instructor's collaboration with the institution, which for some students might amount to collaborating with the enemy. After all, the university as an institution often marginalizes our courses and our students as basic or remedial; also, the university, like all schooling, tends to reproduce the unequal social relations and unjust distribution of power and resources of the larger society. As Trimbur and others noted, collaborative learning grew out of the antiauthoritarian and countercultural mood of the 1960s. But the pragmatic use of collaborative learning to initiate students into academic discourse communities does not seem

very revolutionary. That is precisely the critique leveled at social constructionist advocates of collaborative learning by some left-wing composition
theorists. Trimbur summarized their criticism: "Without a critique of the
dominant power relations that organize the production of knowledge . .
. the social constructionist rationale for collaborative learning may, unwit-
tingly or not, accommodate its practices to the authority of knowledge it
believes it is demystifying" ("Consensus and Difference" 603).

These contradictions and questions have been recognized by those involved in the Forms of Academic Literacy course at the University of Wisconsin-Madison. The academic literacy curriculum for first-year writing was
incorporated into a well-established tradition of collaborative writing classrooms. Professors Nick Doane, Martin Nystrand, Joyce Melville, and Deborah Brandt, along with many graduate teaching assistants, encouraged,
theorized, and studied the writing studio approach. Students were asked
to bring new or revised drafts to most class meetings and to share these
drafts in small groups. At least in its pure manifestations, the writing studio
approach did not involve a content-based syllabus. Students determined
their own writing topics with considerable freedom. The move to a more
focused emphasis on academic literacy did not come all at once. Some
instructors, exercising their pedagogical freedom, introduced specifically
academic assignments, sometimes content-based, into their sections of English 101. Melville began using Bartholomae and Petrosky's seminar on
adolescent change, adapting their six-credit course to the UW three-credit
course. And when Greene became director of first-year composition, he
initiated the Forms of Academic Literacy course.

But neither Melville nor Greene abandoned the collaborative approach
of the writing studio. Instead, along with other instructors, they broadened
the scope of collaborative activities in order to meet the objectives of the new
syllabi. Working with Smith and her students, Greene studied student
collaboration, especially the role of conflict and negotiation that went on in
collaborative planning (see chapter 8, this volume). Greene and Smith took
seriously the project enunciated by Trimbur when he asked composition
researchers to "frame questions that treat collaborative learning not as a
pedagogical technique to be compared to other techniques but as a
'naturalistic setting' that allows researchers to examine language development through social interaction" ("Collaborative Learning" 106). Recognizing the connection between collaborative learning and academic literacy is
only a starting point. We need more studies of what actually goes on in
student writing groups and what effects such collaboration has on the
development of academic literacy. In a course like Forms of Academic
Literacy, we can ask how the use of published texts by scholars and experts
affects writing group talk. Does the imposition of literacy as subject matter
for student writers limit the liberating potential of peer collaboration?

Greene and Brandt discussed their different perspectives on these questions with graduate students teaching the first-year course. Making classroom-based research an ongoing part of the UW-Madison writing program helps keep these crucial questions alive for instructors in institutional programs that otherwise might coopt the radical potential of a collaborative pedagogy.

This is not the place to review the wealth of professional literature about incorporating process and collaboration in beginning writing classes. What I want to emphasize here is that these principles must not be jettisoned or even subordinated to other goals, such as initiating students into academic discourse or teaching students to critique language and literacy. The five principles undergirding the Forms of Academic Literacy course enable one another. Within a social view of writing, teaching writing as a collaborative process, teaching academic literacy, and teaching diversity are compatible and mutually reinforcing. Rose described his ideal of education as "one culture embracing another" (*Lives* 225). The culture of composition teachers, individual students, and the academy can embrace each other through a syllabus that moves beyond an academic fraternity view of initiation by preserving and transforming the tension between students' languages and academic languages. Students' and teachers' diverse cultures can embrace each other, especially in a collaborative classroom where creation of community is a goal. And students' cultures can embrace other cultures, including cultures that may not be represented by people in the classroom, through interaction with texts written by diverse authors. But Trimbur is right to remind us that these goals are utopian and cannot be realized by simply assuming that collaborative learning will lead to consensus, or that it should:

> To develop a critical version of collaborative learning, we will need to distinguish between consensus as an acculturative practice that reproduces business as usual and consensus as an oppositional one that challenges the prevailing conditions of production. ("Consensus and Difference" 612)

The critical version of collaborative learning, Trimbur argued, must recognize the role of dissensus or difference, seeing consensus "not as an agreement that reconciles differences through an ideal conversation but rather as the desire of humans to live and work together with differences" ("Consensus and Difference" 615). The intention of the academic literacy syllabus is to problematize the very notions of literacy and academic literacy so that students can begin to see the sometimes irreconcilable differences in the views of published writers and in the social, cultural, and institutional ideologies that have shaped the lives of experts and students. We must guard against any temptation to employ collaborative learning in a way that pushes students toward uncritical—or even grudging—acceptance of our particular beliefs, even our beliefs in the social construction of knowledge or the value of multicultural literacy. We can insist that our classrooms be sites of participatory learning and mutual respect. But our students may prefer Hirsch's educational program to Rose's or Jordan's; they may not see our society as in need of radical critique or as anything less than a land of academic equal opportunity.

Patricia Bizzell wrote, "Teaching academic literacy becomes a process of constructing academic literacy, creating it anew in each class through the interaction of the professor's and the students' cultural resources" (150). Bizzell called for the development of "a truly collaborative pedagogy of academic literacy"—difficult, she admitted, due to the unequal social power of different professors and of different students within their respective groups (150). Students and professors involved in a course like the one profiled in this book will recognize the difficulties Bizzell acknowledged. Some of them will, we hope, recognize that whatever was done to them in the past in the name of academic or cultural literacy need not bar them from acting through such literacies on their own and their communities' behalf. Writing instructors and their students can bring their experiences into the literacy conversation; as skillful readers and writers, they can challenge the assumptions of that conversation and ask its participants to take account of our society's diverse literacies. That kind of reading and writing is not basic—but it is essential, radical, and attainable, in the very first writing course any university student takes.

WORKS CITED

Bartholomae, David. "Inventing the University." *Perspectives on Literacy,* Ed. Eugene R. Kintgen, Barry M. Kroll, and Mike Rose. Carbondale: Southern Illinois UP, 1988. 273–285.

Bartholomae, David, and Anthony Petrosky. *Facts, Artifacts, and Counterfacts: Theory and Method for a Reading and Writing Course.* Upper Montclair, NJ: Boynton–Cook, 1986.

Bizzell, Patricia. "Arguing about Literacy." *College English* 50 (1988): 141–153.

Christensen, Linda M. "Teaching Standard English: Whose Standard?" *English Journal* Vol. 79, No. 2 (Feb. 1990): 36–40.

Edgerton, Larry. Personal Interview. 3 July 1990.

Fuentes, Carlos. "How I Started to Write." Simonson and Walker 83–111.

Gere, Ann. "Kitchen Tables and Rented Rooms: The Extracurriculum of Composition." *College Composition and Communication* 45 (Feb. 1994): 75–92.

Graff, Gerald. "Other Voices, Other Rooms: Organizing and Teaching the Humanities Conflict." *New Literary History* 21 (1990): 817–839.

Heath, Shirley Brice. *Ways with Words.* New York: Cambridge UP, 1983.

Hirsch, E. D., Jr. *Cultural Literacy: What Every American Needs to Know.* Boston: Houghton Mifflin, 1987.

Jordan, June. "Nobody Mean More to Me than You and the Future Life of Willie Jordan." *Harvard Educational Review* 58 (1988): 363–374.

Lu, Min-Zhan. "Professing Multiculturalism: The Politics of Style in the Contact Zone." *College Composition and Communication* 45 (1994): 442–458.

Melville, Joyce. Personal Interview. 6 July 1990.

Melville, Joyce. "Profiles in Language Diversity: The Case for Grammar Instruction in English 101." *English 101: An Introduction to Academic Literacy.* Department of English, University of Wisconsin. Madison, 1994(?). n.pag.

Nystrand, Martin. *The Structure of Written Communication: Studies in Reciprocity Between Writers and Readers.* Orlando, FL: Academic Press, 1986.

Rodriguez, Richard. *Days of Obligation: An Argument with my Mexican Father.* New York: Viking, 1992.

———. *Hunger of Memory: The Education of Richard Rodriguez.* New York: Bantam, 1983.

Rose, Mike. "The Language of Exclusion: Writing Instruction at the University." *College English* 47 (1985): 341–359.

———. *Lives on the Boundary: A Moving Account of the Struggles and Achievements of America's Educationally Unprepared.* New York: Penguin, 1989.

Simonson, Rick, and Scott Walker, eds. *The Graywolf Annual Five: Multi-Cultural Literacy.* Saint Paul, MN: Graywolf Press, 1988.

Smith, Frank. "Myths of Writing." *Language Arts* 58 (1981): 792–798.

Taylor, Denny. *Family Literacy: Young Children Learning to Read and Write.* Portsmouth, NH: Heinemann, 1983.

Taylor, Denny, and Catherine Dorsey-Gaines. *Growing Up Literate: Learning from Inner-City Families.* Portsmouth, NH: Heinemann, 1988.

Trimbur, John. "Collaborative Learning and Teaching Writing." *Perspectives on Research and Scholarship in Composition.* Ed. Ben W. McClelland and Timothy R. Donovan. New York: MLA, 1985. 87–109.

———. "Consensus and Difference in Collaborative Learning." *College English* 51 (1989): 602–615.

White, Edward M. *Developing Successful College Writing Programs.* San Francisco: Jossey-Bass, 1989.

Will, George. "Education's subtraction from literacy." *Indianapolis Star* 2 July 1995: D2.

Chapter 3

"Only Connect": Sequencing Assignments in the Beginning Writing Classroom

Katherine L. Weese
Hampden-Sydney College

In the previous chapter, Stephen Fox describes how the literacy course evolved as part of the UW-Madison first-year writing curriculum and explores the value of such a course for beginning writers. Linking the course materials to theories of a collaborative pedagogy, he argues that the course provides a way for students to use their own experiences to create knowledge in the classroom and he explores the decentralized role that teachers of the course adopt. But teachers do play a central role in mapping out the course's broad outlines and creating the assignments that will structure the course. In this capacity, they can enhance the course's goal of encouraging students to generate much of the content of the course. This chapter sets forth the details of the Wisconsin course to show how its overall structure reinforces the goal of helping students write with a sense of their own authority.

Beginning writers' educational experience is often at heart a fragmented one, one that does not provide students with an underlying narrative or web of connections that will help them make sense of the role education plays in their lives. The design of a beginning writing course, then, ideally should provide a kind of narrative structure for the students that will encourage them to see their educations in a cohesive way. Any set of course materials will serve these ends more effectively if instructors incorporate them within a well-planned and narrativized course structure. This may seem self-evident, but I want to avoid the idea of sequence as the all-too-standard writing curriculum where students progress from easy tasks to difficult ones, from producing narrative, to descriptive, to persuasive writing, a kind of course design that actually reinforces fragmentation by considering each mode as separate unto itself. Or, as John Schilb pointed out, first-year composition is often characterized by "random controversies routinely unrolled" (179), a model that does not immerse students deeply enough in any one issue that they can begin to see how a controversy (in this case, literacy) can be approached in a variety of ways or understood from different perspectives, or to see how assignments link to one another; he stated that, "when writing courses concentrate ultimately on mechanical training, then the texts and topics ushered into them as content inevitably seem artificial" (178). This nonnarrative approach to teaching (what I have heard some people call a buckshot approach) makes assignments seem like individual fragments, none of which has anything to do with other work in the course. In contrast, the UW-Madison literacy course focuses not on mechanical training, but on theorizing a well-integrated curriculum that will involve students deeply in issues of interest to them so that they can truly contribute their voices as authors to the ongoing conversation about literacy.

To narrativize 101 is to develop a series of assignments (reading and writing, formal and informal) in such a way that a new assignment builds on knowledge gained from a previous assignment and also expands that knowledge, challenging the student to grow further as a reader and writer. The concept of narrative is useful because it incorporates several structural principles that will allow instructors to develop a coherent course. First, narrative depends on the unfolding of events over time. The idea of sequence becomes important, as it should in a composition course design. Second, narrative develops over time not only by pressing forward, but also by looping back: in other words, it repeats. Peter Brooks wrote in *Reading for the Plot*, for example, that narrative:

> must ever present itself as a repetition of events that have already happened
> . . . in order to create plot, that is, to show us a significant interconnection
> of events. An event gains meaning by its repetition, which is both the recall
> of an earlier moment and a variation of it. (99–100)

Coles used similar language when he described the sequence of assignments that make up the Pittsburgh Adolescent Growth and Development course: "the sequence is not a one-way progress through levels of discourse. The assignments are, rather, persistently recursive, looping back to reengage previous reading or discussion, reviewing experience written about earlier in light of fresh theorizing" (Coles 169). Brooks' description of repetition in narrative and the Pittsburgh course design both introduce a third key idea, interconnection. The structure of repetition with variation becomes valuable in a course design insofar as it allows students to see interconnections among assignments.

An integrated approach to a course design seems especially urgent in beginning writing courses because of the typical make-up of such a class. Our country's education system has often poorly served our students, who frequently come from different ethnic backgrounds and whose experience with English may often derive from what Mike Rose called an "atomistic" model of learning (*Lives on the Boundary* 210).[1] This model "quarantine[s]" students who are "diagnosed" deficient in writing skills from other students and from the more integrated types of study in which proficient students can engage; thus it "has been conceptually and . . . administratively segmented from the rich theoretical investigation that characterizes other humanistic study" (*Lives* 210–211). That is to say, remedial instruction, or even the typical high school instruction from which many of these students come, breaks language into its smallest, atomistic elements and promotes the mastery of grammar at the expense of "the vibrancy and purpose, the power and style, the meaning of language that swirls around [them]" (*Lives* 212). It strips away context, and in so doing promotes an inherently fragmented and grossly inadequate way of conceiving language.

The nature of the first-year experience at the University of Wisconsin-Madison and most other large universities surely must be a fragmented one as well. For instance, Rose described a freshman taking notes in lecture:

> People are taking notes and you are taking notes. You are taking notes on a lecture you don't understand. You get a phrase, a sentence, then the next loses you. It's as though you're hearing a conversation in a crowd or from another room—out of phase, muted. (*Lives* 168)

Because the majority of courses the first-year students take at such a large institution as UW are lectures like the one just described, beginning writing students face, on a regular basis, this kind of fragmented understanding of the material they are supposed to learn. They travel from class to class, the structure of the day itself broken into discrete units by the ring of the bell that signals the end of the one unit and the beginning of the next; because students are most often generalists at this stage, registered for introductory lectures in a variety of fields, they likely have little opportunity to grasp fully what is taking place in their various lectures and less still to connect those discrete units to one another, to explore the ways in which knowledge from one course might overlap with or apply to other courses.

---

[1]As Fox pointed out, however, in chapter 2, this volume, many of the students come from White, middle-class backgrounds and many, having done well in English, are surprised to find themselves enrolled in the course. Nonetheless, many have still been taught that the study of English is the study of grammar.

Finally, many of the students are not only new to college themselves but new to the idea of college because many are the first in their families to go to college at all, especially if they are from minority and immigrant backgrounds. As a result, they may experience another kind of fragmentation in that they, like Richard Rodriguez (see *Hunger of Memory*), may feel cut off from their families and their past. There are no role models at home for their new academic pursuits. Rodriguez described the consequences of this break with the past and family throughout *Hunger of Memory*; several of my Mexican-American and Puerto Rican students deeply identify with his views and corroborate his observations about the distance education creates between himself and his family members. Rodriguez commented also on the gap between two radically different settings when he described how the working-class child seeking the education his family never had finds himself

> moving between different environments, his home and school, which are at cultural extremes, opposed. . . . From his mother and father, the boy learns to trust spontaneity and nonrational ways of knowing. *Then*, at school, there is mental calm. Teachers emphasize the value of a reflectiveness that opens a space between thinking and immediate action. . . . Unlike many middle-class children, he goes home and sees his parents in a way of life not only different but starkly opposed to that of the classroom. (46–47)

Drawing on Richard Hoggart's *The Uses of Literacy*, Rodriguez pointed out in the above passage that a feeling of dissociation or fragmentation results when the student moves between an unorganized house where there is no quiet place to study and a rigidly ordered academic setting. Rose's *Lives on the Boundary*, too, is suffused everywhere with a sense of the radical disjunction between students' (and Rose's own) home or community and the academic community.[2]

Precisely because most beginning college writers likely experience one or more of these forms of fragmentation, beginning writing instructors need to provide in their writing courses (which may well be the one course where the students have sustained contact with each other and with an instructor in a small group setting) a kind of structure that will encourage the connections denied by the very nature of the students' encounters with the university. "Only connect," E.M. Forster commanded in the epigraph to *Howards End*, a novel I read as a high school senior and whose

---

[2]See especially *Lives* 114–115. Many students, however, would like to be able to bridge that gap, and many of them object to Rodriguez's rigid insistence on the distance between the two. One of my own students, for instance, wrote in an essay that "family is a source of education, not a hindrance to it." Despite the widely differing physical environments and psychological atmospheres, there are likely numerous ways to help students negotiate the rift.

emphasis on the concept of connecting helped me perceive links among all my classes. In his novel, Forster further drew on the philosophy embodied by his epigraph "only connect" when he described characters in terms of their ability to "see [life] whole" (161). By seeing a writing course thus, we can find infinite ways to connect. When I see the course whole, for example, I see a series of concentric circles, a map of sorts for the course (see Fig. 3.1). As instructors, we often use visual diagrams to represent writing, to "draw" students' papers, and to encourage students to see their work and thereby aid them in developing cohesive essays. If we apply our advice on writing to our own process of planning a semester, we can reap the same benefits: We can envision the course in such a way that we see its plan from beginning to end.

I describe later in this chapter how this diagram maps out the sequence of assignments within the Forms of Academic Literacy course. The major assignments for this course are reproduced in Appendix A; several shorter writing assignments, designed to help students prepare for the longer papers, are reproduced in Appendix B. However, the same general principles can inform virtually any other set of course materials. Coles advocated, for example, that "a semester-long sequence of assignments on a topic of primary interest to [the students] offers an approximation of the experience of sustained immersion in inquiry which gives [professionals'] rewriting its meaning and its context" (Coles 168). The map, then, is offered as a general model that any instructor could adapt to his or her course materials.

LITERACY AUTOBIOGRAPHIES

In the diagram, I begin with extratextual analysis as the innermost circle, the circle around which all other levels of the course revolve. This unit of the course consists of the students' work on their literacy autobiographies, an assignment in which they draw on lived experience outside of what they read in any other authors' texts, or where they draw on the text of their lives. As Kutz, Groden, and Zamel pointed out in *The Discovery of Competence,* narrative is often an undervalued form of writing within the composition classroom, where "it has most often been seen as demanding a less developed form of cognition, one that students should leave behind as they move into 'higher,' more abstract forms of reasoning" (51). Yet as the authors noted:

> when we select details from the flux of experience and shape them into a story, we are also engaged in naming, abstracting from, and restructuring the raw data of the physical world, and in finding its patterns of meaning. . . . [I]t is in our stories . . . that we embed our understanding of more abstract terms like pedagogy. (51–52)

A MAP OF ENGLISH 101

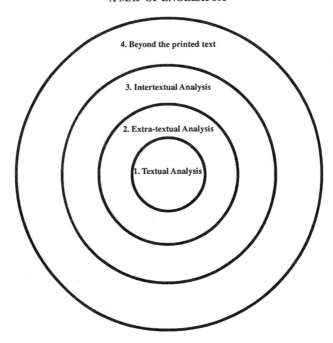

1. Textual Analysis includes summary—what a text says—and "Mining," how language and structure convey meaning. Mining texts can encourage students to think about their own choices as writers; thus this kind of analysis is linked to all the larger circles in that they use this level to write effective papers at all levels.
2. Extra-textual Analysis entails relating readings to personal experience in order to fulfill two goals: helping students think critically about their own experiences and helping them think critically about texts' claims.
3. Intertextual Analysis consists of making connections among the different readings in writing a comparative analysis or a synthesis.
4. Beyond the Printed Text conceives of different social structures (e.g., the university) as a text that students can study through interviews.

FIG. 3.1.

In the UW literacy course, the language of the autobiography assignment encourages students to see narrative as argument. Handled effectively, narrative writing can indeed be both analytical and interpretive. Thus, our assignment directs students to consider how and why type questions; it asks them to "explore the origins of some of the theories that you hold about reading, writing, and language," an activity that requires cause–effect analysis. We ask them to cull out "significant factors and events that have contributed to your development as a reader and writer," a task that re-quires distilling and hierarchizing experiences, a fundamentally interpretive activity. Finally, the assignment asks students to consider "how do your experiences help all of us to understand what literacy means? What sort of environment supports the development of advanced literacy?" These questions require students to theorize broadly from their experiences, to draw general conclusions that define literacy, and to map out the conditions that foster it. To insist that narrative is a less advanced form of writing is to return to the problem of compartmentalizing writing instruction into discrete kinds of tasks, considering different modes of writing as separate stages in the cognitive development of the writer. In reality, most types of intellectually engaging assignments that will interest both instructors and students combine various strategies like narrating, describing, analyzing, and comparing and contrasting. One could certainly imagine, for example, a personal narrative that described events and recounted stories (possibly using some comparison and contrast strategies), that then went on to analyze these accounts as evidence for some claim or generalization, and finally formulated an argument in an attempt to persuade a reader. Although the overall bent of this autobiography assignment might be more personal than later academic assignments, the difference is surely one of degree rather than of kind.[3]

Indeed, we begin the course with an autobiographical essay about literacy not because it is simpler than a strictly academic task, but because it provides a key step toward the analysis required by later assignments. But most important, the assignment allows students to develop their own ideas about literacy, drawing on the evidence of their lives, before they are introduced to professional writers' commentaries and analyses. The student narratives through which they analyze and interpret their experiences of literacy in various communities provide a vital way for them to begin creating knowledge and to theorize themselves what it means to be literate. When they write the autobiography first, students begin with a sense of authorship, a strategy we hope will enable them to adopt a critical stance as they encounter professional authors' ideas.

Central to such an effort is teaching students to value what they bring with them to the beginning writing classroom, rather than disparaging them (as a traditional model for teaching basic writing might) by insisting they are deficient, semiliterate, incompetent. This unit of the course strives

---

[3]For an objection to narrative assignments, see Rose: "We have reason to doubt that work on narration or on description will build in students a repertoire of more abstract and complex schemata, schemata, that is, that are not based on chronological sequences or spatial arrangements" ("Remedial Writing Courses" 121). Yet the kinds of assignments Rose objected to are decontextualized topics like "write about a person who influenced your life," or "describe a favorite place." In contrast, our autobiographical assignment encourages students to employ the kinds of "abstract and complex schemata" that they will need to use in other college writing tasks.

to help students connect their lives at the university to their lives at home, and vice versa. Similarly, Kutz, Groden, and Zamel strove to help students discover, recognize, and value the competencies and literacies they bring to the classroom by incorporating narrative accounts of prior experiences into the course curriculum. They theorized that "we could draw on our students' knowledge of their experience and their competence with language to establish a base for building new areas of knowledge and competence" (88).[4] Within the context of the academic literacy course, this strategy would specifically entail tapping into the literacies that students bring with them to the classroom and using those literacies, their understanding of literacy, and their own experience in writing and reading instruction as material that will allow them to formulate reactions to what professional authors say about literacy. It will also constitute a body of evidence to which students can return as they work on later assignments, weighing their own observations and theories against the professionals' in order to expand their notion of authorship and to speak without simply bowing to the authority of what other writers have already said.

TEXTUAL ANALYSIS AND ITS RELATION
TO AUTOBIOGRAPHY: USING ESSAYS
AND FICTION IN THE WRITING CLASSROOM

After students draft versions of their autobiographies, they begin to encounter other readings as they enter what is marked on my diagram as the second level of the course, loosely termed textual analysis, which consists of two components: first, students learn to summarize a text by figuring out what it says; second, they interpret texts by figuring out how it says, or how language and structure convey meaning. These tasks, of course, are related in the way that content and form are related and hence cannot be separated. Moreover, these strategies for reading texts, although they ask students to recognize features of the text as semiautonomous objects, never stand by themselves. Although all kinds of interpretive stances rely on an understanding of how texts work, close reading skills in and of

---

[4]Kutz, Groden, and Zamel found, however, that artificial tasks assigned in the classroom often stripped their students' narratives of the sense of purpose a naturally told story would entail. They found they had to challenge their assumption "that we could elicit that [new] competence directly through the tasks we designed, allowing students to transfer what they knew from the larger world to the work of the college classroom" (88). In teaching the UW literacy course, however, we find that if students have a vested interest in the subject matter of their narratives—the story of how their literacy developed—we can merge the personal and the academic fairly successfully. Students are also given a very clear sense of purpose for their autobiographies and are told in advance that the material they produce will be drawn on later as they consider professional points of view about academic literacy.

themselves would make a paltry plan for a course without larger considerations about how readers bring an agenda to the text with them. Because a course that stressed merely a formalist approach would not foster critical thinking, close reading becomes a stepping stone to a much broader overall plan, a component part of something much larger than itself. In the diagram, then, there is a fluid boundary between the innermost and the second circles because students bring their own backgrounds as readers and writers to textual analysis, contexts that influence the ways they approach and interpret the texts they read.

Students practice these approaches to reading in the professional literacy autobiographies they read, such as Rodriguez's *Hunger of Memory*. A journal assignment on this text might ask them something like the following:

> You will notice as you read that Rodriguez tells many stories about his experience growing up, experiences that shaped his understanding of his education. You will also notice many places where he stops telling stories in order to comment on his experience, looking back on his past with a critical or interpretive eye. In your journal, write down the page numbers of two such passages where he analyzes the meanings of events or explores their implications for his development. First, *summarize* what he says in each of these two sections. Next, *analyze* the strategies he uses as a writer to help him convey his point. (How does he organize information? What kinds of language does he use? By what means does he hope to convince the reader he's right?) Finally, *give your personal reactions* to his ideas about literacy. Do you agree with his ideas or not? Why or why not? Is his experience in any way like your own? (This assignment is adapted from Bartholomae and Petrosky's "Reading Assignment D," *Facts, Artifacts and Counterfacts* 63–64.)

Such assignments ask students to be attuned to issues of what, how, and so what, and to see clear distinctions among summary and rhetorical analysis and reaction. At this point in the course, a class period might be devoted to comparing summaries and to discussing how individual students' reactions to Rodriguez's work influence their choice of details included in their summary statements (cf. Bartholomae and Petrosky's *Ways of Reading* 2–3).

The assignment fits the general narrative structure underpinning the course. It is linked backward to the students' autobiographical writing, but it also pushes them forward to new kinds of writing: writing about texts. As students shift from autobiographical writing to the kind of reading and writing that will be expected of them in other classes, instructors can highlight how these assignments relate to assignments from other classes. Students can bring in their assignments and make them part of the class discussion as well, analyzing how other tasks from across the curriculum relate to the ones they are asked to complete in the literacy course. Such

an approach further reinforces the narrative principle by helping students
see relationships among writing tasks in the university as a whole.

I use this opportunity to introduce students to some of the conventions
of writing about literature and the complicated textual analysis that accompanies literary studies. Usually instructors value the paper that shows
how form relates to content; faced with the paper that tells how the literary
work reminded students of days they spent with their grandfathers on the
family farm, instructors will tell students that they have failed to complete
the assignment as directed. Having experimented with literary texts in the
composition classroom, I have often adopted this stance, asking students
to learn the conventions of the formal literary analysis. Familiarizing students with different conventions provides a basis for what they will encounter in the field research project; learning the discourse conventions of
English gives an example against which they can measure their findings
when they investigate writing in another field. Thus this type of assignment
fits into the larger narrative of the course in multiple ways.

Yet at the same time, more reader-response-oriented approaches to
teaching readings can provide an entry to the debates in literary studies
about the status of theory in the classroom. Using various interpretive
methods can provide a way to ask students to recognize the limitations of
the formalist readings that academic institutions often stress, masking the
social and political agenda that lurks beneath the surface of the seemingly
innocuous, text-based approach to teaching literature.[5] In light of this goal,
students in some sections of the Forms of Academic Literacy course have

---

[5]I also envision how some of the goals of the beginning writing course can influence my
literature classes as the lines between the two components of the discipline—literature and
composition—become increasingly blurred. Typically conceived as a service element of the
university or college English Department, composition has been relegated to the margins,
only recently coming into its own as a serious discipline. Although many of the exciting new
composition courses and critical studies have adapted much literary theory in theorizing the
discipline of composition studies, literary studies has much to gain by borrowing back some
of these ideas, especially in lower-level courses where, too often, formalist analysis remains
the only kind of analysis. In her introduction to a recent volume that brings together
composition, literary theory, philosophy, and ethnography, Anne Ruggles Gere posited that
the term "restructuring" serves as a better metaphor for the relationship among disciplines
because, unlike the currently used metaphor, "bridge building," it implies that composition
studies, "instead of simply borrowing from a given field, . . . interacts, changing and being
changed" (3). Gere noted that restructuring as a metaphor for interdisciplinarity includes
"reconstructing relations between theory and application" (3). In introductory literature
courses, perhaps most undergraduate courses, literary studies lags behind composition studies
in applying theory to classroom situations. What if introductory literature classes were to
incorporate the cultural studies elements of the beginning writing course we describe?
Although this is not the forum to argue for such an approach in the Introductory Literature
classroom, those of us who teach both literature and composition could perhaps see how
similar approaches to teaching can inform both disciplines.

read Toni Morrison's novel *Song of Solomon* to supplement their readings of autobiographical accounts of professional authors' literacy development.

Morrison's novel is a kind of cultural literacy bildungsroman, rich in examples of how storytelling and cultural texts passed down through the generations (like the Sugarman song) can shape one's view of the world. *Song of Solomon* provides a way to address literacy in a manner akin to Deborah Brandt's view that literacy lies in the ability to connect language to one's own experience and to use language in order to become a better citizen of the world (*Literacy as Involvement*). We study Milkman's journey as a metaphor for becoming literate in one's own cultural history, and I focus on the way this conception of literacy informs day-to-day living and his new-found sense of responsibility to family and community. Although I do ask students to develop close reading habits with the novel and to analyze its strategies (dominant metaphors, motifs, character development, narrative techniques), we also treat many other possible interpretive models: placing the novel within the context of multicultural literacy issues, measuring it against E. D. Hirsch's ideas about cultural literacy (*Cultural Literacy: What Every American Needs to Know*), situating ourselves as readers, discussing which of Milkman's experiences resemble our own and which do not, considering Marxist and feminist interpretations of the novel. How do one's cultural and social background influence the way one reads a literary text? What contexts for reading change the kinds of readings that might be produced? What kinds of interested readings produce particular types of responses to the texts? These are questions that often go unanalyzed and hence agendas remain hidden. Instructors of writing and reading need to address the ways that the context in which the work is introduced (in what kind of course, juxtaposed with what other texts, in light of the instructor's own theoretical sympathies) influences the way in which one reads the work. Making explicit the issues that could give rise to conflicting interpretations, as we do in the UW literacy course, would provide fruitful channels for helping students understand reading processes and ultimately enhance their appreciation of the literary text's potential to evoke meaningful conversations about cultural and social issues.

In fact, Gerald Graff advocated "teaching the conflicts" as a way to engage students more fully in literary analysis; he pointed out that "as readers, we are necessarily concerned with *both* the questions posed by the text and the questions we bring to it from our own differing interests and cultural backgrounds" (42). For him, learning the conflicts and the subsequent "relation to a community" that he developed as a reader "made the intimacy of literary experience possible" (43). Raising these kinds of considerations in the classroom familiarizes students with the nature of academic study within a particular field; it gives them greater access to what we do as professionals. Just as students in science lab courses experience the kinds of research questions that drive those fields, so under-graduates in writing and other courses need access to the complex and engaging ideas that underpin professional investigations. The types of as-signments given in conjunction with literary analysis are designed to show beginning students how university and college professionals approach texts for the larger purpose of acquainting them with the types of questions academics ask across the disciplines.

TEACHING STUDENTS TO READ AS WRITERS

Not only does the literacy course encourage students to recognize the vested interests they bring to their readings, the elements that influence what they find significant in a text (cf. Bartholomae & Petrosky introduction to *Ways of Reading* 2–4 and "Facts, Artifacts and Counterfacts" 9–29), but it also encourages them to read with a sense of authorship. Stuart Greene's concept of mining texts becomes crucial to the literacy course design at this point, in helping students use texts in ways that extend beyond the boundaries of the texts themselves ("Exploring the Relationship Between Authorship and Reading"). To mine a text is to examine it in light of its context, its structure, and its language, with the ultimate goal that the reader will extract from the text its possibilities for informing his or her own writing (or will reject the text's relevance to his or her writing). As Greene put it:

> for this excavation, the miner uses certain "tools" appropriate to the situation to help uncover what is most desired. . . . Such an "excavation" can be a selfish endeavor for it serves the individual in his or her search for "nuggets" of information. (Greene 36)

Yet mining also helps students lay bare the ways social contexts shape an author's purpose and strategies. As he described a course he taught, Greene noted:

> students began mining texts in an ongoing process of reading, analyzing, and authoring that recognizes the social nature of discourse. Each piece of writing that a student reads or writes is a contribution to an ongoing written conversation. To reconstruct the context of a text requires an understanding of how an author frames a response appropriate to a given situation and an author's own purpose. (44)

Students can then consider whether such strategies suit their own purposes: "in reading in the role of writers, students make judgments about the most appropriate way to make their own contribution in writing" (44). Thus, students in the academic literacy course not only draft their literacy autobiographies based on their own experience but they also reconsider those autobiographies in light of professional texts about the same subject matter. Students relate the readings to their own experience for a two-fold purpose: to think critically about their own experiences with literacy and to use that experience to think critically about the readings' claims. In writing their literacy autobiographies, then, they combine these forms of critical analysis to reflect on the development of their uses of language, both academic and otherwise. Most important, mining provides a way for students to approach texts from a sense of authorship and to adopt the stance of authority that we encourage in the literacy course. According to Greene, mining texts can help students to become literate in a way that extends beyond "politely observing what other authors have accomplished in their writing. Instead, students are given the promise of contributing as authors" (45). (See also Bartholomae & Petrosky, introduction to *Ways of Reading* 11–18 and "Facts, Artifacts and Counterfacts" 29–41.)

The informal assignments students are asked to complete encourage this sense of authorship. For example, when students read a chapter of Eudora Welty's *One Writer's Beginnings* ("Listening" 1–39), I ask for the following journal entry:

> This assignment is designed to help you understand how a writer uses a particular type of language to evoke the desired response in the reader. You should use this knowledge in your own writing as well, by making deliberate choices about the quality of your language. Your choices will vary depending upon what kind of paper you're writing, and upon what specific impression you want to create for the reader. For this journal entry, take these two steps:
>
> 1. As you read Welty's essay, describe her language itself. That is, what kinds of words does she use frequently? What feeling do these words create for you? What mental picture do you have of the house she grew up in? Consider also Welty's purpose for writing this piece. What context does she write in? How does her language serve her purpose?
> 2. Now, think about the house you grew up in, and how it relates to your development as a writer. Decide whether or not Welty's language is appropriate for your own experience. Decide what impression you'd like the reader to have of the atmosphere in your house. Then write a paragraph in which you take care to choose words that convey this impression. Be prepared to explain to your group members *why* you chose the language you chose. As you work on your description, think too about your context as a writer. What purpose might you conceive for writing this description and linking it to your beginnings as a writer?

In the context of other courses, reading as a writer would likely mean that students learn to transform source texts for their own purposes, to make their own arguments, rather than basing ideas in personal experience. In the third unit of the course, students write a paper that encourages them to adopt a stance of authority in this manner on an academic topic.

SYNTHESIZING DIFFERENT POINTS OF VIEW

The academic literacy course encourages students to connect the professional texts to one another and to consider their own texts, their autobiographies (which are reprinted and distributed to the whole class), as part of the growing intertext of the course materials. Here we arrive at intertextual analysis, the third circle on the diagram for the course's structure. Morrison's novel and her conception of literacy provide intriguing comparisons and contrasts with other works in the course, and hence reading *Song of Solomon* also takes the course into the third circle, intertextual analysis. Lorri Neilsen's work *Literacy and Living: The Literate Lives of Three Adults* allows for the same broad definition of literacy Morrison embraces, so I ask the students to look at *Song of Solomon* in light of Neilsen's argument that literacy is learning to be at home in the world, learning to be attuned to the events and people that surround one. For example, one such assignment read:

> I asked you last time to think about Milkman's identity and how language, spoken and written, plays a role in shaping his sense of who he is. Lorri Neilsen maintains in her book *Literacy and Living* that literacy is, in part, learning to be at home in the world, being attuned to the people and events that surround you. As you read about Milkman's journey to the South, think about it in terms of how he is fulfilling Neilsen's definition of what it means to be literate. How "literate" is he when he gets to the South? What does he gradually learn about himself and about the ways of the South, and how does knowledge help him function in this world? How does his identity change as a result?

Students then write a more formal, longer paper comparing Morrison's and Rodriguez's views, examining *Song of Solomon* and *Hunger of Memory* in terms of the way the two texts define literacy and the way they treat the connection between literacy and personal–familial–cultural past.

The comparative analysis of these two books provides a precedent for the difficult synthesis paper, which asks the students to synthesize and comment on the views on literacy held by three or four authors in the course. As they move into this second long assignment, where they further delve into the conversation about literacy, they read a number of difficult essays by authors such as E. D. Hirsch, Paulo Freire, and David Bartholomae, which focus on critical controversies surrounding academic literacy and the crisis in American education. Even with their prior writings, we need to help students manage this task, and again careful sequencing within the informal assignments as well as three lengthy, formal papers can help them negotiate this part of the course with success. Thus when one of my students seemed daunted by the synthesis assignment, at a loss as to what the task required of her, I could then point out that she had already done that type of writing in her comparison of Morrison and Rodriguez, a paper she had managed quite successfully. She then had a way of understanding the new assignment in terms of the old: She had to draw on the same strategies she had used earlier, but she would need to consider another author and to highlight her own evaluation of the authors' stands. Similarly, anyone who wanted to teach students to synthesize a variety of views on any topic could help students handle this assignment by first incorporating into the course design critical comparisons of two ideas or two texts.

Thus the synthesis paper actually combines the approaches the students have developed in their comparison of Morrison and Rodriguez and in their literacy autobiographies. Extratextual analysis, or bringing the student's own experience to bear on the course materials, plays a role in the synthesis paper that is central to the course goal of encouraging the students to write with a sense of authorship. As Kutz, Groden, and Zamel pointed out, a traditional guide to research writing portrays research "as different from the other writing and learning students do, as separate from students' personal experience of the world" (117). In contrast, we sequence the assignments in the course in such a way that the research or synthesis paper becomes an integral part and expansion of the writing and learning students have already done; it is linked to their personal experience. Many connections then emerge among the different levels of the course, so that by the time students write the synthesis paper, they are using close reading or textual analysis strategies; they are bringing in extratextual analysis by evaluating the authors in terms of their own experience; and they are drawing on the comparisons they have already made between two authors to examine each text in light of the others.

The synthesis assignment, A Conversation about Literacy, draws on a metaphor Rose used in *Lives on the Boundary*: that literacy means making a contribution to an ongoing conversation. Thus as our assignment instructs students:

> in order to enter the conversation, you need to demonstrate your awareness of what others have been saying, establishing a shared knowledge of issues with your readers. Entering the conversation also means *using* what you know to get people to think about the topic in *new* and interesting ways.

The assignment ultimately asks students to choose one issue related to literacy that derives from their reading of the materials, and "to use the texts you have read *for your own purposes.*" This purposeful evaluation of others' writings about literacy is enabled by the earlier assignments through which students developed their own ideas to play against the professionals'.

We stress this assignment because the synthetic and analytic thinking it requires reflects the nature of research-based assignments students encounter in other courses, assignments they find very difficult. Other assignments from courses across the disciplines can again be introduced at this point, by students and teachers alike. A colleague in the Psychology Department commented to me recently that his students had trouble writing a final lab report in a research design course: The course had introduced them to a variety of sources (research articles) through the term and instructors expected students to draw on this material for the introduction section of their final reports. Almost invariably, my colleague noted, students produced reports that summarized each article in a separate paragraph, in the order in which the articles were introduced in the course. Students seemed unable to synthesize the information and shape it for their own purposes. One of the literacy course's goals, then, is to encourage this kind of writing. Yet as Greene finds in chapter 5, this volume, many complex factors shape a student's ability to complete this type of assignment in an effective manner. With more attention to the ways students read the language of this particular assignment and negotiate its demands, we can better prepare them to write the paper that synthesizes and analyzes information from a variety of sources, the kind of paper they will enounter frequently in many disciplines.

RESEARCH IN THE FIELD: EXPLORING LITERACY IN THE UNIVERSITY SETTING

In the final unit of the course, students undertake a field project. The fourth circle, which I loosely call "beyond the printed text" (or "viewing the university as a text"), continues the trend of progressively opening the levels of the course outward at the same time that new tasks draw on old ones. Here, the students conduct an interview project with a member or members of a discourse community that interests them. They use people as sources in addition to printed materials (they also examine a sample paper that the professor provides them), but they evaluate the source(s) of their information in light of everything they have learned from the course readings. The professor they interview then becomes another kind of text in the intertextual analysis they undertook previously. Having determined in their synthesis papers a perspective on a critical issue in literacy and education, they might bring this perspective to their field project and in effect test it within the discourse community they investigate. In addition, the students learned the discourse conventions of the field of literary studies in the beginning of the course when they focused on literary analysis. They can use that set of conventions to measure the kinds of discourse conventions they discover in the new field they investigate and to see how these conventions might vary from one discipline to another.

The assignment is valuable in that students return to the classroom with a greater understanding of how they might be expected to perform within another field. When students pool their information, the whole class emerges with a sense of the tremendous variety of discourses and the range of conventions that constitute the university. As Rose pointed out, there is a need for a beginning writing program "that alert[s] students to stylistic/rhetorical variation within the university" ("Remedial Writing Courses" 112). At the same time, students bring to those investigations a sense, which has developed all semester, of how they have been positioned as "basic" writers within the university and of how they might challenge that position. The experience helps students connect their experiences as beginning writing students and their larger experiences as college students; if they understand where they came from and how they wound up labeled "basic" writers and how their writing strategies that often have failed them in the past originate, they can better understand how to rethink their strategies. They may very well also encounter conflicts or approaches to literacy that challenge the ideas they have developed through the literacy course. Such conflicts provide further challenges for students as they think about how they might negotiate these differences if they choose to pursue the field they investigate. No matter what the outcome of such encounters with other disciplines, students who have completed the Forms of Academic Literacy course ought to enter other disciplines with a heightened awareness of what it means to read and write in an academic context and a heightened self-consciousness about the choices they make as readers and writers.

I leave the boundaries of this last circle on the map open to suggest the infinite possibilities for applying all the approaches to reading and writing learned in the course to the world at large, beyond the university itself. Thus the narrative for the course is not a linear one, nor does it ever achieve closure. It begins, in fact, before the course begins, stretching back over the students' life experiences and, ideally, it stretches forth beyond the last day of the class as their experiences grow. The structure thus invites the students to extend their knowledge of reading and writing both to other courses and to their lives in general so that they may continually add to the story by drawing connections that spin out in any number of directions.

CONCLUSION

These are not all the connections among the levels of the course (in fact I usually discover more kinds of connections retroactively as the course progresses), but they provide a sense of what I mean by narrativizing the course and they provide an example of what that goal would look like in conjunction with a particular set of materials. I do not mean to suggest that this map is the definitive or only one; rather, I want to point out that any map or whole-semester plan underpinning the course will help both instructors and students to make sense of the course in a holistic way. What matters most is simply that instructors can see the course whole according to their own pedagogical goals, their own vision of a beginning writing class; that they can then decide how they want the semester's assignments to progress; and finally, that they can convey that picture to the students.

No matter how one sees it, letting the students also see the structure is key. Just as Linda Flower suggested in *Problem Solving Strategies for Writing* that writers need their essays to "reveal the inner logic" to the reader (284–294), so instructors of a beginning writing course need to reveal the inner logic of the course to the students or all the hard planning will go largely to waste. Just as we encourage students to be self-conscious about their reading and writing strategies, so instructors should adopt a self-conscious approach to the course, letting the students know why they are doing what they are doing, and how it relates to the larger scheme of things. This is an area in which it is easy to fall short, to assume students will see the emerging logic that structures our syllabi without our needing to remind them at every juncture of the underlying plan. One way of accomplishing this goal would be to write into every assignment a statement of how it relates to the previous assignment. When wording journal entries or informal assignments, it is likewise important to reveal the purpose of the assignment so the students will see how it can help them develop strategies they need for the formal papers and how the smaller assignments constitute purposeful work rather than busy work or reading checks. More important, instructors could spend class time discussing at the beginning of a new segment in the course where that segment is headed, how it draws on or relates to the old material, and how it will pave the way for what comes later. Eliciting students' responses by asking them to explain their understanding of the new assignment and to talk about how it fits in with the previous assignment would be a key move at this point. Instructors could ask what students feel the purpose of the assignment is: Why do you think I am asking you to perform this task? How do you think it might be useful to you in this course, or in your college experience? One could very well diagram the course on the board at these junctures, a strategy that might enable the students to see the plan more fully than a verbal overview would.

Finally, the concept of giving a course a narrative by forging multiple connections among ideas and assignments is hardly new. Yet as Greene's chapter 5, this volume, demonstrates, this goal is often rendered problematic and needs careful attention. A carefully sequenced course design reflects and offers a model for the very kind of activity we encourage in our students' writing. A course that develops an idea or theme by carefully sequencing its treatment of that theme so that it proceeds logically, so that it continually links new information to old, and so that it progressively opens the theme into new and larger realms parallels the manner in which a well-structured paper develops. Moreover, the activity of connecting and forging links in essence underpins the kind of intellectual activity we value. When a student puts two separate things together in a startling yet convincing way, we praise that student's originality and synthetic thinking. Often, connecting serves as a synonym for what we call an original and creative approach in an expository paper. Linking ideas or concepts to one another, linking details to one another, linking concrete details to abstractions—overall, the general pursuit of such connections—lies at the heart of what we want our students to be able to do. The "only connect" approach for beginning writing students thus models both the kind of structure and the kind of thinking we admire and reward in our students' work; by providing that element in our course designs, perhaps we can better enable them to transform texts for their own purposes, to connect their experiences with the ideas they encounter, and thereby to develop a sense of their own authority over the subject matter with which they deal.

WORKS CITED

Bartholomae, David, and Anthony Petrosky, eds. *Facts, Artifacts and Counterfacts: Theory and Method for a Reading and Writing Course.* Upper Montclair, NJ: Boynton/Cook, 1986.

——. "Facts, Artifacts and Counterfacts: A Basic Reading and Writing Course for the College Curriculum." Bartholomae and Petrosky, *Facts, Artifacts and Counterfacts* 3–43.

——, eds. *Ways of Reading.* Boston: Bedford Books, 1990.

Brandt, Deborah. *Literacy as Involvement.* Carbondale: Southern Illinois UP, 1990.

Brooks, Peter. *Reading for the Plot.* New York: Vintage, 1984.

Coles, Nicholas. "Empowering Revision." Bartholomae and Petrosky, *Facts, Artifacts and Counterfacts* 167–198.

Flower, Linda. *Problem Solving Strategies for Writing.* 4th ed. New York: Harcourt, 1993.

Forster, E. M. *Howards End.* New York: Alfred Knopf, 1921.

Gere, Anne Ruggles. Introduction. *Into the Field: Sites of Composition Studies.* Ed. Anne Ruggles Gere. New York: MLA, 1993. 1–8.

Graff, Gerald. "Disliking Books at an Early Age." *Falling Into Theory.* Ed. David H. Richter. Boston: Bedford, 1994. 36–43.

Greene, Stuart. "Exploring the Relationship Between Authorship and Reading." *Hearing Ourselves Think: Cognitive Research in the College Writing Classroom.* Eds. Barbara M. Sitko and Ann M. Penrose. New York and Oxford, England: Oxford UP, 1993. 33–51.

Kutz, Eleanor, Suzy Q. Grodin and Vivian Zamel. *The Discovery of Competence: Teaching and Learning with Diverse Student Writers.* Portsmouth, NH: Boynton/Cook, 1993.

Rodriguez, Richard. *Hunger of Memory.* New York: Bantam, 1983.

Rose, Mike. *Lives on the Boundary.* New York: Penguin, 1990.

———. "Remedial Writing Courses: A Critique and A Proposal." *College English* 45 (1983): 109–128.

Schilb, John. "Cultural Studies, Postmodernism, and Composition." *Contending with Words: Composition and Rhetoric in a Postmodern Age.* Eds. Patricia Harkin and John Schilb. New York: MLA, 1991. 173–188.

BIBLIOGRAPHY

Hirsch, E. D. *Cultural Literacy: What Every American Needs to Know.* Boston: Houghton Mifflin, 1987.

Morrison, Toni. *Song of Solomon.* New York: Signet, 1977.

Neilsen, Lorri. *Literacy and Living: The Literate Lives of Three Adults.* Portsmouth, NH: Heinemann, 1989.

Welty, Eudora. Listening. *One Writer's Beginnings.* Cambridge, MA: Harvard UP, 1984. 1–39.

Part II

CLASSROOM RESEARCH
STUDIES

The Legacy of Schooling: Secondary School Composition and the Beginning College Writer

Nicholas Preus
Waldorf College

In their efforts to write in academic contexts, basic writers in the first year of college fall back on strategies acquired in their years of secondary school. This, of course, is well known, and studies not only demonstrate this contention but also catalog and explain the particular strategies on which students rely. Yet we need more knowledge about those strategies and how reliance on them affects students struggling to enter the world of college writing. Instruction is frequently made difficult because of the horizon of students' assumptions, a "legacy of schooling" (Flower 224) whose boundaries limit the range of possibilities open to student writers; the difficulty is increased by a concomitant unfamiliarity with academic discourse and its conventions (Bartholomae). Students' assumptions interfere with the acquisition of new strategies and hinder entrance to a discourse community. They also impede possible development of a critical stance toward authoritative conventions and ways of knowing (Mortenson and Kirsch 557).

In this chapter, I attempt to extend our understanding of the legacy of schooling by analyzing the responses of students to protocols and interview questions during a paper-writing assignment. I gathered the data from my section of English 101, a basic writing course at the University of Wisconsin-Madison. These data revealed not only the components of a legacy of schooling, but also students' efforts to move beyond them to new understandings. The writing strategies identified here arise from a still common, highly validated practice in secondary schools, even in the post-process-writing era.[1] This practice is not limited to the schools, however; colleges also inadvertently, sometimes explicitly, underwrite the strategies enacted by students such as these.

Analysis of student responses for this study revealed the presence of three powerful constituents of the legacy of schooling: the demand for quantification, the deployment of the generalizing commonplace, and the insistence on a distinction between opinion and material that can be evaluated as either right or wrong. These are components of the standard repertoire on which many first-year college writers, and especially basic writers, rely.

For Linda Flower, that standard repertoire consisted of "writing strategies [freshmen] control with comfort and call up without question" (232). Gist and list involves getting the gist of a text and linking its main points with a simple connecting term or idea. This strategy, Flower said, is the "product of years of paraphrasing, summarizing, and recitation in school" (235). TIA—for True, Important, and I Agree"—involves reading with a filter. Any item registering in these categories is retained for use and anything else is deleted. A "pool of ideas the writer likes, understands, and can elaborate on" is created (235–236), but problematizing voices from texts tend to be filtered out. Students who engage in the third strategy, constructive planning, think about content, goals, evaluative criteria, and design problems in relation to their papers. They look "at their writing as a rhetorical problem and a constructive act" (240). This strategy is powerful and adaptive but clearly not all students use it, and a number in Flower's study relied on more limited processes (242). The Madison data suggested that the occurrence of this strategy was infrequent and that students seemed to fall back on more limited strategies even when they had a sense of how limited those choices were. In at least one case, however, a student's responses show a movement in the direction of constructive planning.

These standard strategies, according to Flower, comprise a robust repertoire that is at the same time "limited, and ripe for change" (229). The legacy of "practiced strategies and strong assumptions" (224) may no longer serve students' needs in college writing because the students have perhaps failed "to appreciate the conflict between those prior assumptions and the unstated expectations of an academic discourse community" (224). Flower identified sites where the standard repertoire comes "into conflict with the demands of the rhetorical situation," places where the repertoire was "hit-

---

[1]Unfortunately, we are all too ready to fix blame for our students' inability on the teachers who preceded us. I do not want to join that particular chorus by suggesting that secondary school teachers are the cause of college basic writers' problems. On the contrary, I would argue that institutional, curricular, and pedagogical forces that are systemic—from lower elementary through graduate programs—contribute to the formation of the responses I discuss here.

ting its limits, failing to deal with inherent problems in the task . . . and failing to meet other expectations for academic sophistication" (232). Her study reveals that assumptions stemming from previous successes in school tasks can prevent students differentiating these tasks from the more "complexly constructive" acts of college writing (233).

The Madison study bears out Flower's analysis; it shows students employing the fundamental strategies she described. At the same time, in the protocols, interviews, and texts of these basic writers, there is also much trouble along the way, many well-learned strategies that can hardly be called strategies at all inasmuch as they tend to disrupt both processes and texts rather than to advance them. Past experiences maintain their hold in unexpected ways in spite of students' struggles to write in a manner less dependent on responses that they are now finding either inappropriate or ineffective in a new academic context.

Flower's catalog of the fundamental elements of students' working knowledge is important to our understanding of where to begin our teaching. In addition, I suggest we consider three other basic issues that every high school and college writing teacher will recognize and that our data show to be common problems embedded in the products and processes of basic writers.

The first of these responses—ubiquitous among first-year college writers—is the concern with quantity: the number of pages, quotations, citations, and sources needed to satisfy what the instructor is looking for. This familiar issue appears whenever a task is assigned and it constitutes a major element in a student's representation of that task.

Students in English 101, after completing an autobiographical narrative unit, began work on a multiple-source analytical–synthetic paper—the type of paper they would encounter in other college courses. For many, it was an anxiety-filled time. In his interview at the end of the process, one student, Tom, said:

It was an experience. It's the hardest paper I've ever had to write so far. But if he [the instructor] is right . . . in saying that this is going to be your typical paper. . . I greatly needed this paper, you know. Because I'd rather have it now in a pass-fail course [than], you know, maybe get a C or D on it. It's good practice, I guess.

Tom's comment expresses his sense of having entered a world of new expectations. But it also reveals the degree to which he thinks in a framework where external motivations and strictures determine his response. Those expectations being unfamiliar, he posed an anxious question very familiar to teachers of writing: "What are you looking for?" During a conference, in response to the instructor's comment that they should set the paper guidelines aside for the moment, he said, "Well, I'm just saying, am I along your guidelines, kind of what you expect so far?" And in response to the instructor's question about a text, he replied, "What are you looking for?" One of Tom's classmates, Sarah, in a think-aloud protocol, said, "So, basically, he's looking for references and quotations that help him understand what you are talking about."

As Peter Elbow remarked, the "basic subtext in a piece of student writing is likely to be, 'Is this okay?' " (81). A concern for what the instructor is looking for generates particular kinds of responses in the students' acts and texts. For one, questions concerning acceptable quantities of elements appear repeatedly as an issue in the interviews and conferences of the students. These concerns reflect their desire to specify measurable items that, when sufficiently provided in the final text, will qualify it for an acceptable evaluation. Years of training in which attention to numbers of pages, citations, and supporting points—coupled with a response to authority that seeks to contain uncertainty by recourse to a hopefully safe and manageable criterion of measurement—produce an overconcern with quantity at the expense of other possible strategies.

In the protocol, Sarah explained what she would find difficult about this assignment: "Finding enough information from each author . . . so that will probably be one hard thing and also this 5 to 7 pages." Later, in the conference with the instructor during the writing process, Sarah asked, "So there is enough quotes in here? Because, like, when we read Tiffany's yesterday, she had like so many quotes. And then I felt like, god, maybe I don't have what he's looking for?" Sarah's concern over quantities—of sources, information, quotations, and paper length—were based on what she took the instructor to be looking for. On the one hand, she tried to reassure herself that there is a measurable quantity of these elements that will produce a successful result; on the other, she was anxious because she did not know what the teacher's, or college's, expectations were. And she was not alone.

In her final interview, Cheri considered whether she had done what the instructor wanted. She replied, "Um, yeah, I talked about three authors. It was five pages." Tiffany responded to a similar question—did you fulfill the goals of this paper—with this answer: "I believe so. I, like, covered the three different authors, plus my opinion." And Tom, the most concerned about quantities, extended his anxiety from expectations and formal elements to the time and effort that would be required to achieve sufficient inclusion of items. In the protocol, he responded to the 5- to 7-page guideline in the assignment, "Impossible—is what I've got to say about that . . . I don't know—it's just—the hardest part I guess is finding enough information to get 5 to 7 pages." Certainly the concern over time is legitimate on the part of an academically at-risk, first-year student. But the sense of Tom's reply is that what is really at stake is the unaccustomed task of searching his texts to find enough information to fill 5 to 7 pages.

Of course, where quantity is the issue, larger concerns, such as a meaningful text, analytical and synthetic moves, a sense of rhetorical purpose, are elided. From the early grades—usually beginning in about Grade 4— through much of college and university, a value is attached to the quantity of elements in writing. In the face of other expectations that are very unfamiliar, even unknown, a student may understandably turn to what she thinks she can control, the quantity of something, in an effort to improve the rating of her product.

Teachers stipulate quantity with the sense that by doing so they will increase the amount of attention a student pays to a certain issue. However, as we have seen, quantity becomes the object of student overconcern as they contemplate finding enough information from three sources. In secondary school settings, numbers of paragraphs will frequently be stipulated in an effort to encourage students to write more extensively, just as later and for the same reason, certain numbers of pages are required for college term papers. The consequences of this kind of quantification can be seen in Tom's reaction to the assigned length of the paper: He found it shocking. His initial attention was focused—and as the transcripts of interviews and the conference show, his continued attention as well—on the length of the paper and the amount of content it will require to fill that length. But Tom had considerable difficulty with the whole assignment and the processes he was asked to enact. Even objective matters such as quantities were daunting for him. Other students in the class, although concerned, seemed to have fewer anxieties over raw length.

All of the students in the study, however, worried about the second element of the legacy of schooling, the *sine qua non* of college writing, the thesis or central organizing idea. A problem of many papers is the thesis that has become a simple commonplace. Students bring with them a tactic for dealing with the central idea that might be thought of as a well-learned use of the "commonplace," as Bartholomae termed it (149–150). Here, however, commonplace may stand for a kind of rhetorical move enacted in response to the requirements of an assignment, a move that students have developed over the course of their experience with teachers and school courses. This is the contention with which it is impossible to disagree, or what might be called the generalizing commonplace. Related to Flower's TIA strategy, or perhaps emerging from it, students seek sources with which they can agree and construct around them a statement, or thesis, with which no one can disagree.

In the English 101 assignment, students were asked to stake out a position on some aspect of the literacy debate, to take into account the views of three other writers, and to construct an argument for their own point of view. Sources in the course had been specifically selected that presented divergent views and contentious positions. Yet the data show that students tended strongly to avoid contention and debate, collapsing or truncating arguments in ways that minimized their differences. Moreover, in their own position or thesis statements, the students also showed a marked tendency toward assertions that could not generate contention. One might think of these as statements formulated specifically to avoid opposition and argument: generalizing commonplaces with which no argument is possible. And yet, even as these are deployed in the paper, they tend to mask the real concerns and positions that students do, in fact, hold on the issues raised by their papers. The data show that students clearly have a stake in the discussion, but frequently they tend to occlude that stake beneath a surface of a vague commonplace.

Cheri proceeded in this manner. Her final paper sets out the following proposition in the introductory paragraph:

> In our society we need to work together to form communication, and we need communication so we can work together. In other words for our society to reach the highest possible level of communication we need the coopera- tion of all of us, and in order for cooperation to occur we need communi- cation amongst all of us. All of the authors we have read have touched this aspect in some way.

Cheri's thesis has its origins in E. D. Hirsch's point that a shared body of knowledge is the basis for the effective communication that, in turn, makes a complex society and a functioning democracy possible (xv–xvii). But Cheri's formulation has dropped Hirsch's contentious assumptions in favor of a more obviously true statement: Communication requires cooperation and cooperation requires communication. The chiasmic form of the state- ment suggests a meaningfulness that it really does not have; it is a self-evi- dent proposition, an assertion with which no one can disagree. Yet at the same time, this is not simply a defensive move. Its appearance is not a function of Cheri's uncertainty about the validity of her ideas and–or desire to conceal or mitigate inadequacy before the scrutiny of an evaluating reader.

Cheri's thesis falls, in part, under Flower's category of a TIA statement. She found, or contrived, a proposition with which she agreed, which she felt she could support, and whose truth claim readers will acknowledge. But there is also more going on here than Cheri's enacting a well-learned strategy for picking ideas out of the reading for use in a paper—Flower's explanation of the TIA strategy. In fact, Cheri did have a stake in this argument and she was quite serious about the importance of her claim. She said in her protocol, "I kind of like this because I like writing about things that are important to society and stuff." In the draft conference, she tried to clarify her point for the instructor:

> You have to cooperate or you need people for input to communicate. Do you know what I'm saying? You need each other's ideas in order to communicate effectively . . . And then, you need to communicate in order for you to be able to work together and get these ideas—do you know what I mean? Everyone needs to be able to say what they feel in order—they need to—you know what I mean . . .

After considerable time discussing the relationship of cooperation and communication and her sources' points of view, the instructor asked, "How did you arrive at this idea?" Cheri replied:

> Um, I don't know. It was kind of related to my last paper. But—I don't know—it kind of—it's important to me. I think it's really true that, you know, things could be better if we did do it. If we shared more, rather than always competing and stuff. [In the last paper] I talk about cooperative versus competitive learning. And it's—I don't really talk about competition in here as much, but, you know, I just try to talk about more like how we communicate together and everything.

Her final paper gives examples from her sources of the importance of communication and working together. And then, in the final paragraph, while summing up the cooperation–communication point, she included this thought, "I personally feel that an environment that encourages working together rather than one that encourages working against each other is significantly better. It may work for some to work alone, but I don't see much sense in it." Here we have a momentary glimpse of the issue that really concerned her, an issue she wrote about in her first project (the literacy autobiography), and one which she was trying to theorize in her analysis–synthesis paper, having read material on the national educational debate. She was concerned that competitive education, to her the norm, is less effective than cooperative education. Specifically, as a first-year, at-risk student at a major university, she was anxious about her status and ability not only to compete but even to survive in a competitive academic environment. Her preference was a more collegial, cooperative learning environment such as she has found, to some extent, in her ungraded, literacy-based, English 101 course.

In conference, she noted that Frank Smith advocated working together with others on one's writing (796), and she said:

> I think what he's saying is, sure it's okay to write alone, but—you know, like what we've been doing in class is helpful, to have each other to give you

ideas and help you get started. It's still your paper, but you're able to have more insight on it with the help of others . . . it opens your mind to more—it makes it a better paper.

Later she commented, "At first everyone was like, 'Five to seven pages, that's going to be hard.' But once we started talking to each other, it seemed more possible."

Cheri had a stake in her paper and the issue with which it deals; her personal investment was, in fact, painfully real. She was concerned about her academic survival and, in the competitive world of the university, she was not at all sure her prospects were good. She felt her chances would be better in a less competitive system, one that was more supportive, collegial, and cooperative. Yet in her final paper, this personal stake was omitted, although it was related to the arguments in the source material encountered in the course (e.g., Mike Rose's *Lives on the Boundary*). And what took its place is a generalizing commonplace that fails to stake out a position, followed by a series of examples in ostensible illustration of the commonplace.

There are two factors operating here. One is surely an authority issue, a history of experience with the scrutiny of evaluating teachers that produces her tentative and guarded assertion. Another, however, is her inexperience with writing analyses, or with writing papers in which one's own point of view is an acknowledged lens through which events, texts, and other points of view are critically examined.

In spite of 20 years of process-centered writing curricula in the schools, this kind of analytical project is seldom undertaken. Instead of encouraging critical constructions of meaning in which the student writer is a stakeholder, instruction often focuses on the expressive nature of writing and the processes by which it can be encoded in text. Expressiveness may be an important aspect of the writing experience, but what seems to happen in the schools is that a dualism develops between report writing and expressive writing. This polarity, as we shall see later in this chapter, becomes embedded not only in writing but in the reading and discussion of literary texts as well. It becomes the familiar dichotomy between what is right or wrong and what is considered opinion. But before we turn to that issue, we need to look briefly at other thesis statements from the class and the ways in which they put into practice the strategy of the generalizing commonplace with which one cannot disagree.

Sarah's paper circled around the commonplace idea that "communicating and understanding are important." A corollary to this idea for her is that miscommunication can cause a lot of conflicts. This is where she began to sort out her point for the paper, but her early draft caused her problems, "I don't really have an argument in here . . . I mean there's one statement in here that I say I disagree with, and this is why. But I don't make an argument out of it." She identified her problem as not being able to "find examples that tie into the problems of miscommunication."

The consequence of starting with the generalized commonplace, as writing teachers know all too well, is that formulations of this sort allow neither analysis nor argument. Sarah recognized this problem. In conference, she read the draft and remarked that it was "boring." But with the instructor's help, she was able to see the significance of what she wrote about an experience in Martinique:

> They couldn't understand me and I couldn't understand them. I felt like they were being so rude to me, just because I was different culturally. When communicating, your culture background can cause some miscommunication. And miscommunication can cause a lot of conflicts.

The instructor asked what happened to this idea in the rest of the paper. Sarah said she lost it.

By the time of her final session with the interviewer, when the paper was complete and handed in, she seemed to know the main point of her paper, "When you're communicating, your culture background can cause some conflicts, which causes miscommunication. And miscommunication causes conflicts. I think that's basically it, just that communication is like real important." At first, she was able to state her idea: Culture can cause conflict. But then she seemed to feel she was mixing up the order of things and tried to correct herself: Miscommunication causes conflict. Finally, unable to hold onto the first idea, she lapsed back into the generalizing commonplace: Communication is important.

The paper itself oscillated between restatements of the commonplace accompanied by illustrative examples and her more insightful proposition that cultural misunderstanding can generate miscommunication and conflict. She struggled through the revisions to maintain her focus on the cultural aspect of her argument, but seemed frequently pulled into restatements of the commonplace. The paper remained in conflict as it tried to establish itself firmly on the grounds of the more productive idea, but often fell back into more general and less contentious formulations. The struggle, of course, is a sign of Sarah's progress.

> [The instructor] he kind of showed me how to take a sentence and really dig into it. And like use that sentence as the main idea and the digging into it as your text. Instead of just stating that one little sentence, [your reader] being someone that you know won't know what you mean.

As we see in these remarks, she had begun to work with the idea of rhetorical purpose: You must do something besides state an idea because someone might not know what you mean. She perhaps had also begun to think metacritically if she meant that what you dig out of your sentence, or main idea, is your text. In any case, she seemed to be pulled forward by her increasing understanding of college writing. To be sure, there were frequent lapses into secondary school strategies, but this is all part of the struggle to produce meaning.

The generalizing commonplace is a function of a context that values consensual formulations. Secondary school classrooms are, for the most part, inimical to contention and divergent views.[2] It is not so much that schools are agents of authoritarianism as that they simply have too many tasks to which they must attend. Student-to-teacher ratios are far too high, especially in English–language arts, and both schools and teachers must deal with situations they are scarcely equipped to handle. This, of course, is not news. Even in a changing climate of writing instruction, and despite all the good intentions of writing teachers, sheer numbers dictate some system of mass processing students through lessons and courses. Small disruptions in this system—such as the contentious views of an individual or small group of stakeholders—can threaten the process and its production of performance and predicted outcomes—learning objectives, regents' exams, SAT scores. What is required, then, is consensus. There must be agreement that systems will be maintained and regulations followed; there must be agreement that certain forms, processes, and commonplace ideas constitute identifiably acceptable writing.

By contrast, college and university writing instructors often ask writers to challenge, question, and problematize conventional formulations, to produce analytical writing and to stake out positions, to construct meaning out of one's reading, thinking, and experience. Students have seldom, if ever, been asked to undertake tasks such as these. If these tasks have even been acknowledged in their secondary schools, students have still been implicitly told that they must practice their formal skills with commonplace ideas before they will be ready to progress to the higher demands of college.

General commonplaces are valued because they allow for concentration on formal matters; they can be quickly identified as acceptable and familiar positions for a student paper so that the teacher's real work—on structural and mechanical matters—may commence. The content of the paper forms a backdrop to formal concerns where there are so many apparent problems that need attention if the student is to achieve acceptable writing. There are few English teachers who, under the load of students, papers, and both

---

[2]In my time as a high school English teacher and as a college supervisor of student teachers, I seldom encountered real argument or contention taking place in English classrooms. Where I did find this kind of activity was in ability-tracked honors and AP classes, a situation that might bear further inquiry.

institutional and community expectations, do not knowingly, if regretfully, sacrifice opportunities for developing divergent viewpoints and individual difference among their student writers.

Tom was a product of this kind of system. He struggled to survive at the university, deploying every strategy he could to produce success, as we have seen in his efforts to quantify aspects of the performance. His was an instance of a paper that had the possibility of avoiding the generalizing commonplace: There was a personal stake in his writing and he attempted to argue from his position. But the force of his school training compromised his ability to frame his argument effectively in a fashion that allowed him to use his sources for his rhetorical purpose.

Tom was unequivocal about his position. He wrote in his introductory paragraph, "It's best to be the 'average' person rather than being either above or below the average line." He then elaborated his view, "My idea is to eliminate remedial classrooms. I feel strongly about this, because I've experienced friends that have been remediated, and they are outsiders." And later, near the end of the paper, the thesis was elaborated further:

> Being mainstreamed greatly increases a person's social life as well as the knowledge part of it. Now don't get me wrong, I'm not saying that truly stupid people should be just mainstreamed. Along with this, they should be offered opportunities and programs somewhere along the line to help out. I just don't think remediation is needed that segregates all underclass students together.

Clearly, Tom had a stake in this argument. Although he did not acknowledge it either in his papers or his interviews, he was, in fact, in a remedial setting at the time he was writing the paper. English 101 is a basic writing course. Perhaps he felt like an outsider among his peers or had recent memories of high school and of the problematic status of remediated students. In any case, he was vehement about his opposition to remedial tracking, "I think that remediation is a stupid way of helping out our educational underclass."

His strategy in the paper was to summarize bits of source material where he saw his theme appearing, actually trying to carry out what he understood analysis and synthesis to be. But, in an attempt to shape the sources to his purpose, he invented positions for the authors that they actually do not hold or advance. In his protocol, he responded to the assignment's call to "use your skills of summary and analysis":

> Um, this part, I don't think will be that bad. Summaries are pretty easy, as far as I'm concerned. It's just basically a conclusion of all the material, with one main idea. Whereas, analysis is many main ideas. Analysis—we've been doing a lot of that in class lately.

Tom went on to collect his sources using what Flower described as the gist and list method, identifying general ideas in passages and selecting them for use (235). In the end, his paper contained summary unrelated to the point and he got sources wrong partly because he misunderstood them and partly because he did not read one text. Yet, Tom began the process of using sources for his argumentative purpose. And in doing so, he revised his paper in such a way that it was based less on a generalizing commonplace and more on making a claim. His first draft began with a statement of purpose: "The separation between public and private life is what I will concentrate on." This has the potential to generate the commonplace paper, a series of illustrations of separation, but Tom soon found himself, because of his personal stake, entering a discussion of remediation and its problems.

Tom's problem was that his thesis and argument—a series of repetitions of the thesis and faulty elaborations of it—remained at the level of assertion. In other words, they were opinions, often illogical, that arose from personal experience. Tom had not thought about his being implicated in the problem he identified, although he was passionate about the opinion he expressed. He had no experience of moving from passionate opinion to claim-making. Nor had he thought much about remediation as it is actually practiced, or as his sources presented it. His was a gut reaction to the very notion of marginality that remediation represents.

In fact Tom's thesis and argument, although not falling entirely into the vague and general commonplace, fell victim to the third common residue of secondary school training: the emphasis on opinion and its confusion with interpretation and analysis. Or, more specifically in the terms of secondary school experience, the pervasive distinction between what is right or wrong and what is opinion.

Teachers of first-year college students frequently hear the question, "This is just our opinion, right?" What follows from the teacher is often an explanation of what constitutes analysis and interpretation as they are practiced at the university. But the students are really asking: "Is this comment or piece of writing going to be evaluated?" Frequently the question is accompanied with another query: "This can't be right or wrong, can it?" They are asking the teacher to make a distinction in an assignment between what can be judged right or wrong and what is outside the domain of judgment, an individual's opinion. If the task falls under the first category, one set of strategies will be employed by the students; if it falls under the second, another, much less guarded and restrictive set of actions will occur.

In secondary school classes, this distinction is fundamental and normative. On one side of the equation are all of the products that can be judged right or wrong. In writing classes, these products are usually some kind of report. Reports are useful for processing large groups of students through writing classes because they can fairly easily be assessed in terms of two criteria: formal concerns and the quantity or quality of factual material accumulated and summarized. Reports fall victim less frequently to the generalized commonplace than attempts at analysis and interpretation. They are quickly assessed for reliability and thoroughness of information presentation. And they reveal students' processing of factual information via summary and paraphrase—what Flower referred to as recitation: The student collects, organizes, and recites information (233).

The report, whose degree of right or wrong may be judged in reference to these criteria, is distinguished from tasks on the other side of the equation, those that ask for one's opinion. These opinion assignments are offered for two purposes. The first is to encourage and to provide an arena for expressive writing. And, considered broadly, we might include all imaginative writing in this first category. Here students are allowed, out of their own experience, to write entirely from an individual point of view without having to turn to any other authenticating sources. What springs from their thoughts and lives may be expressed. Usually in the schools, these exercises are matched with practice in writing one or another of the imaginative genres: poem, short story, play (dialogue).

The other purpose for opinion-based writing is to reduce the effects of evaluation. In an effort to generate writing from students that is less guarded and restrictive—or rather that is less apt to fall victim to a problematic overconcern with formal matters to the exclusion of meaningful writing—teachers will indicate that the assignment is to be based on students' opinions. This is an attempt to "free up the writing process," as one high school teacher told me, "and to remove the threat of assessment" so that students will write more and write more thoughtfully.

The opinion paper is rarely permitted to be pure opinion, however. Usually students must back up their opinions with information of one kind or another. In an effort to encourage analytical writing that incorporates a point of view, rhetorical strategizing, and interpretation of substantive information, teachers have adopted a back-up-your-opinion formulation. A typical instance of this kind of writing is the persuasive essay, often included in unit or term planning. A student is asked to choose a topic on which she has an opinion. The essay then presents a case, a persuasive argument, for the student's position on the matter. Frequently, these assignments are also framed in a way that exposes students to larger concerns and debates (e.g., capital punishment) in order, as an additional objective, to involve young people in national issues.

What often emerges in the opinion paper is what Flower referred to in her TIA strategy: The writer finds ideas with which he agrees (235). This is more than a simple tactic for selecting information, however. The way one backs up one's opinion is to find sources and facts with which one agrees—or that agree with one's position, as students more frequently frame it. In other words, my opinion and material from others who agree with my opinion, constitute the substance of the argument in the persuasive essay.

This kind of writing is so common that it is taken for granted as an effective way to move students toward a more desired kind of writing, analysis. But, in fact, it seems to have other consequences as well. The study shows college students frequently invoking opinion as a strategic move that will satisfy the requirements of their paper. But they also know that opinion must be backed up by sources that agree with them. Finding sources that agree with one's own position constitutes one of the major concerns of these writers. For example, Tom went so far as to invent positions for his sources that he then used as support.

Tom said, "And I really—I guess what I should do is I should get a definite opinion down." In Cheri's first protocol, she represented the writing task before her as consisting of, "I guess kind of giving our opinion to—incorporating our opinion into what the writers are thinking." Tiffany too, in her first protocol decided that in the early stages of her writing, she must "find one of those main things that they [her sources] all have in common and then figure out which one you have the most opinions or feelings about so that you're able to write about it." She had to make sure that "it's something that I can agree or disagree on, that I have some opinions about. Because if I don't have any opinions about it, then it's going to be awful hard to show my point of view." With the paper completed and handed in, Tiffany remarked, "I like, covered the three different authors, plus my opinion. And I put them all together into a paper with a conclusion and introduction."

Opinion, in other words, is represented as a major expectation of writing in the context of school. In terms of the legacy of schooling, opinion represents the student's position that because it is opinion cannot be right or wrong. Once opinion is established, the remaining task is to find sources that agree with this opinion, to back up the opinion, to demonstrate that others share the opinion and thus to validate it.

In her protocol, Sarah responded to the assignment's suggestion that she present her own point of view as she worked with the ideas of others: "Well, there's probably going to be some disagreements in the paper meaning that if you don't agree [with] that person." Agreement or nonagreement was for her, in the beginning at least, an issue. She was unsure whether sources that disagree with each other, or, more importantly, with her opinion, were problematic or not.

Later, in the same protocol, she linked writer–source agreement with what she later considered to be a different kind of flaw: the appropriate number of quotations. When there is too much quoted material, the reader cannot tell if the writer agrees with her sources or not, "And like her paper was just quotes . . . It's not really even a paper, discussing an opinion or anything . . . when it's quotes, it's hard for the reader to really understand if you agree with them or you don't." Sarah here revealed the familiar dichotomy between right–wrong and opinion, but in a manner that shows she was trying to move beyond the well-learned impulse to quantify right elements of a paper. She knew that a paper dominated by quotations was not what this assignment demands. A college paper discusses a writer's opinion and the sources that agree or disagree with the writer's opinion. About quotations, she said, "I mean you don't want it full of quotations, but more of your own ideas."

In her final interview, Sarah discussed how she came up with her main idea (cultural miscommunication causes conflict). The interviewer asked, "How did you arrive at that?"

> One, by my own experience and also with reading through some of the authors—with them talking about communication. Basically they all agreed with me. I don't really have an argument in my paper. But, because they all agreed that communication in certain different ways . . .

Although the project was completed, clearly this was not the end of the matter for Sarah. She was beginning to see that opinion itself might be problematic and that something called argument is now valued. Sarah began her paper with an anecdote illustrating cultural miscommunication. In the conference, she considered what she had done:

> It's not, like, factual stuff. It's more like a story. I feel like I'm just like giving quotes and then I'm saying what they mean, what I think that they mean, and then give my opinion . . . I mean, I could be wrong and it might look different to someone else, but I feel like that's just kind of like what it is . . . I mean, I haven't really—I don't really have an argument in here.

She was struck, for the moment, by a new distinction between opinion and argument, and was not able to see how point of view informs and directs argument. Yet she showed that she was beginning to move beyond the distinction between report and opinion. She knew how to report the specific details of an anecdote, and she gave her opinion, but when she considered a reader with a different point of view who might see the facts differently, she realized that she did not have an argument—a way of persuading the reader that her interpretation of the facts was valid.

Sarah had made a step here in her understanding of the analysis paper. It was beginning to be visible to her that a writer analyzes facts from a point of view and constructs a persuasive argument with evidence that will make that point of view compelling. In the end, she claimed that the paper did not have an argument after all, but the final interview continued to demonstrate that she was moving beyond the report–opinion dichotomy.

> [At first] I decided that I would take—I'd state my viewpoint in the beginning and then I would take an author, state their viewpoint and then say if I agree, disagree, why, why not, and why my reader should agree with what I'm saying. And so I did that with three authors and then had my summary—conclusion stuff. Um, I started doing my paper and I kind of thought—God, this is so boring. . . . So our class discussed a lot about trying to make our papers interesting . . . And so, when I put my story in the beginning, it gave me things to refer back to and made it more interesting, rather than just facts, kind of like an anecdote to it or whatever. So, I kind of stayed with that. And getting my quotations was just basically reading through stuff, trying to find quotations that referred, you know, to what I was talking about. Or if it didn't, you know, maybe if there was a difference of view—write it because that would be good to show why I think they should agree with me. And I don't know—I mean—it just kind of came to me as I wrote.

At the end of the project, in other words, Sarah had not only moved away from reporting, she was considering reader response (it's boring), talking with members of her group, making a rhetorical move to adjust to that response (include a story), and in addition to finding writers to agree or disagree with, finding source material that might represent a different point of view. This source material was useful because she could use it to show readers why they should agree with her point of view. And she resolved the problem of quotations, realizing that what was needed was "more of your own ideas." Sarah has begun constructive planning as Flower termed it (240): Thinking about goals, evaluative criteria, and design problems in the paper, but she has had to see through a powerful component of her former training to do so.

In the early think-aloud protocol, Sarah said she remembers having only written a research report and some book reports. She said that she did not know "the difference between summary and analysis," although because of the class, she now does. She knows, furthermore, that opinion giving is not sufficient; there must be sources with whom one agrees or disagrees. By the end of the project, she knew there was a reader whom she must interest and persuade, and she was aware that she must use sources, even ones with which she disagrees, to make a case that will persuade an actual reader. Her final product is not perfect; she still has some way to go before she will be able to write a successful paper for introductory literature. But she is on her way.

What is the legacy of schooling in Sarah's case? We can see it in her concerns at the beginning of the process:

finding enough information from each author . . . choose your three authors
. . . five to seven pages . . . dig into these books and see what they're trying
to tell us . . . And write down what they said and their ideas and write down,
you know, how you feel, and if you don't agree, state why. And set it up in
a paper.

In other words, her legacy is quantifying, reporting, stating a commonplace,
and opinion giving. But, as we have seen, she moved from these well-
learned understandings toward reader awareness, rhetorical purpose, and
argument.

Cheri shares with Sarah this legacy of schooling and her thesis, too, was
a generalizing commonplace. But at the end of her final interview, Cheri's
response to a question indicated she had not really begun the breakthrough
to constructive planning in her own paper. She was asked if she thought
the paper was her own idea. She replied:

I don't know if it's, I would say, my whole own idea. You know, Hirsch has
some ideas and Smith. I agree with their ideas, but to say they're my own—
like, hey, I thought of these—but I agree with them. So I guess, it kind of
is my own idea throughout the paper, but I don't know.

Cheri was still framing her project in terms of TIA, finding sources with
which she agreed, appropriating them as her own and attempting to make
out of them an acceptable thesis. This process resulted in a paper that did
not include her real position or stake in the issue and a topic that permitted
no real disagreement. Sarah, on the other hand, began with a TIA strategy,
but found the result boring and moved on to issues like reader interest,
divergent points of view, and a paper that incorporated her own ideas.

Sarah's progress was made possible, in part, by putting the legacy of
schooling on the table for discussion in the class. Students quickly became
aware of the limitations under which they had usually written. Bringing a
new set of options and strategies into view is not easy, however. As we have
seen, there is much confusion, recursive movement back and forth between
new and old knowledge, and lapses into familiar and comfortable strategies.
These, of course, are not errors but part of the acquisition of new knowledge and new literacy. What is important to note here, however, are the
components of students' legacy of schooling. These are powerful and familiar strategies, as Flower indicated (242). And they are the consequences
of writing instruction that itself is impinged upon by institutional demands
that limit its form and possibilities.

This instruction is neither wholly the product of the secondary schools
nor are teachers, at whatever level, wholly responsible for perpetuating it.
College instruction that underwrites quantifications, generalizing conten-
tions with which no one can disagree, and report–opinion dualisms con-

tributes to the difficulty students experience in making the transition to academic literacy. For the most part, college and university courses expect more of their students although because of their experience in certain disciplines, students may misinterpret what is expected of them. Writing center instructors will know, for example, that students writing in the social or hard sciences frequently have to write reports. Clearly, these texts serve specific functions in those domains. But they can also inadvertantly leave the impression that synthetic writing is somehow the extraordinary demand of a few disciplines and can confirm students' sense that the research paper or report is the standard for writing at the university.

Students' confusion over expectations arises from the perfectly normal problem of making the transition to academic writing, but it can also be exacerbated by teaching that emphasizes reporting at the expense of other operations. This kind of teaching is not attributable to neglect; writing teachers fall back on familiar strategies too. Both secondary- and university-level teachers are often driven by institutional constraints to adopt teaching practices that do not foster real attention to writing and that do not encourage and nurture difference, divergence, or contention. For one thing, it takes time to attend to students' real struggles. And, of course, time, to institutions, is money. In a climate of downsizing and section-cutting, we as teachers may manage our increasing loads by falling back on our own well-developed strategies, requiring easily evaluated quantities, allowing generalizing commonplaces to pass while we assess formal issues, and if we find we are reading papers in which students have nothing to say, assigning an opinion paper.

WORKS CITED

Bartholomae, David. "Inventing the University." *When a Writer Can't Write.* Ed. Mike Rose. New York: Guilford Press, 1985. 134–165.

Elbow, Peter. "Being a Writer vs. Being an Academic." *College Composition and Communication* 46 (1995): 72–83.

Flower, Linda, Margaret J. Kantz, and Kathleen McCormick. *Reading-to-Write: Exploring a Cognitive and Social Process.* New York: Oxford UP, 1990.

Hirsch, E. D., Jr. *Cultural Literacy: What Every American Needs to Know.* Boston: Houghton Mifflin, 1987.

Mortensen, Peter, and Gesa E. Kirsch. "On Authority in the Study of Writing." *College Composition and Communication* 44 (1993): 556–572.

Rose, Mike. *Lives on the Boundary.* New York: Penguin Books, 1990.

Smith, Frank. "Myths of Writing." *Language Arts* 58 (1981).

Chapter 5

How Beginning Writing Students Interpret the Task of Writing an Academic Argument[1]

Stuart Greene
University of Notre Dame

Rose, Rodriguez and Hirsch have raised many interesting questions about the education system in this country, questions such as what will be taught, who will decide, who will be taught, how will it be taught? But all of these questions focus around one thing, what Hirsch called cultrual literacy. He defines it as "thnetwork of information that all competent readers posses" (50). All three authors agree, in one way or another, that our education system is the cause of an increased cultural illiteracy among the people of this country, particularly with the people who are at the stage of their secondary and post-secondary education. The result of this increase has produce an increase of students who are unable to meet the level of cultural literacy set by the school. The difference between these authors is that although each knows what the general problem is, each has his own idea of where the problem is specifically coming from and his own way of solving the problem.

In this excerpt from the introduction to a beginning writing student's paper (the paper is reproduced in its entirety in the appendix to this chapter), the student establishes the importance of certain questions that find their source in E. D. Hirsch's conception of cultural literacy. He maintains that different authors agree that the educational system in the United States is not working, and he points out that each author has a

---

[1]This study was funded by the National Council of Teachers of English Research Foundation. Portions of this chapter appear in Greene, "Making Sense of My Own Ideas," and are reproduced with permission from Sage Publications.

different idea about how to solve the problem.[2] This student presents his questions and concerns in a clear and direct way, thus setting up the discussion that will follow. We expect a review of the issues and what each of these authors has said. What may be less clear is what this student thinks about the issues he discusses. Given the way he frames this essay, what would you infer was the assignment he was given? To write a summary of the issues he has read about? To include his own ideas? To analyze and synthesize information from sources? For me, a key question is how this writer interpreted the task he was given and the story that lies behind this text. What prompted this writer to focus on these three authors and the issue of cultural literacy? Were there other choices that he might have made? What does he leave out?

The purpose of this chapter is to address these questions in the context of a study designed to explore how 15 beginning college writers both interpret and negotiate academic writing tasks that require them to integrate their own ideas with the ideas of others. This research focused on an ethnically and culturally diverse group of 15 students who spent the term reading and writing about the topic of literacy, one that gave them an occasion to explore their own practices as readers and writers. The task of creating a text from other texts can provide a window on a problem that is not unique to beginning writers, but that has become increasingly more a part of beginning writing instruction (e.g., Bartholomae and Petrosky, *Facts, Artifacts, and Counterfacts*): how to mediate and make sense of different and conflicting voices within a shared conceptual world. To synthesize information marks an important intellectual step in which an author represents a community of writers and their abiding interests, not simply the interests of a single author.

Although educators have come to value students' ability to analyze, synthesize, and integrate others' ideas within their own intellectual project (cf. Bartholomae, "Inventing the University"), few studies, specifically with beginning writers, have looked closely at the motives, decisions, and actions that influence students' thinking as they read to write in school. In fact, despite an increasing concern with integrating reading in the remedial writing classroom, Glynda Hull and Mike Rose pointed out that "we make inferences about what students learn or don't learn with limited knowledge" (140). But if we are to help beginning writers learn to think critically, then we will need to know more about how students struggle with con-

---

[2]As a number of educators have suggested, the labels used to describe students' abilities as writers, such as underprepared, remedial, and basic, are all problematic (e.g., Fox 65–68; Rose, especially 167–204). Following Bartholomae (*Teaching Basic Writing*), I use the term *beginning* to talk about student writers who may be adept at thinking through and solving problems but who lack the options that might enable them to apply what they know flexibly and appropriately in different rhetorical situations.

flicting discourses as they construct their own experiences and advance their own rhetorical purposes as authors.

In studying students' approaches to this reading-to-write task, I asked three primary questions: (a) How did the instructor represent the task of writing an essay based on different sources of information and the process of writing in the classroom? (b) What are some possible ways that student–teacher interactions can influence how students negotiate and construct meaning in reading and writing? and (c) What were students' interpretations of writing an essay based on sources; that is, what sorts of knowledge and experience would they draw on as primary sources of information in fulfilling this task? Together, this knowledge and experience can include (but is not restricted to) the texts they read for class and students' ways of reading and writing related to their social and intellectual backgrounds. More specifically, as James Banks pointed out, students' knowledge consists of the concepts, explanations, and interpretations that derive from personal experience at home or within their community; facts, explanations, and interpretations that are disseminated through mass media; and the kinds of generalizations and interpretations that students find in school, including textbooks and teachers' lectures (6–10). Although students may adopt a particular stance, conveying what might be construed as their own ideas in authoring a text, the ideas they hold are expressions of shared commitments and beliefs that are rooted in class, race, and gender.

In what follows, I develop an account of how we might begin to draw connections between the mind of individual students and culture and ethnicity. Once we ask how writers—who are also readers—construct meaning, then the interaction between personal intentions, ability, and conventions becomes the subject of inquiry. The way each force shapes the other remains a compelling and open question to both researchers and teachers interested in building a sociocognitive theory of meaning making. Of particular interest to my study of authorship is to reveal the decision-making points that can enable us to understand the hidden logic that motivates what a writer does, a logic that may be only partially apparent to a teacher or reader. These decision-making points are part of a larger theory of negotiated meaning (Flower, *The Construction of Negotiated Meaning* 36–84) that can bring into focus how individual writers reflect on competing demands and alternatives, develop an awareness of options, and weigh these options in the face of conflict. It is in the face of conflict, both the inner voices that compete for a writer's attention and those voices outside the writer—that negotiation appears.

Such a view of negotiated meaning provides a basis on which to examine some key assumptions that are deeply held in our field and so ingrained as to be tacit. For example, theorists (e.g., Bruffee; Clarke; Trimbur, "Consensus and Difference") tend to equate conversation with knowledge construction, observing what effect conversation has on its participants—how the attitudes and ideas they bring to social interaction are being challenged, reaffirmed, or perhaps ignored as they simultaneously interpret, fail to understand, or resist what is said. We also assume that students' voices play an essential role in learning as does the teacher's in giving shape to the structure of social interaction. After all, social processes mediate individual cognition, as Vygotsky's sociohistorical studies suggest. Vygotsky argued further that selves must be accounted for in terms of these social processes and in terms of communication. An analysis of classroom discourse can provide one way to explore these assumptions, enabling us to understand why students make the choices they do in reading to write and gain some insight into the struggle that is involved as they try to give expression to others' ideas in their own unique ways (Nystrand and Gamoran, "Instructional Discourse"). But how students construct meaning and give expression to their ideas also depends on the ways in which they *negotiate* the conflicting voices, "contradictory opinions, points of view and value judgments" that are very much a part of their prior linguistic, social, and cultural experiences (Bakhtin, "Discourse in the Novel" 281). Therefore, we cannot necessarily assume that what students learn is a function of the social interaction that occurs within a classroom. Moreover, to ignore the role that individual cognition plays in writing is to deny agency (i.e., the active, constructive power of individual writers) and students' unique sociolinguistic backgrounds that influence how they approach academic writing.

There are indeed limits to emphasizing the individual as a locus of meaning because we can lose sight of the larger cultural and institutional pressures that influence how writers compose. After all, as Barbara Rogoff observed, an "individual's efforts and sociocultural arrangements and involvement are inseparable, mutually embedded forces of interest" (27). And Henry Trueba pointed out that "intellectual development is socially and culturally based, and that what happens in the home, school, and local community . . . is crucial to understanding the learning processes and academic achievement" of all students (279). Still, as Glynda Hull and her colleagues suggested, without the promise of a more fine-grained analysis of students' experiences as readers and writers, "we risk losing sight of the particulars of behavior" (322). Seen in this way, taking a microperspective has both practical and theoretical significance in that a study based on close observation can provide a window on moments of decision making, conflict, and negotiation, each of which can have an enormous impact on a writer's performance of difficult tasks, can provide insight into the interplay of cognition and context, and can invite further observation-based theory building (e.g., how does the process of negotiation work in different contexts?).

By looking closely at individual writers' process of composing and their texts, we can provide an important link between the private and often unpredictable acts of mind and the form, style, and expression of students' ideas within a rhetorical situation. We may assume that a writer's interpretation is a stable, integrated image of a task, but writers often change goals and strategies throughout the process of composing because of their conflicting sense of who they are writing for: the teacher as examiner, an interested reader, their peers and the like (Greene, "The Role of Task in the Development of Academic Thinking" 59–62, 71; cf. Freedman). This kind of conflict provides some sense of how complicated the process of writing can be for beginning writers. The implications of such a study are significant for those who teach because with this knowledge we can begin to understand the reasoning behind the choices students make as they attempt to adapt and transform the ideas of others into their own idioms.

An Analysis of Classroom Discourse

An important part of my discussion of authorship is a brief, but representative excerpt of classroom discourse from a 50-minute discussion of the assignment the instructor gave his students: to write an essay about literacy. Throughout the term, the instructor tried to provoke discussion in class about writing and the issues students wanted to focus on, rather than present information about writing; in this excerpt his approach is no different. Here we can begin to see the ways in which language provides students with an important source of information about the kind of talk that is valued and what is legitimate to talk about in writing their essays. Specifically, the analysis that follows addresses a key question in this study: What are some possible ways that student–teacher interactions can influence how students negotiate and construct meaning in reading and writing?

A regular observer in this class, I took field notes and audiotaped each class during a 15-week semester. I also used various process-tracing methods, including retrospective protocols and cued questions in order to understand students' evolving interpretations of the task they were given.[3] And, finally, I read the literacy autobiographies that all of the students in the course wrote for class in order to learn about their experiences as readers and writers in different institutional and cultural settings.

The instructor of the course was a doctoral student in literature who had an advanced degree in education.[4] His teaching was highly rated by both faculty and students and he had a great deal of experience working with

---

[3]Although I did not participate in class discussions, it could be argued that I played a key role in the students' writing. Think-aloud protocols and interviews prompted these six students to give accounts of writing that they would not have otherwise provided (Swanson-Owens and Newell).

[4]The instructor is Nick Preus, who writes about these students' legacy of schooling in this volume. With Jeffrey Wiemelt, he provided much insight into students' writing.

diverse groups of students struggling with basic literacy skills. In addition to having taught remedial students in high school and college in rural areas of the Midwest, he had taken courses in composition theory and attended a weekly colloquium on the teaching of writing designed to meet the needs of at-risk students. Unlike the students in his course, some of whom were economically disadvantaged and were the first generation in their family to attend a university, he grew up in a family of educators. In fact, both his parents and grandparents were college teachers and administrators from small-town Midwest environments. And like his immediate family, the instructor had attended a Lutheran college where the sons and daughters of Midwest farmers, small-town businessmen, and ministers could get an education. It was established to serve the needs of the rural, working community.

The starting point for the students' analysis of literacy was a literacy autobiography that focused on a wide range of potential topics for their writing: the role language (including talk) played in their family and different social groups; how reading and writing figured into their relationship with their friends at various stages of their lives; the kinds of reading and writing they had done in school; the significant memories they had of successes and failures; and the role reading and writing played in developing their identity. These students shared their autobiographies in writing groups, began to formulate their own theories about what constitutes literate practice, and read such works as Richard Rodriguez's *Hunger of Memory*, Mike Rose's *Lives on the Boundary*, E. D. Hirsch's *Cultural Literacy*, and excerpts from Eudora Welty's *One Writer's Beginnings* and Alice Walker's *In Search of Our Mother's Gardens*. About midway through the semester, the instructor asked students to write an argument that focused on an issue, question, or problem that was in dispute and that sought to further the class's understanding of literacy. For example, one could raise the question (as one student did) of how the notion of cultural literacy could exist within a climate of multicultural diversity and then provide an argument explaining why such an issue needed more attention than it had been given in either class discussion or the reading. The students were told that they could base their essays both on their own experiences (e.g., their literacy autobiographies) and the reading. Although students might be engaged more authentically in some social project or one in which the students selected their own sources based on a problem or issue they identified, the task in this class represented the kind of writing that students are often asked to produce in other courses across the curriculum. Such a task also provided a form of instructional scaffolding, one that engaged students in generating new knowledge through discovering what others had said before they turned to a final project in which they developed an essay based on self-selected sources.

The instructor said in class that he wanted his students to write an argument in order to give them an opportunity to explore an issue in a focused way. They would have 4 weeks to complete their essays. The main statement of the assignment he gave them was this:

> In writing your essay, I would like you to discuss an issue related to literacy that has come up in the readings, class discussions, or in your autobiography. Construct an argument that stakes out your position on the issue and that also reveals your understanding of what others have said about this issue. Try to show why your view is the one with which we should agree.

In an interview, he explained that he had five specific goals in mind when he designed this assignment: (a) to expose his students to different and conflicting perspectives on a critical controversy, (b) to teach them how to appraise a writer's argument, (c) to see links among different arguments in a variety of source texts, (d) to learn how to narrow a topic and formulate a controlling idea or point of view, and (e) to help students learn how to interweave their own ideas with relevant information from sources. Although students in an academic context are not often invited to include their own ideas in writing an argumentative essay (Higgins), the instructor placed a high value on students' personal engagement with issues related to their own literate experiences in different social contexts.

In class, he read a one-page assignment aloud, emphasizing that his students should "play with the ideas of the other people [they had] been reading"; that they should "formulate their ideas . . . [their] own point of view . . . and set up an argument that is based more on conflict [than] agreement"; "choose an issue that is interesting to you"; "map out [your ideas]"; "play ideas off one another"; "set up a dialogue"; and "use sources to create a discussion." He also posed the following questions that he wanted them to consider throughout the process of writing their essays: Is there a clear problem or issue (i.e., something in dispute) that motivates the essay? Is it held in focus? Does the essay help clarify the problem or issue? Does it go beyond the sources to make an original claim?

In the discussion that immediately followed the instructor's remarks, one student, John,[5] observed that both E. D. Hirsch and Richard Rodriguez touched on the idea of cultural literacy in their writings, but John wondered if Mike Rose had done so as well in *Lives on the Boundary*.[6] When the

---

[5]All students' names are pseudonyms.

[6]At the risk of simplifying the ideas presented by these three authors, I'll give just a thumbnail sketch of what these authors focused on in their respective texts in order to provide some sense of the issues the students in class had talked about. In his book *Cultural Literacy*, E. D. Hirsch argued that educators need to establish a common culture or canon of texts as a core of background knowledge for those who are not enculturated or who are inadequately enculturated within literate society. In an autobiographical work, *Lives on the Boundary*, Mike Rose provided, among other things, a probing analysis of education in America, describing in some very poignant terms the difficulties students face when they try to enter an academic community that they do not really understand. Rose also suggested

instructor responded to John's question about how Rose's discussion of
literacy fit in, he (i.e., the instructor) raised questions that invited his
students to participate in the conversation ("What do you mean?") and
that were motivated by his attempts to clarify a point ("Tell me again,
what's the problem"?). As illustrated in a brief, yet representative, excerpt
of classroom discourse, he also tried to reframe the problem that students
were working on to keep the conversation going, although much of the
burden of sorting out the meaning of such words as information remained
with the students. The ellipses here and in excerpts from retrospective
protocols represent pauses unless otherwise noted.

John: Hirsch and Rodriguez sort of talked about minorities possessing
        information . . . (pause) actually I guess uh yeah Hirsch and
        Rodriguez I guess Rose did too.
Inst: Tell me again. What's the problem?
John: Minorities possessing information.
Inst: Possessing infor . . . (student interrupts)
John: Yeah, information which is . . .
Inst: How do you mean that?
John: How do I mean it?
Inst: Yeah. What do you mean?
John: Well (laughs), which is essential for minor . . . for improving
        social and economic status. (His voice goes up as if questioning.)
Inst: OK, crucial for social and economic advancement. How could
        we . . . work Rose into the discussion? (Silence for 5 seconds)
        OK, let's back up. Minorities possessing information. It's crucial
        for advancement. Now what do you mean by information?

What begins as a conversation between a student and his teacher evolves
into a relatively open discussion among the students who coconstruct
knowledge, as shown in the excerpt below, about the role that information
(or knowledge) can play in the lives of minority students.

Beth: They don't possess it or they do?
John: They do.

---

that developing a core curriculum will not necessarily create the sort of equity in culture
and society that Hirsch seeks (see especially 233–238). Finally, in his autobiography, *Hunger
of Memory*, Richard Rodriguez explained the conflicts he experienced as a nonnative speaker
of English who desperately sought to enter mainstream culture, even if this meant sacrificing
his identity as the son of Mexican immigrants.

Inst: But . . . you're saying that Hirsch and Rodriguez are saying that minorities need to have a certain kind of information?

Beth: Yeah.

Inst: In order to advance. Is that right?

Beth: Yeah.

Inst: And you're saying that Hirsch and Rodriguez say that?

Beth: Well yeah.

Inst: OK.

Carol: I don't understand the concept.

Inst: You don't understand the concept? Let's rework it.

John: You want me to state it in a different way?

Inst: What are we getting at?

Jesus: Aren't we saying minority people need more information about culture so that they can further their lives? I mean like Hirsch and Rodriguez needed to know more about you know their own cultures so that we will be better off in society.

John: Sure. (He concedes the point and the class laughs.)

Inst: That's an example. What's the point, right? How do we phrase it so that it does make sense? Are we getting tripped by the word information? Is that the problem?

Vuong: Knowledge.

Inst: Knowledge. Do you like knowledge better? Is this what you're saying? Or is it different?

Vuong: Well, that could be.

John: But is it? (laughs)

That both students and their teacher frame questions, expecting active responsive understanding and anticipating such an understanding in return, infuses such talk with a dialogic quality (cf. Bakhtin, *Speech Genres*, 69, 91, 94). In this way, the students and their instructor begin to create a jointly negotiated context that influences the kind of thinking that can occur within this classroom (Nystrand). The issues students discuss are not given, but are constructed through the give-and-take of social interaction. And the students' roles require that they actively participate in the making of knowledge and meaning. In fact, the students not only help to maintain the conversation, but insure that it develops in a way that begins to reflect their own ideas about what they are trying to understand ("Aren't we saying minority people need more information about culture so that they can further their lives?").

This kind of talk appears quite different, I think, from more traditional approaches to teaching in beginning writing classrooms, where discourse is often structured around a teacher's question, a student's response, and a teacher's evaluation (see also Hull et al. 302–306; Mehan; Nystrand and Gamoran 263–64). Such an instructional sequence attempts to foster students' acquisition of given information; knowledge is not constructed, but received, so that students play a passive role in learning. So powerful is this schema for doing school that some students in this class may have believed that their instructor was testing what they knew rather than exploring possible answers to a student's question. In fact, when he asked the first student, John, what he meant, John answered tentatively, trying to determine if he had the "right answer" that his instructor might have been searching for. "What do you mean," the instructor asked. "Well," the student responded, "which is essential for minor . . . for improving social and economic status [?]." Thus, students like John must often negotiate the seemingly conflicting discourses that ask students to recite given information, on the one hand, and that invite students to inquire into unresolved issues to advance the conversation, on the other.

It is important to recognize what students say and how their words are received. In this case, the instructor does not seem to respond to John and Vuong in the same way that he does to both Beth and Jesus. John's repeated statement ("minorities possessing information" for survival) is followed in each instance by a probing form of a question ("what do you mean?"). At the same time, when Beth asks a question (minorities "don't or do" possess information), the instructor rephrases her question ("you are saying") and turning the question into a statement (the writers are saying that "minorities need to have a certain kind of information," that is, they do not have information for survival, as John has been asserting). When Jesus repeats the instructor's reading established by the paraphrase of Beth's question in the form of a rhetorical question beginning with a we, the instructor again lets it go without any probing. One might wonder, then, if these students' interpretations of task is influenced by the instructor's seeming willingness to accept and develop some students' "own" meanings while persistently probing the meanings of other students.

How these students interpret the writing task they have been given depends on the context of particular events in class and the language used, a language that also lives on the boundary of other contexts and that is saturated with different and often conflicting values and beliefs (Bakhtin, "Discourse in the Novel" 281–84; Volosinov 102). Words such as "argument," "minority education," and "cultural literacy" that become important reference points in the class discussion about how to write an essay about literacy enter from different contexts permeated with others' interpretations, thereby complicating students' attempts to both construct and negotiate meaning.

For many of the students, this way of talking about texts and ideas in class can be removed from their social and intellectual backgrounds (e.g., their home communities), so that they may have viewed this discussion from an outsider's perspective. Although the instructor tries to bring his students inside the textual world he constructs with them, the discussion remains focused on the texts his students have read, not their own experiences as they might have expressed them in their literacy autobiographies. The discourses of home and school are treated as separate and discrete, at least implicitly, even though these conflicting voices may persist in the minds of the students who must negotiate a stance in their writing about what they think and feel about the issue of literacy. As Min-Zhan Lu observed, it is difficult to keep these two worlds separate ("From Silence to Words"). In addition, even though the students read works by Welty and Walker, the students were not encouraged, in this excerpt anyway, to think about how those authors' ideas might have contributed to the discussion about cultural literacy. What is left *un*said in this discussion is as important as what is said in thinking about how students might interpret the task before them and in thinking about their role as authors.

Still others may have also felt left outside of the conversation, particularly those students who suffer the anxiety that perhaps they do not belong. Such a response may very well have been reinforced by the reading, which included repeated images of students who feel they are outside of language, who have been silenced and marginalized, and who struggle to be accepted in a community that values a certain way of thinking. Rose underscores the dislocation that occurs when students (like himself) begin to cross educational boundaries. And he considers that all he achieved may have been a "ruse." Although recognizing that a life of the mind could somehow foster "competence" and lead him into the world, Rose also suggests that "this was all very new and fragile" (47). As Vuong, the student who wrote the essay that appears at the beginning of the previous section put it in a retrospective protocol, "Rose . . . he gives you an idea of what is happening to people . . . happening to some of the students who are not prepared. And I just feel . . . and it makes me think of whether I'm really that prepared or not."

Interpreting the Task of Writing an Argument

If we are to understand how students internalize the voices that enter from different contexts and how they negotiate a path through the ideas of others, then we need to go beyond this kind of close reading of classroom discourse, accounting for the complex web of meaning that writers construct. We need to hear our students' voices. Listen for a moment to John, the student who initiated the class discussion of whether Rose's analysis of literacy fit in with Rodriguez' and Hirsch's arguments about cultural literacy. In a retrospective protocol describing how he interpreted the task, John paused after reading the first few words of the assignment, particularly when he considered what it might mean to enter a conversation or dispute the assertions of the authorities he has read: "First of all," he said, "I feel that it's . . . that's the hardest part because I think it's going to be hard to so called 'speak' in this paper with these other writers, such as Hirsch, Rose, and Rodriguez. That's going to be pretty difficult."

To illustrate further the problems that can complicate beginning writers' attempts to contribute their own ideas in creating a text from other texts, I return to the student whose essay I began to analyze earlier. I chose to discuss Vuong, a Hmong student, as a case example because the problems discussed here typify the conflicts that other students in this study of 15 beginning writers confronted in writing their essays. Although this illustration does not represent the processes that these other students engaged in, Vuong helps to show the ways in which interpreting a writing task is situated in a broad context of understanding.

Vuong came to the United States when he was 5 and is the first generation of his family to attend public school in this country. In the literacy autobiography he wrote for class, Vuong mentioned that he was never really encouraged to read very much, explaining that his parents were "never well educated." But he developed over the years a sense that school and learning English could be essential sources for his success. In the ninth grade, his first year of high school, he was placed in ESL classes in science, English, and history because his test scores on English were quite low. By his second year, he had only one ESL class and had been placed in mainstream classes, except for English. In his last 2 years of high school, he took both an introductory course in writing, as well as a class in intermediate writing for native speakers. In these classes, Vuong wrote comparison papers, argumentative essays (e.g., "Why television is better than going out into the stadium and watching the real game"), but mostly he wrote reports that entailed doing some research. His previous teachers encouraged him to include his own ideas, but the primary emphasis was on the details of writing, that is, how to format the paper, including footnotes and bibliography.

Vuong's First Impressions of the Writing Task. After participating in and listening to the class discussion about cultural literacy, Vuong provided, in a retrospective protocol outside of class, the following impressions of what he thought the task required. With the written assignment before him, he thought aloud, explaining that the task appeared to require him to integrate his interpretation of the reading with his own opinions, to use examples, and to take a position by first comparing and contrasting the arguments of three different authors:[7]

> So he wants us to write about the authors that we've been reading about
> . . . he wants us to get the main point of view of different authors and to
> discuss whether they agree with each other or they don't agree with each
> other and to pick out something from these three authors that is most
> important to you and try to get a position . . . which author you think is
> most closest to your idea . . . pick the authors that most agree with you and
> try to tell your reader and convince them that your point is the right one
> . . . or is the most logical. He did want us to give examples of what the
> authors that we're going to choose say about their idea. Also he wants us
> to express our opinions of what these authors have seen.

Appropriating some of the language from the assignment—to use examples and express an opinion—Vuong interpreted the task in a reasonable way. He was simply doing what he believed he was asked to do and provided some structure to a relatively open-ended task of writing an argument. A further analysis of his initial impression of the task also reveals Vuong's understanding of the nature of academic work, particularly the emphasis he placed on the authority of both the teacher and the authors he has read. It is, after all, his teacher who sanctions what he writes:

> *He* wants us to write about the authors that we've been reading about . . .
> *he* wants us to get the main point of view of different authors and to
> discuss whether they agree with each other or they don't agree with
> each other. . . . *He* did want us to give examples of what the authors . . .
> say about their idea. (emphasis added).

And although recognizing the possibility of including his own ideas, Vuong saw that the source of his ideas resides, for the most part, in the texts: "pick out something from these authors" and "express our opinions of what these authors have seen."

Thus, even though the instructor appears to have invited students to adapt the sources they read for their own purposes as authors, Vuong's interpre-

---

[7]On the day that the 15 students received the assignment in class, I met individually with six participants in the study and asked each student to read the assignment from start to finish, commenting and thinking aloud into a tape recorder as they read. Immediately after they finished thinking aloud about how they might go about writing the essay for class, they were then asked a series of cued questions designed to gather further information about these students' interpretations of the task (e.g., Do you have a sense of what you want to write or the point you want to make in this paper? and What's important to you in accomplishing this task?). I also interviewed the instructor of the course on two occasions in order to understand the learning goals of the course and the goals of the assignment he gave them.

tation reflects a fundamental tension between two versions of what it means to write in school, a tension that seems implicit in the wording of the assignment: to demonstrate an "understanding of the reading" and to "stake out [a] position." On the one hand, students are often asked to reproduce information, revealing that they have done the reading for a single reader: the teacher as examiner. On the other hand, students in a university setting are also expected to orchestrate different points of view in developing an intellectual project of their own, one that foregrounds their ideas within an ongoing conversation. The differences are anything but trivial when students set out to write and try to determine their role as writers in completing an unfamiliar task of creating a text from other texts or when they do not feel that they are a part of the conversation. Here Vuong appeared to rely on a well-learned strategy of comparing different authors, thereby making an unfamiliar task familiar, and eventually found a way to enter this scholarly discussion about literacy in the United States.

However, Vuong built a very different representation of the task when he considered his own experiences. Like Richard Rodriguez, Vuong revealed a profound concern about how his own assimilation in Western culture and Christian values would affect his relationship to his family, his traditions, and the language that defines who he is. In fact, we learn from the account that he provided immediately after his retrospective protocol that he wanted to write about cultural literacy because of the impact the reading had on him as a student trying to succeed in school and as someone coming to terms with his cultural identity:

> [The reading] has more meaning to me than what I've read during high school. It relates to me so much . . . Rodriguez tells about his separation of his parents coming further from his parents because of education. . . . I've been finding that it's not only me, but it's becoming more in general for Asian students . . . for my nationality. It's that as we become more educated we go further apart from our family and our traditions. We become more assimilated into the American culture . . . for some American kids this won't mean too much. [O]ur class comes from a middle class, so they are not familiar with these books here. And they can't relate very well to these books when I talk to them a few of them. But for a person who is assimilating into American culture this is a big problem. So for this paper I'm trying to get a more . . . an increased understanding of what cultural literacy really means.

Here Vuong focused more on his own identity than the authors' ideas when he shifted his sense of audience from his instructor to his peers. Moreover, the source for writing seems to derive from a sense of conflict he identified between his own cultural background and the other students in class, not from what the instructor wants him to do (e.g., "He did want us to give examples of what the authors . . . say about their idea").

From Interpretation to Text. What is most striking about Vuong's text is the extent to which he maintains the separation between the discourse of school and home. He did not talk about his own concerns about assimilation and ethnic identity. Nor did he mention the conflict that he felt between his reading of *Lives on the Boundary* or *Hunger of Memory* and his sense that the other students did not seem to understand the full import of these books. Instead, he focused primarily on what the authors said about cultural literacy, which is consistent with his very first impression of what he might write about—that the task required him to talk about other people's ideas. In this, he demonstrated the power of his initial impressions of how he might write his essay and a legacy of schooling that places a great deal of value on recitation of received ideas. The reading clearly shaped his point of view and motivated his discussion of cultural literacy so that he subordinated his own ideas to those discussed by published authorities.

The opening paragraph helps to indicate the topical structure (see, for example, Witte, "Topical Structure and Writing Quality") of his essay, one that focuses on the authors he has read and his statement of a problem: the lack of agreement about how educators will deal with the apparent failures of the American educational system. I italicized those phrases that indicate that the topical structure (i.e., what each sentence is about) of Vuong's essay is organized around the ideas of the authorities' he has read:

> *All three authors agree,* in one way or another, that our education system is the cause of an increased cultural illiteracy among the people of this country, particularly with the people who are at the stage of their secondary and post-secondary education. *The result of this increase* has produce an increase of students who are unable to meet the level of cultural literacy set by the school. *The difference between these authors* is that although each knows what the general problem is, each has his own idea of where the problem is specifically coming from and his own way of solving the problem.

What follows this introduction is a summary of the authors' positions. Vuong used the sources to structure his essay and sought some sort of consensus among these different authorities:

> *These authors* go about arguing their points by first defining who is the culturally illiterate, then onto why the school system is at fault, and finally give their solution to the problem. *Rose's suggestion* is "more opportunities to develope [their] writing strategies . . . to talk about what they [had been] learning. . . . to let [them] in on the secret talk" (193–194). . . . *Hirsch believes* that the most culturally illiterate people are the young generation of Americans in high school. *Hirsch states,* "During the period 1970–1985, the

amount of shared knowledge that we have been able to take for granted in communicating with our fellow citizens has also been declining. More and more of our young people don't know things we used to assume they knew." (51). *He is saying* the school system is not doing enough to increase cultural literacy in this country and as a result many of the American people cannot communicate at the same level as they once did.

Having summarized for several pages the positions of the different authorities he read, Vuong brought into focus some of the unanswered questions that plague educators and policy makers, establishing, at least momentarily, his own stance about affirmative action and bilingual programs only in the final paragraph:

> I agree with Rose the most. Rose understands that there is a problem among students who are trying their best to increase their cultural literacy; therefore, we must help them as much as possible. Rodriguez beleives that these people must be helped, but who should be helped? Who are really the minorities? . . . . Yes, there is a need to define the people who need help the most so that they could be helped, *but when bilingual programs are not supported I disagreed* [emphasis added]. Rodriguez' mistake is that bilingual programs in the 70's are not like the ones in the 80's. I think that if he could see how much bilingual programs have changed and helped people he would change his mind.

Identifying with Rose's position, Vuong also began to clear a path of his own by refuting Rodriguez's analysis of these programs with an implicit reference to personal experience and suggesting that Rodriguez's line of argument may be misguided. This kind of rhetorical move enabled Vuong to fall back on the familiar strategy of comparing different points of view, as illustrated, yet he went beyond such a strategy by providing an alternative to Rodriguez's argument, signaled by the conjunction *but.* That is, despite Rodriguez' attempts to underscore the potentially adverse effects that affirmative action and bilingual programs may have for minorities, Vuong sees the value of helping students in any way possible, perhaps because of his own progress in school as an ESL student in high school. Thus, with the knowledge gained from Vuong's protocol and literacy autobiography, there appears to be an interesting subtext that suggests how Vuong constructed meaning in his own experience through the stories others told.

When he read Vuong's final draft, the instructor remarked that he was impressed with Vuong's attempts to analyze and synthesize the different positions on cultural literacy. But he also noted that it was sometimes difficult to distinguish between Vuong's point of view and the authors'. For example, one must ask if assertions like these represent what Vuong believed as well:

The system is at fault because it permitted affirmative action and bilingual programs to prevent the majority of the minorities to have quality primary and secondary education. This is what Rodriguez believes affirmative action is doing to nonwhite students, ". . . admissions committees agreed to overlook serious academic deficiency [just fulfilling their status quo,] . . . [such as] barely able to read, . . . to grasp the function of a sentence, . . . [to] compose a term paper . . . [which is causing] those students with very poor academic preparation, [to have] few complete their course of study." (154–55)

As successful as Vuong seemed to be in interweaving different and often-times conflicting points of view, for the most part he avoided the commit-ment that assuming an authorial role might entail. At least as it was estab-lished in the questions that the instructor asked his students to consider when they wrote their essays.

Still, it may be too easy to see what may be missing from Vuong's essay; what is more difficult and necessary is to understand that what he has written has both a history and a logic. If Vuong did well in school, it may be because he learned to accommodate other people's ideas. In fact, it was unusual that he was able to move from an ESL track to the regular classes in high school, perhaps shedding further light on his tendency to assimilate. Indeed, he had figured out strategies that worked and his move-ment to regular classes is testimony to that; in this essay, however, he was asked, if only implicitly, to challenge the words of authorities he has been taught to trust. Moreover, if his prior experiences tell us anything about Vuong, it is that he was a good student who was torn by his desire to assimilate into Western culture and his belief that he must retain his ethnic identity as a member of the Hmong community. The result is a text that demonstrates Vuong's understanding of some key issues and his ability to restructure information through juxtaposing different writers' ideas in a unique way, instead of one that develops a personally authored discourse that speaks to what it means to be caught between two cultures.

In the end, Vuong's interpretation of the writing assignment he was given and the text he wrote did not differ markedly from the other students in this study. Analyses of other students' texts showed that even though these students felt they could incorporate their own ideas in writing their essays, when they actually wrote their papers they based their work primarily on the sources they read. Moreover, these other students organized their essays in the form of a comparison, each paragraph focusing on a different author. Like these other students, Vuong saved his opinion for the last paragraph, but I would speculate that his reasons for doing so may be quite different. In this case, he did not think anybody else in the class was going to understand his experience with bilingual classrooms.

The one exception was Jesus, who organized his essay in the form of a problem analysis. To point up the nature of this contrast, I would like to turn briefly to Jesus as a second case example, focusing on his background as a student and then examining both his initial interpretation of the task and the topical structure of his essay.

Born in Puerto Rico, Jesus had been outside his country on a number of occasions to visit family and to go on vacation. His family, well-educated and upper middle class, speaks only Spanish, although as Jesus pointed out in his literacy autobiography, he has had few occasions to speak English, except for English classes in high school, where he did little writing. In fact, he observed that from the time students enter the first grade in Puerto Rico, they tend not to use English outside of class. "The language of everybody is Spanish." Moreover, even though he wrote papers in Spanish, including some research papers, he pointed out that he "never had the experience of analyzing an article or subject and give my views about it." As a consequence, it is possible that Jesus was less aware of the dominant discourse of schooling (i.e., recitation) that shaped Vuong's experiences with reading and writing. Finally, for Jesus, learning English has been a frustrating experience. He saw English as the language of others. Spanish, he asserted, is "his language."

Jesus' First Impressions of the Writing Task. Jesus' interpretation of the writing task revealed that Jesus was aware that he needed to represent the points of view of other writers and that his own experiences were a legitimate and essential source for writing. Picking up on the instructor's suggestion that the students in class should "play ideas off one another" in setting up a dialogue, Jesus understood that he needed to represent other authors' positions faithfully, on the one hand, and use the reading to support his own argument, on the other. More than summarizing what others have said, Jesus believed that he should establish a rationale for discussing a particular point of view. For example, in the retrospective protocol he provided immediately after receiving the assignment, Jesus suggested that:

> In [an] analysis you have to summarize because you need to know what his [the author's] main point is but you need to set up an argument . . . your argument. Maybe agreeing with him but why you agree with him . . . you know supporting your argument. It's not only saying yes that's true but if it is true explain it or the implications it will have.

For Jesus, the genre of writing what he interpreted as an analysis seems to authorize him to take a position, although, like Vuong, he foregrounded the authority of the teacher as well in his protocol: "He wants us to formulate our own ideas." At the same time, Jesus also recognized that he must do something more than simply agree or disagree with the authorities he has read.

Interpreting the task as one in which his own ideas can be the source of his essay and in which he can challenge the ideas of these authorities,

Jesus identified an implicit problem in E. D. Hirsch's argument about cultural literacy. In his protocol, he wondered, "How can we achieve the 'standards.' That's a quote from Hirsch. And you know he refers to it as the standards that we must have. But how can we achieve that in a cultural diversity?" At this initial stage of writing, Jesus framed a series of questions that helped him to generate ideas. "Who," he asked, "will decide what changes are in minorities' best interests?"

Like Vuong, Jesus is also aware that the other students in class will read his essay. This fact provided a strong motive for Jesus to take up the issue of how cultural literacy can exist in the face of cultural diversity. Neither Vuong nor Jesus believed that the other students in their class entirely understood what was at stake in discussing such issues as cultural literacy. In an interview, Jesus pointed out that "they [many of the other students in class] come from a world apart and don't know how to deal with the things they don't have to worry about but I think they should know what's happening." Thus, in conceptualizing this task, Jesus believed that writing this essay could give him an opportunity to teach others about cultural diversity and the problems that arise when educational reform ignores diversity.

From Interpretation to Text. In keeping with his initial impressions of how to write this essay, Jesus summarized Hirsch's notion of cultural literacy for two apparent reasons: in part to reestablish what his readers (i.e., his instructor and the other students) already know, and in part to use this shared knowledge of cultural literacy as a point of departure for his own rhetorical purpose. For Jesus, cultural literacy represented an untenable position, particularly when one "consider[s] the environment of cultural diversity that prevails in most regions in the United States," a point he began to make at the end of the introduction to his essay. Here he explained how cultural literacy has been defined and then complicated the issue he raises with an emphatic "but," calling attention to a key problem:

> To be able to read and write are merely skills rather than effective thinking and analysis. These involve the possession of general and shared knowledge that will enable understanding and comprehension of common topics or issues. This is often called as cultural literacy. It is defined by E. D. Hirsch in his article "Cultural Literacy" as "the possession of basic information needed to thrive in the modern world." But what should be the contents of this "general and basic information" is an issue among educationalists and other education-concerned people these days. Considering the environment of cultural diversity that prevails in most of the regions of the United States, now this issue increases debates and discussions.

Although Hirsch's ideas serve as a starting point for this discussion, Jesus set out to explore a fundamental tension between cultural literacy and cultural diversity. In the second paragraph, he set the agenda for his essay, focusing on a set of relations, not a topic or author:

> I intend to explore this relation between cultural literacy and cultural diversity and how minorities are highly involved and affected. Their participation in the completion of the cultural literacy "standards" is limited and yet is entitled by their social, cultural and economic status.

Jesus fulfilled the promise of these introductory remarks in the remainder of his essay, providing a detailed discussion of Hirsch's understanding of cultural literacy. He also discussed Rose's and Rodriguez' concerns with culture, but the topical structure of his essay suggested that the summaries of these authorities' arguments existed in the service of Jesus' attempts to problematize the idea of cultural literacy. In writing his essay, he begins to adapt, even transform, the information he has read into the basis of an argument. I have italicized those phrases that foreground the topical structure of Jesus' essay and that help to show that Jesus' concerns as an author motivated his explanations of others' ideas. In fact, references to the authorities he has read are often embedded in parentheses:

> *The idea of a shared and general knowledge possessed by the citizens of a nation or a country* will work effectively if everyone has and/or receives the same educational or background information. . . . In order to clearly define the relation between cultural literacy and cultural diversity, *it is important to understand the connection between background and cultural knowledge and literacy.* . . . To be culturally literate, "*a citizen must be able to grasp the meaning of any piece of writing addressed to the general reader*" (Hirsch, 12). . . . *Our national culture* changes over the years. . . . *The environment in which people interact* has changed; now *cultural diversity* prevails in our nation. *The experience of being separated from the rest because of differences in cultural and social backgrounds* is not a good one. *Setting equality in the knowledge and information possessed by students across the nation* is impossible.

Rather than seek consensus or focus on the authors (e.g., "Rose said" or "Hirsch suggests"), as other students in this study did, Jesus not only established why it is necessary to "understand the connection between background knowledge and cultural knowledge and literacy," but he explained why the arguments supporting cultural literacy are problematic in his conclusion.

> The basis of a culture can be stated. Not the culture of the United States 50 years ago but the culture of the United States of today: a nation encountering many challenges not only in education but in politics, sciences, etc., a nation that serves as a home for people from many parts of the world, from many cultural, class, racial and ethnic differences. They have the right

to be respected, accepted and known by others. Through multicultural education we can assure that their rights are been respected.

Although Jesus did not explicitly state that this is his opinion, such a statement comes full circle, reminding us of the argument in the introduction where Jesus told us that "the completion of . . . cultural literacy standards is limited and yet is entitled by their [minorities'] social, cultural and economic status." Therefore, it is not difficult to distinguish what Jesus believed from what the authorities he has read argue, as it was, at times, in Vuong's essay.

Conclusion: Implications for Teaching and Research

I want to close by suggesting that the problem of assuming an authorial role, particularly as it is revealed in the case example of Vuong, may be all too familiar, although the problem may have different origins. We may invite students to develop an intellectual project of their own and "participate in arguments that are specific to a particular group," but students like Vuong may be reluctant to take on what Min-Zhan Lu called "the burden of participation" ("From Silence to Words" 445). After all, she pointed out that conventional modes of argument that we expect students to use exist prior to and outside of their experiences. Students are also more likely to exclude any discourse (e.g., home, school, or community) that might interrupt the unity and coherence of another, so that they "forget the discourse of the one when they cross the boundary dividing them" (Lu, "From Silence to Words" 445).

Higgins' research on argumentative writing, conducted in an inner-city community college, also contributes to our understanding of the extent to which beginning writing students are willing to assume the role of authors, particularly insofar as they are willing or able to include their own ideas. The drafts of an argument that students wrote showed that they rarely included personal experiences and ideas outside the assigned sources to support their claims in their texts; instead, they frequently tacked on a personal opinion paragraph at the end of their papers much as Vuong did. When she interviewed students in her study, Higgins discovered that they used their personal experiences to understand and relate to source concepts so they might paraphrase them better in their texts. Some students relied exclusively on personal beliefs and experiences when evaluating source ideas for inclusion in their papers, only choosing to cite evidence that they themselves had experienced or agreed with on a personal level. Perhaps most telling was that the students in her study explained that they had excluded any references to personal experience from their texts because they were afraid of digressing from the assigned materials and ruining the organization that the source texts provided them. Her interviews show that students negotiated the urge to use their own ideas by using them to choose concepts but then excluding them from their texts or by separating their own ideas in an unrelated summary paragraph, which they had learned was acceptable in their reading course.

As Higgins and others demonstrated, when we examine students' processes of composing—the thinking that often remains hidden behind the texts they produce—we find that an even better predictor of what students will do is the task they give themselves. It follows that we need to pay attention to the dynamic interplay between individual writers and the social interaction that can influence the form and expression of their texts. This means observing how writers negotiate the constraints, conflicts, and alternatives that present themselves in the face of a community's (e.g., home or academic) conventions, on the one hand, and writers' own personal goals on the other. After all, individual writers' understanding of the social purposes for writing is influenced by a legacy of schooling and culture that may come into conflict with a current model of instruction. As a consequence, students may very well resist developing a rhetorical purpose of their own, not because of some deficit, but because they lack the options that might enable them to use what they already know flexibly and appropriately in a new situation.

When we shift the terms of instruction from *recitation*, asking students to review given information, to *dialogue*, inviting them to enter an intellectual conversation, we force our students to rethink, perhaps transform, their understanding of what it means to write in school. Such a change can be uneven because students' ability to adapt what they know is influenced by so many complicating factors. As Anne DiPardo has observed, "only over time can . . . students begin to integrate new influences and understandings, to move beyond initial conflict and uncertainty toward" new ways of thinking (7). Thus, it is one thing to talk about the need to encourage beginning writers to forge a voice of their own and to confront conflicting ways of using language; it is quite another to teach beginning writers to assume the role of authors who can position and reposition themselves in relation to different values and ideas (cf. Lu, "Writing as Repositioning" 20–21).

At the very least, we need to make our instructional models explicit, providing occasions for students to explore and discuss the social roles they believe they can assume in their writing and in classroom talk (e.g., critic or decision maker). Given the importance of how students interpret a writing task, we can help beginning writers to determine whether it might be appropriate to include their own ideas and to reflect on why it might be appropriate to do so in a particular situation (cf. Flower, "Negotiating Academic Discourse" 222–23). Specifically, we can offer guidance throughout the entire process of writing, first asking students how they would interpret a task and then discussing possible options for writing. In this case, it may have been instructive for Vuong and John ("I think it's going to be hard to so called 'speak' in this paper with these other writers") to listen to Jesus' interpretation of the task in order to see that there are different and equally legitimate ways to complete the same writing assignment. Jesus provided an alternative interpretation, revealing that he was aware that he needed to represent the points of view of other writers in "set[ting] up an argument." By seeing the legitimacy of such an approach, students can begin to see the possibility of establishing a sense of agency and can expand their repertoire of strategies for composing. But it is equally important for us to recognize that students of different racial or cultural backgrounds may be using the same "student" strategies (e.g., write a comparison, "put your 'I believe' paragraph at the end") for different reasons. Vuong may have been reluctant to talk about bilingual education until the end of his paper because of what he felt the other students in class seemed to understand about multicultural issues in education. On the other hand, Jesus, who also felt differently from the other students in class, was able to use his awareness of political and language conflict to spin out a strong argument.

We can also share with students the transcripts of retrospective accounts such as those discussed here. By reading transcripts, students can see how others approach the problem of establishing an intellectual project and translate their understanding into actions they can take in creating a text from other texts. In this way, students are encouraged to reflect on their own decision-making process as readers and writers relative to how others navigate through difficult decisions, set goals, and choose certain paths. Perhaps most important, students' discoveries about themselves can help us see that there are things that they do that can make a difference as they attempt to contribute their own ideas as authors.

Further, we can analyze sample essays (e.g., from previous semesters) in class by examining how a writer interpreted the task, discussing the consequences of taking such an approach, and considering alternatives (Penrose 62–64). Writers' texts are not simply translations of their impressions of how to perform a task, but these impressions are the realization, development, and visible form of some of the choices and decisions writers make in organizing and selecting information (cf. Witte and Cherry 30–33). Thus, it is possible to examine the introduction to Vuong's essay, as I did earlier, and infer that he believed he should rely on the reading he was given as the primary source of his ideas. In contrast, Jesus' introduction reveals an understanding of the task as one that required him to use his own ideas as the organizing principle of his essay. The question worth raising with students is whether each approach is appropriate given their impressions of how to go about writing an argument.

In the final analysis, the goal of teaching students to be authors, I want to suggest, is not to initiate students into communities by teaching forms and conventions, nor should we necessarily see authorship as a developmental construct where an authorial role is measured in terms of membership in a discipline. Instead, we can help beginning writers learn to make a contribution to an evolving dialogue by appropriating the voices of a community and reaccentuating these voices into their own unique idioms, as Jesus was apparently able to do (cf. Bakhtin, "Discourse in the Novel" 293–94; Ritchie 172–73). Success in writing would depend on students' ability to ask and answer questions, acknowledging the authority of written texts and knowing when to question them. If learning is an intertextual process of creating links between one's own ideas and a social network of knowledge that constitutes and defines the work of a community, then those who become engaged in the "arguments that are specific to a particular group" must learn to adapt their discourse to a rhetorical situation that is shaped by historical and social forces. To do so means understanding the function of different genres as responses to rhetorical situations and the patterns of reference that establish one's authority in writing (Devitt).

Rather than avoid the kind of conflict that complicates the process of writing for our students, we can begin to use that conflict constructively in helping them develop a stance and see that they are responsible for generating, transforming, as well as preserving, knowledge (Lu, "From Silence to Words" 445, 447). But with a willingness to assume an authorial role, students must also come to terms with authority—their own authority and the authorizing principles in both text and context that influence what writers say and how they communicate their ideas. If students like Vuong are unwilling to challenge the authority of published writers or the conventions that exist prior to and outside of their own experiences, then perhaps the starting point for inquiry and analysis should be the problems they identify as important in projects they develop.

The literacy autobiography that students wrote in this study was one such starting point. We can validate students' ideas in another way as well by encouraging students to use and cite their peers' work. At the same time we can help instill the need to evaluate the quality and relevance of any source in developing an argument. In this way, we can provide students with a curriculum that integrates personal experience and reading in order to stimulate learning. And by doing so, beginning writers may be more willing to take on the "burden of participation," particularly if the process of inquiry is integrally related to their experiences at home, in their community, and at school.

Yet helping students to expand their repertoire of strategies so that they can assume an authorial role is as much a social issue as it is cognitive. The role writers adopt is the result of a complicated process of negotiating the power relations inherent within certain social forces and the inner voices that shape writing (Flower, *The Construction of Negotiated Meaning* 282–84). Meaning is always located simultaneously in teacher–student, student–student, teacher–class interactions, and between these various levels of classroom interaction (Bloome and Bailey 189). Although researchers (e.g., Nystrand and Gamoran 282–84) claim that student engagement and commitment occur when writing, reading, and talking are vehicles for active inquiry, we still need to look closely at the extent to which the social conditions within a classroom encourage students to be authors. For example, what kinds of reasoning do the questions we ask in class promote? What kind of talk will foster students' willingness and ability to adapt and transform information for their own purposes as authors?[8]

Further studies need not be limited to the social relations developed within the classroom context. Instead, we can find ways to connect students' social and cultural backgrounds to their performance in class, the instructor's reception of students' personal meanings, the differences in the construction of the task by each student and the differences in the actual writing. Making these sorts of connections can complicate our understanding of why some students assume the role of authors and others do not.

To build robust theories of the kind of thinking that will enable students to become authors, we need to look closely at both the social and cognitive factors that influence student learning. By examining their attempts to make sense of and write about others' ideas in context through close, systematic observation, we can begin to see the cognition that motivates students' performance in school. With teaching and research, then, lies an important challenge: to make our students' thinking visible, seeing their choices as part of a living process that ordinarily remains hidden from view.

APPENDIX
COMPLETE TEXT OF THE WRITING ASSIGNMENT

Synthesis Paper: A Conversation of Thinkers

Our next project is the writing of a paper that will allow you to formulate your ideas about literacy and to enter a conversation with the writers we

---

[8] A number of educators have observed that a legacy of essayist literacy (Olson) has led students to see texts as complete, self-contained, and objective, not open to challenge (e.g., Farr 4–14; Trimbur, "Essayist Literacy" 72–75). As a consequence, students often become deferentially literate (Newkirk), that is, politely observing what other authors have accomplished in their writing. For a discussion of this problem and approaches to teaching students to read critically through the use of models, see, for example, Greene ("Exploring the Relationship Between Authorship and Reading" 42–51) and Haas (30–31).

have been reading. You will be able to present your own point of view as you work with the ideas of others. As I have suggested in class, you will need to use the skills of summary and analysis, as well as your ability to synthesize concepts and set up an argument.

Here is the process. You have read books by Rose and Rodriguez and excerpts from the writings of Hirsch, Walker, and Welty. You have also written a literacy autobiography. Choose an issue that is related to literacy that has come up in the readings, class discussions, or the literacy autobiographies. Choose something that is interesting to you, something you have opinions or feelings about. It is always easier to write about a subject that you feel is important.

Examine what different writers say about this issue. Dig in the texts to find ideas that you consider relevant and useful. Note pages where the writer deals with the issue; do things like write down important points, quotations, and ideas of your own regarding the author's position.

On paper, map out the relationships of the writers to one another regarding this issue. As you do this, keep thinking about what your position is in relation to theirs.

Construct an argument that stakes out your position on the issue and that also reveals your understanding of what others have said about this issue. Try to show why your view is the one with which we should agree.

This paper should be 5 to 7 pages long, and double-spaced. All drafts are to be workshopped, with copies made for the group.

For [the next class], please bring a paper proposal of about one page, in which you explain what issue you have chosen.

VUONG'S ARGUMENT

Importance of Cultural Literacy*

Rose, Rodriguez and Hirsch have raised many interesting questions about the education system in this country, questions such as what will be taught, who will decide, who will be taught, how will it be taught? But all of these questions focus around one thing, what Hirsch called cultrual literacy. He defines it as "thnetwork of information that all competent readers posses" (50). All three authors agree, in one way or another, that our education system is the cause of an increased cultural illiteracy among the people of this country, particularly with the people who are at the stage of their secondary and post-secondary education. The result of this increase has produce an increase of students who are unable to meet the level of

---

*Both Vuong and Jesus' argument appear in their unedited form.

cultural literacy set by the school. The difference between these authors is that although each knows what the general problem is, each has his own idea of where the problem is specifically coming from and his own way of solving the problem.

These authors go about arguing their points by first defining who is the culturally illiterate, then onto why the school system is at fault, and finally give their solution to the problem. Rose believes that the cultrually illiterate are those who have been unprepared by their high school and as they proceed to a post secondary education, they will be marked as being "remedial" or an "outsider". Rose uses Marita, a UCLA Freshman, as his typical culturally illiterate person and as an example of what can happen to students like her. He tells that on her first writing assignment for college, discussing Bronowski's writings, Marita was accused of plagiarism by her English TA. Marita sees nothing wrong with her report, because in her view she has put down all the sources she used. But because her high school did not prepare her to properly use quotations, she misquoted it. Rose reading the paper stated, "I couldn't know if she had likted directly or paraphrased the rest, but it was formal and dated and sprinkled with high-cultural references, just not what you'd find in freshman writing" (180). This is what Rose said about Marita's assignment, "Marita's assignment assumed . . . an ability to slip into Bronowski's discussion, a reserve of personal experience . . . [that she could relate to], a knowledge . . . the kinds of stylistic moves you'd find in those New Yorker essays . . . the solution Marita used marked her as an outsider and almost tripped the legal switches of the universtiy" (181). It seems to me that Maritatried to do her assignment the best way she knew how, but because of her inability to perform as the university expected, a university cultural literacy, she almost failed. So what is the solution to become culturally literate at this level?

Rose suggestion is "more opportunities to develope [their] writing strategies . . . to talk about what they [had been] learning. . . . to let [them] in on the secret talk" (193–194). What Rose is saying is that we need all levels of school, including universities, to have special programs—tutorial and bilingual programs—for these people, instead of labeling them, as they did Marita, and kicking them out. By doing this a more culturally literate society will be more likely to emerge.

Rodriguez believes that the culturally illterate are the minorities. He agrees with Rose that the education system is the cause of the decline of cultural literacy, but unlike Rose, he is arguing that the system is addressing aid to the wrong group of students. What the system considers as minority is actually Blacks, Hispanic American, American Indians who have been well educated, cultural literate, and have the means to better themselves. He gives himself as an example, stating, ". . . I wa not really more socially disadvantaged [a minority] than the white graduate students in my class.

. . . I was not disadvantaged like many of the nonwhite students who were entering college, lacking good early schooling" (147). He is arguing that the definitions the system makes are wrong and should be changed to people of different race who lack a good early education, and cultural literacy.

The system is at fault because it permitted affirmative action and bilingual programs to prevent the majority of the minorities to have quality primary and secondary education. This is what Rodriguez believes affirmative action is doing to nonwhite students, ". . . admissions committees agreed to overlook serious academic deficiency [just fulfilling their status quo,]. . . . [such as] barely able to read, . . . to grasp the function of a sentence, . . . [to] compose a term paper. . . . [which is causing] those students with very poor academic preparation, [to have] few complete their course of study" (154–155). Rodriguez is saying that as that as the need to fill status quo to satisfy the minority population increases, less and less is being done about to improve primary and secondary education. By not improving there two ares of education, fewer people, including whites, will be able to continue onto a post education because of their lack of cultural literacy.

The second thing Rodriguez feels is a problem and must be changed is the bilingual programs. He feels that bilingual education is permitting "non-English-speaking children, many from lower class homes, to use their family language as the language of the school" (11–22) and is preventing these studetns from "speak[ing] the public language of los gringos" (19). In other words he feels that bilingual education prevents students from learning what other students in the main-stream classes are learning, therefore, causing them to become more culturally illiterate.

Hirsch beleives that the most culturally illiterate people are the young generation of Americans in high school. Hirsch states, "During the period 1970–1985, the amount of shared knowledge that wer have been able to take fro granted in communicating with our fellow citizens has also been declining. More and more of our young people don't know things we used to assume they knew." (51). He is saying the school system is not doing enough to increase cultural literacy in this country and as a result many of the American people cannot communicate at the same level as they once did.

His idea for this problem is to set up education in this country that will teach children "current mainstream culture". Such current mainstream culture as "Adam and Eve, Cain and Abel, Noah and the Flood, David and Goliath, . . . Humpty Dimpty, Jack Sprat, . . . Paul Bunyan, Sleep Beauty, etc. . . ." (64). When should they start learning all this? "Preschool is not too early for starting earnest instruction in literate national culture. Fifth grade ia almost too late. Tenth grade usually is too late." (62). What Hirsch is saying here is that there is a time when it is best to begin, but also there is a time when it is too late to begin.

My postion on what the authors are saying is that I agree with Rose the most. Rose understands that there is a problem among students who are trying their best to increase their cultural literacy; therefore, we must help them as much as possible. Rodriguez beleives that these people must be helped, but who should be helped? Who are really the minorities? I do agree with him that there must be a clear definition for who is considered a minority. Yes, there is a need to define the people who need help the most so that they could be helped, but when bilingual programs are not supported I disagreed. Rodriguez mistake is that bilingual programs in the 70's are not like the ones in the 80's. I think that if he could see how much bilingual programs have changed and helped people he would change his mind. But Hirsch I'm not sure about, because he feels that the younger generation are the only ones with a chance of having an increase in cultural literacy. The older generation have no chance of every having this. I think this idea is too idealistic and absolete because you can not close one eye to the present and open the other to the future. The past, present, and future are all related and must be looked at, at the same time, to improve the future. Although these authors may have some similar ideas I agree with Rose's ideas the most.

JESUS' ARGUMENT

Cultural Literacy and Cultural Diversity

To be able to read and write are merely skills rather than effective thinking and analysis. These involve the possession of general and shared knowledge that will enable understanding and comprehension of common topics or issues. This is often called as cultural literacy. It is defined by E.D. Hirsch in his article "Cultural Literacy" as "the possession of basic information needed to thrive in the modern world." But what should be the contents of this "general and basic information" is an issue among educationalists and other education-concerned people these days.Considering the environment of cultural diversity that prevails in most of the regions of the United States, now this issue increases debates and discussions.

"No modern society can hope to become a just society without a high level of universal literacy" (12). This statement of Hirsch certainly implies a need for cultural literacy, but my main purpose is to explore how cultural literacy "standards" can be achieved in an environment of cultural diversity. In this research work, I intend to explore this relation between cultural literacy and cultural diversity and how minorities are highly involved and affected. Their participation in the completion of the cultural literacy "standards" is limited and yet is entitled by their social, cultural and economic status. Supporting my work, E.D. Hirsch's article "Literacy and Cultural Literacy" will set the debate about cultural literacy, its demands and implications. Also, Richard Rodriguez's "Hunger of Memory" and Mike Rose's "Lives on the Boundary" will support the arguments in favour of and against multicultural education.

The idea of a shared and general knowledge possessed by the citizens of a nation or a country will work effectively if everyone has and/or receives the same educational or background information. The "standards" of literacy required by a modern society, referred to by Hirsch, have been increasing in our developed world, but not a the same speed. American literacy has not increased: it is lacking in the completion of these "standards" (Hirsch). High levels of cultural literacy brings a number of implications that go far beyond simple facts and statistics but to greater economic prosperity, social justice and effective democracy (Hirsch 2). As Hirsch says "the chief function of literacy is to make us masters of this standard instrument of knowledge and communication, thereby enabling us to give and receive complex information orally and in writing over time and space" (3).

In order to clearly define the relation between cultural literacy and cultural diversity, it is important to understand the connection between background and cultural knowledge and literacy. People from different cultural backgrounds posses information such as customs, traditions and facts particular to them that differ from those of other members of other cultural backgrounds. Despite this difference, literacy among these people involves general knowledge possessed by all the members that will enable them to communicate effectively and deal with new ideas, events and challenges (Hirsch 10,11). There is a difference in terminology but they are closely related one to the other. If people are literate in a democracy, they "can be entrusted to decide all important matters for themselves because they can deliberate and communicate with one another." In other words, illiterate people will live under the incomprehension and the lacking of prosperity (Hirsch 12).

To being culturally literate, "a citizen must be able to grasp the meaning of any piece of writing addressed to the general reader (Hirsch 12). By this, Hirsch means that possessing the specific and necessary information any citizen makes one able, let's say for instance, to read and understand a newspaper article. The only way to spread this information is through our schools, Educational systems should ensure the instruction of this shared knowledge. This instruction must start in the earliest grades (Hirsch 28). The components for education should not only be critical thinking and basic skills (reading and writing) but also include facts that "a child entering a new culture must have" (Hirsch 28). Such facts not only include "stable elements" of a culture, such as history dates, authors and geography, but also "current mainstream culture" (Hirsch 28). But what should be taught from our current world?

Our national culture changes over the years. Arts and terms exposed 50 years ago are different from those exposed today. Also, the environment in which people interact have changed too; now cultural diversity prevails in our nation. Now, you can enter in any common classroom and find children from different ethnic and cultural backgrounds, Latin Americans, Asians, Native Americans, Blacks, and so on. They possess two cultures, the one shared with others, the American, and their own. They and their respective cultures have the right to be accepted and respected. In order that their cultures should be accepted and respected, they must be known and studied by others. These are the basis of multicultural education.

The idea of multicultural and bilingual education appeared years ago. The right of a child to maintain his own and family language as well as learning a new language is being respected. But it is not a matter of just language; it is a matter of culture. Language is a distinction of a culture; a culture is a distinction of a language. They cannot and should not be separated.

Rose believes that cultural backgrounds are closely related to the opportunities and performance of students in college and in the world around them. This is true since their success will depend on the possession of an information and background knowledge that will able them to adapt and do better. He says that "it was harder, at first glance, to see how profoundly a single assignment or a whole academic career can be affected by background and social circumstances" (177). Working in the Tutorial Center, he made tutoring more effective by not trying to focus on the failure, but to see beyond it to the causes. In most cases, the causes of failure were related to the lack of background information due to differences in cultural and social backgrounds.

The experience of being separated from the rest because of differences in cultural and social backgrounds is not a good one. Neither is the experience of being yourself assimilated to a new culture, sacrificing your own. There is a place between. People should not block themselves and go to the extremes. Bilingual and multicultural education will allow students of any background to "close the boundaries" that class and cultures erect unconsciently. Spreading knowledge and information from different cultures will not only permit students from those cultures to adapt more easily and securely, but will create a new vision of community that will end the ignorance and incomprehension.

Different form Rose, Rodriguez believes that assimilation is the only solution. "What I needed to learn in school was that I had the right—and the obligation—to speak the public language of los gringos" (Rodriguez 19). Not just sacrifying his language, he sacrified his culture and his family. With bilingual and multicultural education, this "difference between classroom language and the language of home" will not be so drastic and will allow an easily transition and adaption. By no means I am saying that one's own culture should be forgotten in order to be part of a new one. This is not strictly necessary. Many people that truly maintain their own culture and live and perform in another culture are doing great. Failure is being misperceived. Class and culture are not the only causes for failure since many other great factors affects people that struggle in learning (Rose 205).

The claim of bilingualists is to ensure that students obtain "the skills of the classroom crucial for public success" in their own family language (Rodriguez 34) this will able them to obtain the skills necessary while not losing their sense of individuality—"their ethnic heritage and cultural ties" (Rodriguez 34). When the individual is clear about what he is, what he wants and how he should obtain it, no difference will hold him from obtaining it. In contrast, Rodriguez says that only when I was able to think of myself as an American, no longer an alien in *gringo* society, could I seek the rights and opportunities necessary for full public individuality" (27).

Setting equality in the knowledge and information possessed by students across the nation is impossible. But, the basis of a culture can be stated. Not the culture of the United States 50 years ago but the culture of the United States of today: a nation encountering many challenges not only in education but in politics, sciences, etc., a nation that serves as a home for people from many parts of the world, from many cultural, class, racial and ethnic differences. They have the right to be respected, accepted and known by others. Through multicultural education we can assure that their rights are been respected.

WORKS CITED

Bakhtin, Mikhail. "Discourse in the Novel." *The Dialogic Imagination.* Trans. Michael Holquist and Caryl Emerson. Austin: U of Texas P, 1981. 259–422.

———. *Speech Genres and Other Late Essays.* Trans. V. W. McGee. Austin: University of Texas Press, 1986.

Banks, James A. "The Canon Debate, Knowledge Construction, and Multicultural Education." *Educational Researcher* 22 (June–July 1993): 4–14.

Bartholomae, David. "Teaching Basic Writing: An Alternative to Basic Skills." *Journal of Basic Writing* 2 (Spring/Summer 1979): 85–109.

———. "Inventing the University." *When a Writer Can't Write.* Ed. Mike Rose. New York: Guilford Press, 1985. 134–165.

Bartholomae, David, and Anthony Petrosky. *Facts, Artifacts, and Counterfacts.* Upper Montclair, NJ: Boynton/Cook Publishers, Inc., 1986.

Bloome, David and Francis M. Bailey. "Studying Language and Literacy through Events, Particularity, and Intertextuality." *Multidisciplinary Perspectives on Literacy Research.* Ed.

Richard Beach, Judith Green, Michael Kamil, and Timothy Shanahan. Urbana, IL: NCRE & NCTE, 1992. 181–210.

Bruffee, Kenneth. "Collaborative Learning and the 'Conversation of Mankind.' " *College English* 7 (November 1984): 635–652.

Clark, Gregory. *Dialogue, Dialectic, and Conversation*. Carbondale, IL: Southern Illinois University Press, 1990.

Devitt, Amy. "Intertextuality in Tax Accounting: Generic, Referential, and Functional." *Textual Dynamics of the Professions: Historical and Contemporary Studies of Writing in Professional Communities*. Eds. Charles Bazerman and James Paradis. Madison: University of Wisconsin Press, 1991. 336–357.

DiPardo, Anne. *A Kind of Passport: A Basic Writing Adjunct Program and the Challenge of Student Diversity* (Research Report No. 24). Urbana, IL: National Council of Teachers of English, 1993.

Farr, Marcia. "Essayist Literacy and Other Verbal Performances." *Written Communication* 10 (January 1993): 4–38.

Flower, Linda. "Negotiating Academic Discourse." *Reading to Write: Exploring a Cognitive and Social Process*. Linda Flower, Victoria Stein, John Ackerman, Margaret Kantz, Kathy McCormick, and Wayne Peck. New York: Oxford University Press, 1990. 221–252.

————. *The Construction of Negotiated Meaning: A Social Cognitive Theory of Writing*. Carbondale, IL: Southern Illinois University Press, 1994.

Fox, Tom. "Basic Writing as Cultural Conflict." *Journal of Education* 172.1 (1990): 65–83.

Freedman, Sarah W. *Response to Student Writing* (NCTE Research Report No. 23). Urbana, IL: National Council of Teachers of English, 1987.

Greene, Stuart. " 'Making Sense of My Own Ideas': Problems of Authorship in a Beginning Writing Classroom." *Written Communication* 12 (1995): 186–218.

————. "The Role of Task in the Development of Academic Thinking through Reading and Writing in a College History Course." *Research in the Teaching of English* 27.1 (February 1993): 46–75.

————. "Exploring the Relationship between Authorship and Reading: A Study of Classroom Research." *Hearing Ourselves Think: Process Research in the Classroom*. Ed. Ann M. Penrose and Barbara Sitko. New York: Oxford University Press, 1993. 33–51.

Haas, Christina. "Beyond 'Just the Facts': Reading as Rhetorical Action." *Hearing Ourselves Think: Process Research in the Classroom*. Ed. Ann M. Penrose and Barbara Sitko. New York: Oxford University Press, 1993. 19–32.

Higgins, Lorraine. *Argument as Construction: A Framework and Method*. Unpublished Doctoral Dissertation. Pittsburgh, PA: Carnegie Mellon University, 1992.

Hirsch, E. D. *Cultural Literacy*. Boston, MA: Houghton Mifflin, 1987.

Hull, Glynda and Mike Rose. "Rethinking Remediation: Toward a Social-Cognitive Understanding of Problematic Reading and Writing." *Written Communication* 6 (April 1989): 139–154.

Hull, Glynda, Mike Rose, Kay L. Fraser, and Marisa Castellano. "Remediation as a Social Construct: Perspectives from an Analysis of Classroom Discourse." *College Composition and Communication* 42 (October 1991): 299–329.

Lu, Min-Zhan. "From Silence to Words: Writing as Struggle." *College English* 49 (April 1987): 437–448.

————. "Writing as Repositioning." *Journal of Education* 172.1 (1990): 18–21.

Newkirk, Thomas. "Young Writers as Critical Readers." *Understanding Writing: Ways of Observing, Learning, and Teaching*. Ed. Thomas Newkirk and Nancy Atwell. Chelmsford, MA: Northeast Regional Exchange, 1982. 106–113.

Nystrand, Martin and Adam Gamoran. "Instructional Discourse and Student Engagement." *Research in the Teaching of English* 25 (October 1991): 261–290.

Nystrand, Martin. "Dialogic Instruction and Conceptual Change." Paper delivered at the Convention of the American Educational Research Association, San Francisco, CA, April 1992.

Olson, David R. "From Utterance to Text: The Bias of Language in Speech and Writing." *The Harvard Educational Review* 47 (August 1977): 257–281.

Penrose, Ann M. "Writing and Learning: Exploring the Consequences of Task Interpretation." *Hearing Ourselves Think: Process Research in the Writing Classroom.* Ed. Ann Penrose and Barbara Sitko. New York: Oxford University Press, 1993. 52–69.

Ritchie, Joy S. "Beginning Writers: Diverse Voices and Individual Voices." *College Composition and Communication* 40.2 (May 1989): 152–174.

Rodriguez, Richard. *Hunger of Memory.* New York: Bantam Books, 1982.

Rogoff, Barbara. "Conceiving the Relationship of the Social World and the Individual." *Apprenticeship in Thinking.* New York: Oxford University Press. 25–41.

Rose, Mike. *Lives on the Boundary.* New York: Penguin Books, 1989.

Swanson-Owens, Deborah and Newell, George. "Using Intervention Protocols to Study the Effects of Instructional Scaffolding on Writing and Learning." *Verbal Reports in the Study of Writing.* Ed. Peter Smagorinsky. Beverly Hills, CA: Sage Press, 1994.

Trimbur, John. "Consensus and Difference in Collaborative Learning." *College English* 51 (1989): 602–616.

———. "Essayist Literacy and the Rhetoric of Deproduction." *Rhetoric Review* 9 (1990): 73–86.

Trueba, Henry T. "Culturally Based Explanations of Minority Students' Academic Achievement." *Anthropology and Education Quarterly* 19 (Dec. 1988): 270–287.

Volosinov, V. N. *Marxism and the Philosophy of Language.* Cambridge, MA: Harvard University Press, 1973.

Vygotsky, Lev. *Thought and Language.* Revised ed. (Alex Kozulin, Trans.). Cambridge, MA: M.I.T. Press, 1986.

Walker, Alice. "Saving the Life That Is Your Own." *In Search of Our Mothers' Gardens.* New York: Harcourt Brace Jovanovich, 1983. 3–14.

Welty, Eudora. "Listening." *One Writer's Beginnings.* Cambridge, MA: Harvard University Press, 1984. 1–39.

Witte, Stephen P. and Cherry, Roger. "Writing Processes and Written Products in Composition Research." *Linguistic Approaches to the Study of Written Discourse.* Vol. 1 of Written Communication Annual: An International Survey of Research and Theory. Ed. Charles Cooper and Sidney Greenbaum. Beverly Hills, CA: Sage, 1986. 112–153.

Chapter 6

Intertextuality, Genre, and Beginning Writers: Mining Your Own Texts

Marie C. Paretti
Recognition Research, Inc.

Mining, as both Weese (ch. 3, this volume) and Greene ("Mining Texts") developed the concept, provides a useful metaphor for understanding how students can interact with texts as writers rather than simply as readers—that is, when students mine texts, they engage actively with them to understand structure, language choice, and rhetorical strategies, as well as concepts, in order to inform their own writing. The text becomes a resource adaptable to the student writer's own purposes. But whereas most of the research in this area concerns how students make use of texts by other writers, in this chapter I consider the ways students use their own texts. To that end, I am adapting the idea of mining and filtering it through M. M. Bakhtin's theories about identity formation and on the development of one's own voice in the presence of many other voices (*Dialogic, Speech Genres,* and elsewhere). Bakhtin's framework provides a way to talk about how students can use their own writings to foster a sense of authority.

In particular, I focus here on the relationships between students' informal writings and their formal essays. In our efforts to help students gain a sense of their own authority and use writing as a way to add their voices to an ongoing conversation, we often include a variety of writing opportunities in addition to those essays geared toward formal academic discourse. My students, for instance, keep journals, participate in e-mail discussions, write in-class responses, and so on. Such informal writings, we hope, provide places where students can express their own ideas, saying what they think or feel without worrying about formal constraints. When

I require response journals or ask students to join discussions over e-mail, I do so with three primary goals in mind:[1] (a) to provide students with spaces to express themselves in writing and so foster their own sense of authorship; (b) to teach them to respond critically to other texts; and finally (c) to allow them to work out their own ideas in an unstructured, informal space so that when they turn to formal essays, they can bring a strong sense of their own positions and ideas to help shape their academic discourse. This chapter addresses the last of these goals, exploring if and how students use their own informal writings to author formal essays by asking three central questions:

1. Most simply, do students recognize the differences between the various kinds of writing they do, and the advantages and limitations of each form?
2. Are they able to make use of their informal writings to help develop their essays—that is, can they mine their own texts?
3. What can we as teachers do to help students use these different types of writing to develop their sense of authority as writers?

WRITING IN THE CLASSROOM: FORM AND FUNCTION

My interest in this area has grown out of both my experiences as a teacher and my reading of other teachers' experiences. A number of journal articles, course anthologies, and academic texts take up the subject of informal writing in one form or another—most notably, student journals and e-mail discussions. And according to the research, these nontraditional forms serve an almost infinite array of ends. Reader response journals can foster reading skills by allowing "students who are actively engaged in reading [to] also actively engage in thinking and feeling" and can provide a place for them to "make connections between what they read and their own lives" (Youngblood 46). As such, reader-response journals "[stress] personal encounters with the subject and not traditional academic discourse" (Leahy 109). Alan Cooper wrote of a complex scheme to help students develop their writing skills in which journals progress from being a place for "anything [students] like" to a place to work out "an identifiable thesis" (347). Journals may also function as group documents, as in Maurice O'Sullivan's class. The whole class keeps a single journal in which students not only write out their own reflections on the texts at hand but also respond to one another's comments. Such a journal "opens up new lines of inquiry,

---

[1]Certainly there are a variety of other reasons for informal writings; these reasons are simply the ones that are primary in my composition classrooms.

draws reticent students into class discussions, and encourages frequent syntheses and re-evaluations" (289) as it disrupts the teacher–student dialogue and enables students to talk more freely to one another. O'Sullivan's group journal (1987) actually stands as a kind of precursor to the e-mail discussion lists that have more recently made their way into the classroom. Over the past five years, e-mail has become an integral part of many writing classes. The possible implications of e-mail range from its importance as a genre unto itself because of its widespread use in professional and corporate workplaces (Hawisher and Moran) to its ability to "offer opportunities to enrich the writing of students by affording them the audience of their peers and an authentic sense of purpose" (Spitzer 64). Class e-mail lists, as Joyce Kinkead reported, can provide a place that is "quick, convenient, fun and a release for creative writing," thus counteracting students' hostility and dread toward writing itself (338). In Kinkead's classes, e-mail discussions "encourage students to produce text" (339). In her experience, "electronic mail is intrinsically motivating" (341) and, like O'Sullivan's group journals done the old-fashioned way (i.e., with pen and paper), helps draw out the quieter students. E-mail can also enhance peer review by allowing students to send their drafts to one another, giving the reviewer time to comment, at his or her convenience, on the writing in detail and produce more thoughtful responses than those typically possible during in-class peer review sessions.

Yet despite the number of articles supporting various types of informal writing, little research has been done to uncover how students actually use these informal writings when they turn to assignments that ask them to enter the academic discourse about a particular topic. Do students, when they find their own voice through journal entries and e-mail discussions, know how to bring that voice, that sense of authority, into the academic conversation?

A BAKHTINIAN APPROACH

To begin to understand the relationships between students' texts and examine the ways in which traces of one text appear in another, I want to turn first to the work of Bakhtin as a lens for this investigation. Three concepts from Bakhtin are particularly useful here: genre, utterance, and dialogism.

Genre

One way to talk about the different types of writing students do in a classroom is to consider them as separate genres. In Bakhtin's framework, a genre is not simply a formal structure but an epistemological framework—different genres provide different ways of knowing. In *The Formal Method*, for example, Bakhtin and Medvedev explained that "human consciousness possesses a series of inner genres for seeing and conceptualizing reality" (134). Thus the formal constraints typically associated with the concept of genre are only one piece of a larger epistemological system. Turning from these inner genres to the more traditional literary use of the term, Bakhtin and Medvedev went on to explain that "the genres of literature enrich our inner speech with new devices for the awareness and conceptualization of reality" (134). For Bakhtin "genres are really forms of thinking" (Morson and Emerson 280). Work in composition theory takes a similar view, expanding the notion of genre beyond mere form, as is evident in Carolyn Miller's seminal 1984 article, "Genre as Social Action." Miller treated genre as embedded in the social situation in which it participates, and as such the term includes not only formal structures but also intended actions, context, and motive. In her words, "genre becomes a complex of formal and substantive features that create a particular effect in any given situation" (153). In a 1993 issue of *RTE* devoted to genre, Aviva Freedman noted that when students learn to adopt a particular genre, they begin to "construe certain phenomena in roughly the same way that other actors in the field construe them" (229), reinforcing the social and situational nature of genre.

This understanding of genre as a way of knowing provides insight into one of the central values of having students develop a single idea in multiple genres (i.e., journals, e-mail posts, essays). These genres potentially provide students with a richer understanding of an idea because students can use one genre as a way to step outside the epistemological framework of another. Gary Morson and Carol Emerson noted the ways in which this concept of outsideness plays a critical role in understanding for Bakhtin. In Bakhtin's terms, "In order to understand, it is immensely important for the person who understands to be located outside the object of his or her creative understanding—in time, in space, in culture" (Bakhtin, quoted, in Morson and Emerson 55). The view from outside enables understanding otherwise not possible. Different genres, then, may in fact provide students with a way to move, at least in a limited way, outside a subject by providing multiple epistemological lenses. As a result, students may emerge with a fuller, more nuanced understanding than if they had written only in one genre, particularly if their texts do in fact inform one another and evidence the kind of dialogic interaction explained later in this chapter. This notion in part forms the foundation of William McGinley and Robert J. Tierney's premise in "Traversing the Topical Landscape." In exploring the relationship between writing and learning, they emphasize the value of "different forms of reading and writing . . . [as] 'traversal routes' or cases through which an individual can explore a given content domain" (250). By providing students with multiple routes through a topic, they suggested, we enable them "to orchestrate [their] engagements dynamically according to particular needs" (265) and enhance their ability to learn.

Utterance

The second key concept from Bakhtin is utterance, which provides a way to talk about each individual journal entry, e-mail post, in-class response, and so on. For Bakhtin, the utterance itself—rather than the word or the sentence—is the unit of analysis. An utterance is the complete expression of one speaker[2] to another; as such, it begins when the speaker begins talking, ends when the speaker finishes, and includes the external conditions surrounding the words spoken. The boundaries of the utterance are "determined by a change of speaking subjects" (Bakhtin, *Speech* 71). Most importantly, the utterance is unrepeatable, even when the words used in two different utterances are identical (Bakhtin, *Speech* 108). Linguistically identical utterances are still distinct from one another because of their relative positions in time and space. In terms of this study, each text produced by a student—each journal entry, each e-mail post, each essay—constitutes an utterance spoken by students to themselves, their peers, or their teacher.[3] Bakhtin's approach thus allows us not only to reflect on the recurrence of a particular phrase or idea at various points in a student's work but also to understand the differences between those recurrences. Utterance allows us to move beyond noting repetitions because even if two utterances contain some of the same sentences—perhaps even word for word—they are not identical because the conditions in which they are uttered change. And the nature of those changes is critical to understanding the relationships among the texts of a single writer.

Dialogism

The final concept in Bakhtin that I find useful here is dialogism, which provides a way of talking about the presence of prior utterances in any new utterance. Dialogism has made its way into composition theory discourse in a number of different forms in recent years, designating everything from a dialogue between two specific individuals to a dialectical

---

[2]I am using speaker as Bakhtin does to refer to both speakers and writers.

[3]The student may, of course, show a given text to any number of individuals, and many composition classes successfully encourage students to write for those outside the classroom—campus administrators, newspaper readers, congresspersons, and so on. But by and large the student, the rest of the class, and the teacher form the primary audiences in the classroom used in this study.

approach to history. The term is a slippery one even in Bakhtin. As Morson and Emerson pointed out, it appears in at least three different contexts in Bakhtin's work: as a global worldview, as a property inherent in all utterances, and as a contingent property (opposed to monologism) that may or may not appear in a given utterance (130–31). The most significant, for this chapter, is the one I want to focus on: what Morson and Emerson considered "the first sense" (131), in which every utterance is dialogic because it automatically enters into dialogue with what came before it. As Bakhtin explained, every speaker:

> presupposes not only the existence of the language system he [sic] is using, but also the existence of preceding utterances—his own and others'—with which his given utterance enters into one kind of relation or another (builds on them, polemicizes with them, or simply presumes that they are already known to the listener). *Any utterance is a link in a very complexly organized chain of other utterances.* (*Speech* 69, italics added)

Every utterance enters into dialogue—consciously or unconsciously, directly or indirectly—with what has come before it. Texts, even texts produced independently of one another, are interanimating. In describing the act of writing about a given subject, Bakhtin explained that:

> [i]nstead of the virginal fullness and inexhaustibility of the object itself, the prose writer confronts a multitude of routes, roads and paths that have been laid down in the object by social consciousness. . . . For the prose writer, the object is a focal point for heteroglot voices among which his [sic] own voice must also sound; these voices create the background necessary for his own voice. (*Dialogic Imagination* 278)

This notion of an already existing body of utterances surrounding an object is implicit in the metaphor of academic writing as a process of entering a conversation—when one writes, one steps into a moving stream. Interestingly, though, most work based on Bakhtin has centered on the preceding utterances of others. Yet in *Speech Genres,* as quoted (69), Bakhtin made it clear that one also enters into a dialogic relationship with one's own texts, and it is the nature of that interaction that I explore in this chapter.

THE COURSE: ENGLISH 101

To answer those questions, I studied the work of several students in my Beginning Writing course. The course itself was required of incoming freshmen who scored below a certain number on a multiple-choice grammar–reading comprehension exam. The class was graded on a credit–no credit basis and although required of those students failing the placement exam did not count toward their graduation credit requirement. Student writing in the course consisted of journals, e-mail posts to a class mailing list, and essays set up as compilations of several short papers. In beginning the study, I assumed that each of these types of writing (except for the short and long essays, which I grouped together) constituted a separate genre. The journals were to be informal, semiprivate documents destined only for the student and myself, and the purpose was to provide students with a place to think through their ideas. The e-mail list provided a more public, but still informal, forum for students to exchange ideas with one another and carry on discussions outside of class. Although I was included on the mailing list and received all posts, I did not participate on the list in an effort to encourage students to talk to one another rather than to me. And finally, the essays and short papers were to be formal documents subject to revisions based on comments from both peers and myself, as well as the students' own developing ideas. Students read one another's drafts in small groups and for the first two essays, we produced a packet containing everyone's final draft. That packet then served as additional reading material for the course. At the end of the semester, I had students evaluate, in writing, their own efforts and gains from the course. In addition, for this study, I interviewed several students and asked them to provide a retrospective view of their work over the course of the semester.

STUDENT TEXTS: THE FALLACY OF GENRES

The premise of this research rests in part on the fact that the kinds of writings I assigned represented different genres—different ways of knowing, different audiences, different purposes, different discourses. Certainly they represented different forms—journals could be hand-written, emphasized personal engagement, and were less subject to the rules of grammar and mechanics; e-mail posts appeared on the screen only, ostensibly written to other students yet loose in terms of structure and expectation; formal essays followed a much more defined pattern and were expected to fit the terms of academic discourse. However, as I began to read more deeply into genre theory and watch the progress of my students' writing, I became less and less convinced that these forms *automatically* belong to separate genres.

Miller's definition of genre centers on the social context, on "the action it is used to accomplish" (151), and for many of my students, each of these types of writing was used for the same purpose: to enable them to pass the course. Witness the fact that several students, because of computer phobia, never even got around to using e-mail because they calculated that they could pass the course without it; in a pass/fail course there is no risk of a lower grade based on one or two failed assignments provided all other work is done adequately. Moreover, several students who did attempt to use e-mail waited until the end of the course. One student came to me in the last week of class to ask for help in sending messages. Another called the first morning of finals week to explain that the computer had just "eaten" five responses she had tried to send, and wondered what would happen to her grade if she did not rewrite them. Again, because the course was pass–fail, failing to submit those responses did not in and of itself cause her to fail. For both of these students, at least, the e-mail discussion list was simply another medium for school-based writing, necessary to please the teacher and make the grade. Underneath these two end-of-the-semester requests is the implication that I, not their peers, was the intended audience because the class itself was virtually over and the students were getting ready to leave for the summer.

Similarly, students may have used their own journals primarily to satisfy the course requirements and provide me with material to grade. In our interview, for instance, Sara[4] dismissed the value of writing in her journal and made it clear that the journal was simply another requirement. In one of her last entries of the semester, she wrote partway through the entry, "I already pointed out why I support immigrants coming to the US [the topic of the essay she was writing at the time]. I don't have to repeat them over and over," implying the journal itself was more a waste of time than a resource. Moreover, Sara explained, both in an interview and in her written self-evaluation, that she was frustrated with her essays because she "didn't express my innermost feelings. I [wrote papers] because it's a requirement not for my own desires." When I asked her if she found that she could express more of her own feelings in her journal, she shrugged and looked skeptical, although she said that it was possible to some extent. Essays and journal entries, although different forms of writing, apparently did not serve different functions for her.

For a student like Kurt, on the other hand, the similarity between journals and essays lies more in tone. Despite that fact that journals are informal and supposedly personal, whereas essays are more formal and public, Kurt's essays continually drifted back into the more casual, personal tone of his journal. His journals (although they were brief) allowed him to express his feelings, often very antagonistic and judgmental, on controversial topics such as premarital sex and AIDS. His essays, and particularly one on reverse discrimination, carry the same sense of unguarded personal expression. He wrote, "there is still that lower class white group out there who work just as hard as blacks and other races, yet still gets the cuts on him cuz he's white."

---

[4]All students' names have been changed.

Later he wrote, "Asians, hispanics, blacks, japs, jews, etc. all want equality as well as whites," revealing, in the racist slang, his inability to recognize the difference in tone needed between a private journal and a public essay. Although the essay, designed to be a formal argument based on outside research, does contain some limited statistics to support his claims, by and large it centers on his own opinions of the topic—his 4-page formal argument contained eight "I feel" or "I know" statements. As a result, the line between essay and journal blurred quite a bit.

All that is not to say that journals, e-mail, and essays are never separate genres. Certainly some of my students used the genres for different purposes. Instead, I want to emphasize here that they are not automatically or inherently different. The ability to distinguish differences may in fact be particularly important for beginning writers; that is, if all school-based writing falls into the same category for them, that may limit their ability to take advantage of the epistemological differences between genres in a way that enhances their knowledge of the subject and their ability to assert their own voice in the academic conversation. Clearly, we need to do more research to understand how students—and especially beginning writers in relation to more experienced ones—perceive the various forms in which they write. And as beginning writing teachers, we need to recognize that inability to move among genres and consequently in our teaching make the uses of these different modes explicit. We cannot simply assume that more writing is inherently good without teaching students how to take advantage of the genres available to them. For the kinds of writing required in school to become separate genres, students need to take control of those writings and develop their own sense of purpose and audience for each.

INTERTEXTUALITY: FROM UTTERANCE TO UTTERANCE

Students' inability to distinguish between genres, however, is only one element in this study, shattering one of my initial premises but not necessarily invalidating the central question concerning the relationships between multiple texts by the same student. Even if journal entries, e-mail posts, and essays do not represent separate genres as Miller, Bakhtin, and others use the term, they do represent separate utterances. Each still forms "a link in the chain of utterances" Bakhtin described (*Speech* 69), and hence forms the background against which new utterances emerge. To understand the possible interactions among students' own utterances, I want to examine two students, Carla and Sara. I interviewed each student and asked them to give retrospective accounts of their composing process for a particular essay. The interviews occurred a week after the essay was completed in Carla's case and the day after the essay was completed in Sara's case.

Carla: Compensation and Resource

Carla's second essay, which involved describing and analyzing a community, focused on her home church in Milwaukee, Ephesians Missionary Baptist Church. In her case, the journal, the interview, and the essay itself presented vastly different views of that discourse community. Although brief, the journal entries focus more on the personal aspects of church life. At one point, for instance, she wrote:

> I meet a lot of good friends there. They are like sisters to me. My pastor is like my grandfather. Sts. [Sister] Todd, his wife, is the mother of the church. That is everyone answers to her, you know, like in the household family.

She went on to include a narrative account of Pastor Todd praying for her and functioning as a kind of father figure. In our interview, she went into even more detail, describing how close she was to other church members and how much she missed that group of people.

Her essay, in contrast, was virtually devoid of personal references. Although one of her pre-essay short papers also emphasized the fact that "everyone is either a brother or a sister, e.g. Sister Paretti . . . ," in the final essay this concept appeared only in her last sentence. There, after explaining more of the factual details about the church—what happens in services, what the church doctrines are, what the pastor's official role is—she ends with the statement, "We are all brothers and sisters working toward the same goal . . . Eternal Life." Interestingly, however, she chose to title the essay "Ephesians: My family in Christ," implying that the church's role as family was central to her membership there. In her notes from a brainstorming session in which I asked students to write down a series of possible titles, along with some details for each one, Carla's ideas included "My Family in Christ," "The Spiritual Family," "Initiation of the Baptist Family," and "Ephesian's Family Reunion." Again, family emerged as a key concept for her in this informal space. Under "My Family in Christ," she jotted down ideas such as "what makes this/them your family in Christ, what unites this family, is their [sic] a common goal, who's in charge/control" and so on. Her final essay focused largely on the latter topics and failed to explore what makes this group of people a family.

Clearly, for Carla, the formal essay did at least have a distinct form separating it from the more informal journal and brainstorming work. In our interview, she acknowledged the differences: "It's hard for me to express myself really in words," she explained, saying that when she talked she could use examples to clarify her point but that she did not feel comfortable doing that in writing. "I know how to write it [the personal information and examples] down but I don't want it to be a run-on or a fragment." She noted, "I knew it was like a family but I didn't really know how to explain it." In part, then, her fears about grammar and the appearance of her essay led her to omit information that she felt much freer expressing in other forms. At the same time, she also found herself governed by what she thought other students expected. When I asked her why she did not include the more personal material from her journal in her essay, she said, "I didn't think it was part of the paper. I figured they'd [her classmates—the defined audience for the paper] just want to know mostly about the Baptists." As a result, she explained, she focused on making sure the doctrine and the services would be clear to someone who had never been to a Baptist Church before. She noted that the drafts we looked at as a class all stayed away from personal issues, and consequently she herself "kind of shied away from saying what is [her] family."

In this case, then, Carla's own previous utterances provided a place to express ideas she felt did not belong to the essay. But she was not able to use those journals as a source for the essay or a place to develop ideas. She did not, that is, mine her own texts in any direct way. Instead of allowing her space to work through ideas that she could later include in the essay, the journal effectively counteracted or compensated for the limitations of the essay form. And although such compensation is useful in that it did allow her to express herself, as her teacher I find myself questioning whether or not it served to develop her sense of authorship because she still felt unable to assert her own ideas and interpretations in her essay. The essay remained in the realm of reportable facts.

Interestingly, although Carla wrote little on the e-mail discussion list, her essay explaining the beliefs and practice of her church did provide the background for a response posted about a week after the whole class had shared their essays. One student on the list raised the question of premarital sex and Carla responded. At the end of her response explaining, in nonreligious terms, why she felt sex outside marriage was wrong, Carla closed by saying, "I suppose because of my religion this is my belief." When I asked her, without referring to that particular post, if her formal writings had any relation to her writings on e-mail, she referred back to that comment: "Yeah [they were connected] cause I wrote, 'because of my religion this is my opinion.' " When I asked, purely speculatively, if she thought she would have included that comment had it not been for the class reading her essay, she was not certain. "I probably wouldn't have thought of writing 'because of my religion,' " she explained, but because everyone knew from her essay that she was a Christian, she felt comfortable including the comment. In that case, one utterance—the formal essay—created the necessary context for information supplied in a later utterance on another topic. This scenario suggests that multiple genres, particularly those shared among students, can serve to create context, making a writer known to her classmates so that she can comfortably express her own position more clearly and explicitly in later works.

Sara: Parallel Lines of Thinking

Sara's case stands in direct opposition to Carla's in many respects. While Carla wrote very brief journal entries and only one or two brief e-mail posts and had consistent trouble developing her essays sufficiently, Sara wrote extensively in both her journal and on e-mail and developed her ideas in detail in each of the three essays. Moreover, Sara's journals and essays covered nearly parallel material, particularly for her third essay. The third essay required students to present an argument and use outside sources to back up their positions. Sara chose to use her journal to record her responses to several of the articles she read for her essay. Three of the four articles she wrote about in her journal she also cited explicitly in her essay, whereas the fourth article, although not cited in the paper, dealt with similar issues. In contrast, her e-mail posts covered topics that she considered separate issues—premarital sex and racism. She didn't "want to do the same thing" over and over in each place, she explained. When I asked if she thought her comments about racism on the e-mail list could be related to her essay, she conceded that they might be but insisted on seeing the essay as really focusing on a separate topic. In other words, she saw these utterances as distinct, rather than as part of a chain, and could not create a framework where each utterance might somehow enhance, develop, or challenge those before it.

Ironically, however, despite the obvious connections between her journal and her essay, in our interview Sara insisted she did not use her journal at all in writing the paper. She described a very detailed writing process in which, over a period of several days, she would jot down ideas on scraps of paper as they came to her. She would then type up all those ideas and begin numbering them to create some kind of order for her paper. When she had everything numbered, then she knew she had a basic structure for the essay and could begin writing. As she drafted her essay (on the computer), she had only photocopies of the articles she wanted to use (with underlining, highlighting, and marginal notes to indicate key passages and topics) and her numbered notes. When I asked if she referred back to either the journal or the short essays, she replied, "I don't have short papers [i.e. there with her as she writes]. I don't have the journal because I know what's going on. I know what I remember." I then asked if she thought that writing about the articles in her journal had helped her at all, and her answer was still tentative, allowing for the possibility but really discounting its impact:

> Me: Do you think the short papers and journal help you think about the ideas in [the essay]?
>
> Sara: More or less yes. But you know, see . . . I don't know about other people, but once you have the assignment, when you're reading the article of course you think about what I'm gonna write. . . . So automatically I think about it . . . personally I don't need journals or anything.

For her, the journals, by and large, were a way of fulfilling the assignment and she was not entirely sure why I had assigned them.

Despite her inability to see the connections, though, her journals covered much of the same material developed in her essay. She wrote in her journal about the "aging, undertalented work force" in the United States, about the need to use immigrants' expertise to help us "compete in the international market," about the tendency of immigrant (particularly Asian) children to excel academically, and about the fact that "immigrants *do not* steal the job . . . [but] create the job." Each of these became a major point in her final essay. In moving from journal to essay, however, she began to substitute outside authorities for personal experiences to substantiate each of those beliefs. For instance, in her journal she wrote:

> I've many talented and excellent friends in high school whose parents got their PhD in U.S. and eventually found a job then stay [sic]. Their parents push them hard and they work hard. They all perform very well in high school.

In her essay, in contrast, to substantiate the academic success of immigrant children she wrote:

> [Reich] said that only among Hmong children, almost no one drops out, the high school graduation rate are close to 100 percent and they are heading on to college or technical school. On the other hand, the American children have higher drop out rates. . . . Reich claims that, "13 out of 17 valedictorians in Boston high schools last spring were immigrants or children of immigrants . . ." (Andrews & Roberts 36).

What existed in her journal as opinion based on experience appeared in her essay as fact grounded in academic authority. But she herself did not recognize the ways in which she was using the journal, like Carla, to record ideas not permitted in the formal essay, at least in her definition of it. Moreover, as we discussed the essay, Sara expressed her own frustration with it—not because she didn't consider it good writing but because she was not able to express what she really felt. The essay just contained information rather than feelings. When I asked if she thought she had been able to write more of her own feelings in her journal, she was ambivalent. Again, she acknowledged that she had perhaps done some of that, but still the journal remained a negligible requirement for her rather than a place to think through ideas or say the unsayable. Her journal, at least from her perspective, offered her no new ways of conceiving of her subject, no new information to draw from to develop her essay. As a result, it did little to contribute to her own sense of authority as a writer, or her own willingness to insert her voice into the academic dialogue.

The same is true, I think, of her understanding of e-mail. Although she wrote earlier in the semester about racism and the fact that people's abilities are prejudged according to their race or ethnicity, she did not seem to relate that to her essay, at least in her retrospective account of the writing process. At the same time, when I asked her, in our interview about her third essay, if she thought racism was responsible for some of the prejudice against immigrants, she talked at length about how being an immigrant meant she had to work harder to prove herself capable. As a result, I am led to believe again that the connections are there between the various pieces of her writing, but that she did not know how to use them effectively.

CONCLUSION: THE NEED FOR EXPLICITNESS

For both Carla and Sara, multiple forms provided the potential to view the same idea from a number of different viewpoints, to stand outside, as Bakhtin might say, and so enhance their own understanding of the subject. Multiple viewpoints are embedded in the various texts they submitted to me. But although we can follow the traces of one text throughout the writing that follows it and examine some of the shifts that occur, neither of these students recognized the potential usefulness of those traces. And although I believe that writers do not need to be conscious of everything they do—that is, we cannot know what these essays would look like without the journal writings or the e-mail posts, and the traces are there whether students recognize them or not—I also believe that the more conscious writers are of the resources available to them in their own informal writing, the richer all their writing and their understanding will be.

If Bakhtin, Miller, and those who follow them, are correct in viewing genre as an epistemological framework, then to help students locate and develop their own voices we as teachers must foreground how students can use informal writings as source material for their essays. That foregrounding, it seems to me, must go beyond simply telling students what journals or e-mails are for. It means using these informal texts as part of the course reading material and analyzing the ways each genre constructs knowledge.[5] It means talking explicitly about what we learn by comparing and contrasting an e-mail entry to an essay draft or a journal entry. Through such discussions, students can begin to understand their own language choices and ideas and at the same time recognize their own authoritative voice in a conversation in the same way they recognize the voices of published writers. It also means modeling for students concrete ways to take a journal entry and use it as the basis for an essay by incorporating other voices, rather than starting with outside sources and incorporating the journal in, or, as Carla did, leaving the journal out altogether. In order for the various kinds of writing in our composition classes to function as genres in the terms set out here, we need to treat them as such explicitly in our classes and discuss the way ideas in one utterance influences ideas in another. In doing so, we offer students the opportunity to enhance their own learning. Student writers' ability to "traverse the topical landscape" in the ways McGinley and Tierney posited depends largely on our ability as teachers to function as tour guides for the trip.

WORKS CITED

Bakhtin, M. M. *The Dialogic Imagination.* Trans. Caryl Emerson and Michael Holquist. Ed. Michael Holquist. Austin: U of Texas P, 1981.

———. *Speech Genres and Other Late Essays.* Trans. Vern W. McGee. Ed. Caryl Emerson and Michael Holquist. Austin: U of Texas P, 1986.

Bakhtin, M. M., and P. N. Medvedev. *The Formal Method in Literary Scholarship: A Critical Guide to Sociological Poetics.* Trans. Albert J. Wehrle. Baltimore: Johns Hopkins UP, 1978.

Cooper, Alan. "Daily Writing for Peer Response." *College Composition and Communication* 37 (1986): 346–348.

Freedman, Aviva. "Show and Tell? The Role of Explicit Teaching in the Learning of New Genres." *Research in the Teaching of English* 27 (1993): 222–251.

Greene, Stuart. "Mining Texts in Reading to Write." *Journal of Advanced Composition* 12 (1992): 151–170.

Hawisher, Gail E. and Charles Moran. "Electronic Mail and the Writing Instructor." *College English* 55 (1993): 627–643.

Kinkead, Joyce. "Computer Conversations: E-Mail and Writing Instruction." *College Composition and Communication* 38 (1987): 337–339.

Leahy, Richard. "The Power of the Student Journal." *College Teaching* 33 (1985): 108–112.

McGinley, William, and Robert J. Tierney. "Traversing the Topical Landscape: Reading and Writing as Ways of Knowing." *Written Communication* 6 (1989): 243–269.

Miller, Carolyn. "Genre as Social Action." *Quarterly Journal of Speech* 70 (1984): 151–167)

---

[5]E-mail discussions may in fact be easier to use in this context because they already exist in the public domain. Using journals would require bringing in sample journal entries or perhaps asking students to assess their own journals in the terms outlined here in ways that still protect the privacy of those texts.

Morson, Gary Saul, and Caryl Emerson. *Mikhail Bakhtin: Creation of Prosaics.* Stanford, CA: Stanford UP, 1990.

O'Sullivan, Maurice. "The Group Journal." *The Journal of General Education* 38 (1987): 288–300

Spitzer, Michael. "Local and Global Networking: Implications for the Future." *Computers and Writing: Theory, Research, Practice.* Ed. Deborah H. Holdstein and Cynthia L. Selfe. New York: MLA, 1990. 58–70.

Youngblood, Ed. "Reading, Thinking, and Writing Using the Reading Journal." *English Journal* 74.5 (1985): 46–48.

Chapter 7

The Dialogic Writing Conference: Negotiating and Predicting the Role of Author

Jana French
Valparaiso University

That writing is a dialogic process, a "return to conversation" (Bruffee 641), is now a widely accepted concept. Although usefully foregrounded in any writing course, this concept may be of special interest in beginning college writing pedagogies because it demystifies academic discourse, couching it in terms of an oral activity already familiar to students who may find themselves "outlanders" (Bizzell 164) to the culture and conventions of the university.[1] One way to dramatize the dialogic nature of the writing process is through one-on-one, student–teacher conferencing, which renders literal the conversation between writer and audience.[2] Conferencing can give students insight into the discursive construction of texts by fore-

---

[1]Although students from residually oral subcultures have historically been underrepresented at universities, they are often overrepresented in beginning writing courses. A dialogically informed approach to writing could tap these students' oral competencies and use them as a basis for discussing the rhetorical moves valued in academic discourse. For a discussion of the basic differences between literate and residually oral cultures, see Walter J. Ong (31–77).

[2]This is not to say that conferencing removes the institutional barriers between the student and instructor. I am reminded of John Trimbur's concern that we remember the authority that accompanies our positions as writing teachers in a university setting; as "representative[s] of the academic community" (105) that our students are trying to join, we may not be the "real" audience we ask them to write for. On the other hand, we are in the position to use our authority—which derives not only from our representation of the academy, but also from our participation in the interpretive community of the classroom—to guide their reconception of authorship.

grounding talk as a means to knowledge production; at the same time, it offers teachers insight into what Stuart Greene, in chapter 5 of this volume, called the "hidden logic" (chap. 5, p. 87, this volume) that informs the choices writers make en route to authorship. This chapter returns to the case examples used in Greene's discussion of task representation and interpretation (chap. 5) to analyze the relationship between conferencing and student authorship. By examining the dynamics of the writing conference—the roles assumed by the student and instructor, the kinds of talk produced, and the changes effected (if any) in the student's conception of rhetorical objectives—I mean to demonstrate that conferencing can extend and enrich the dialogue established in the writing workshop while allowing us to observe the student's relationship to the writing task. To this end, conferencing can accomplish two things: (a) encourage the student to negotiate the role of author, and (b) help the instructor predict whether or not the student will successfully assume that role.

As we have been defining it in this volume, authorship involves both the contribution of new ideas to some preexisting academic conversation and the transformation of that conversation toward the fulfillment of one's own rhetorical purposes. This formula is complicated when we consider it in light of M. M. Bakhtin's analysis of the discursive construction of texts. Bakhtin argued that texts are constituted by the interaction between "authoritative" and "internally persuasive" discourses. Whereas each is an amalgam of ideological viewpoints and cultural values, "authoritative" discourses are associated with allegiance to received, or official, points of view and "internally persuasive" discourses with the combination of previously assimilated, unofficial discourses. Because the rhetorical context for this discursive contest is constantly shifting, the dialogue remains "open" and "infinite," perpetually finding "newer ways to mean" (342–346). It is in this sense (and this sense only), I believe, that we can say authorship involves the contribution of new ideas. What we mean, of course, is not "new" in the sense of blank-slate originality but rather newly dialogized; that is, engaging old or established (that is, previously dialogized) ideas in new ways or contexts. Insofar as it is a transformative activity, conscious and deliberate dialogization is a sign of authorship.

Conferencing can model the dialogics of authorship by foregrounding the discursive play in a writer's developing text and by making the writer aware of the competition between official and unofficial discourses in his or her developing draft. This applies whether the authoritative discourses are voiced by an instructor (in a conference discussion or marginal comments), peer (in workshop talk), or published source (as is the case when writers are asked to analyze or synthesize the written ideas of others). Indeed, in any of these writing situations, the student-author's voice can be conceived as that which mediates the contest between official and unofficial discourses and ideally transforms it into a new synthetic whole.[3] This transformation was the goal of the literacy synthesis assignment that provided the basis for Greene's study.

The synthesis assignment required students to take a position on an issue related to literacy while demonstrating familiarity with the scholarly debate surrounding that issue. This was no easy task. However, as well as being stymied by the complexity of the assignment, students in the study seemed constricted by previous schooling in comparative forms of writing and the subsequent consensus of their current interpretive community that a neatly segmented version of the five-paragraph essay would best meet the needs of the task. Five out of six of the students, including Vuong, while demonstrating comprehension of their source authors' ideas, failed to integrate a personal stance in their final papers. This response to the assignment (which presumably mapped onto an organizational format already in the students' heads) certainly fulfilled the combinatory aspect of authorship; however, it did not meet the second, transformative criteria primarily because it focused on the authors rather than their ideas. Only one student, Jesus, organized his paper around a problem of his own definition, engaging his three sources in a dialogue that subsequently transformed their ideas into a new synthetic whole. What follows is a comparative analysis of Vuong's and Jesus's conferences that seeks to explain why Jesus was the only student in the study to successfully move into the role of author.

Several questions inform and focus my analyses of Vuong's and Jesus's conferences:[4] What does the writing conference tell us about the discursive contexts each student is negotiating as he responds to the various writing tasks required by the synthesis assignment? How does the relationship between the student and instructor affect the student's composition choices, including the extent to which he is able (or willing) to take on the role of author? To what extent is the student aware that he is or is not authoring his text in the sense that we have defined the concept? Although I do not mean to cast the instructor in the role of analyst—as

---

[3]This essential state of dialogization, which arguably informs all textual production, undercuts the notion of an authentic voice that students are often urged to locate through exploratory prewriting and drafting. A better option may be to sensitize students to the plurality of voices at play in their developing drafts and to the social and ideological contexts within which these voices speak. Authorship becomes a manageable role, I would argue, once students reconceive voice not as an intrinsic thing to be found but as a product of the interaction of many voices, which they have been assimilating since birth. As Bakhtin described it, "our speech is filled to overflowing with other people's words, which are transmitted with highly varied degrees of accuracy and impartiality" (337).

[4]The conferences were conducted approximately 1 week before the final paper was due and were audio taped by the instructor. These audiotapes were then transcribed, providing the data that I have reproduced in this chapter.

Patricia Bizzell reminds us, basic writers do not need "therapy" but rather "critical training" in identifying and addressing the matrix of factors keeping them outside the conventional classroom (112)—it is clear that conferencing offers a unique opportunity to observe and better understand all that a student brings to an assignment that conditions his or her task interpretation and fulfillment. To this end, and as the following examples show, conferencing also provides an opportunity to engage students in a meta-analytical dialogue about task interpretation and fulfillment and about the role that authorship requires them to play.[5]

CASE #1: VUONG

Vuong's opening comments during his conference indicated that he had a basic grasp of the synthesis assignment. He understood that his purpose was to set the three authors he had chosen in relationship to one another, demonstrate familiarity with their ideas, and focus his discussion on a particular issue in the literacy debate. As he explained to the instructor, he had chosen to focus on Hirsch's concept of cultural literacy.[6]

R: Well, I'm trying to stay in track with what I wrote. I said that the three authors that I would be writing—[Mike] Rose, [Richard] Rodriguez, [E. D.] Hirsch—would have something in common. They blame the educational system for the problem of cultural literacy—lack of cultural literacy. The difference between the three authors is that they have their own way of how to solve the problem, define what specifically is the problem and solve that problem from the definition of the problem.

I: So that their solutions are supposedly the ones that will change the educational system so that that cultural literacy will increase.

R: Right.

I: Good. So how do you set this up in the paper?

R: Well, I'm trying to—I already stated that—what their position on what I'll be talking about. And so I take an author, get his viewpoints,

---

[5]Bartholomae and Petrosky described the demands of academic composition in terms of "textual performance," a kind of rhetorical posturing through which students might "reimagine themselves as readers and writers" in the academic community (8). This metaphor of role playing suggests that a degree of artifice is essential to the achievement of authorship, if not to the activity of writing in a much broader sense; this concept is potentially empowering for basic writers because it emphasizes that authorship is learned and not, as one of my former students put it, "inborn."

[6]Throughout my analysis of the conferences, I will use the conventional abbreviations for interviewer (I) to denote the instructor's speech and respondent (R) to indicate that of the student writer.

define what his viewpoint on that—what the specific problem is, give an example and explain that. That will be pretty much the pattern for the two other authors. And then, I would agree or disagree on the three authors, on some of their points.

I: Kind of as you go along. Once you've set up their arguments, then you'll say something about those arguments from your point of view?

R: Um, I'll do that in one—in the last part.

Vuong's neat segmentation of the project ("I take an author, get his viewpoints, define what his viewpoint on . . . the specific problem is, give an example and explain that") cues us as to the most difficult part of the assignment: the integration of the writer's own ideas. His proposed organizational scheme, which is really a modified version of the classic five-paragraph essay, can be understood as an attempt to balance what he saw as his primary purpose—the reproduction of the authors' main ideas (authoritative discourses)—against the riskier and more difficult task of incorporating his own (internally persuasive) viewpoint. Vuong's decision to save his own ideas for the end of the paper rather than integrating them in a dialogue with the experts indicates how sharply he distinguished between official and unofficial discourses and suggests that he intended to keep them separate in the paper, perhaps for the sake of clarity.

That Vuong believed his primary task was to reproduce the authors' arguments was evidenced by his desire to manage the mass of information that each offers. He was clearly frustrated by his inability to contain and control all the ideas struggling for representation in the emerging draft and seemed distressed, as well, by the internal discursiveness he was beginning to perceive in each author's argument.

R: But the problem is, trying to get there from here—setting them up so I can—just getting their viewpoints is pretty hard because they have so many good points and sometimes it conflicts with what they're saying. Also it's getting hard to understand what they're saying.

I: Yeah, that's interesting. Why is that? Can you think of a place where that—

R: Where they conflict?

I: Yeah. Are you saying that they are conflicting with themselves or with each other?

R: Sometimes—I know that they conflict with themselves for what is the specific problem—how to solve that. That is what I know. But, I'm getting kind of—there is a minor problem—minor confliction between the author—within the author.

Vuong seemed to believe that his role as author was to account for contradictions that he perceived within and among the three writers. Indeed, the understatement of his phrasing during this exchange—"there is a minor problem—minor confliction . . . within the author"—indicates embarrassment at what he has discovered (and perhaps at his audacity in pointing it out, as well). Unable to conceptualize the conflicts as potential points of entry into dialogue with the authors, he saw them instead as disruptions to his organizational strategy: They are incongruities to be resolved rather than sites rich with discursive potential.

Vuong went on to identify one specific contradiction in Rodriguez's argument against bilingual education:

> He's opposing bilingual education, but he also wants a higher education for the disadvantaged people. But then he's—but, I'm thinking, how could he do this? . . . Because bilingual [education] is to help people, of disadvantaged background, who aren't able to learn or have the ability that a mainstream teacher would expect from them.

At the instructor's affirming "yeahs," Vuong then identified a significant point of conflict between Rodriguez and Rose: "And bilingual education would let [these people] into what Rose is saying—the secret talks—to let them into some of the secret talks . . . And that's not what I see in Rodriguez."

Here, it is worthwhile to pause to examine the roles the student and instructor adopted, for while Vuong may have had a rather passive concept of authorship, he at this point took the lead in the conference, not only justifying his organization of the paper but correctly identifying what was frustrating his progress. Indeed, by pinpointing a contradiction in one of his sources (Rodriguez) and a conflict between sources (Rose and Rodriguez), he had just taken a step toward a more dynamic conception of authorship. In an effort to steer him toward these conflicts and get him to grapple with their implications, the instructor encouraged Vuong's intuition that it was paradoxical to argue against bilingual education while supporting higher education for "disadvantaged" students. Here, the instructor took a direct approach, praising the writer's insights but also giving him license to expose Rodriguez's contradictions; specifically, he explained that Vuong need not "make Rodriguez internally consistent." This represents a critical moment in the conference because it marks a shifting in the instructor's tone. Having just asked a series of following (as opposed to leading) questions to prompt the student's talking his way into a controlling idea, the instructor suddenly adopted a didactic tone, which urged Vuong's reconception of the task as well as his role as author: "I mean if [Rodriguez is] not consistent or if there are problems in the way his views

go together, then there are problems. And your job is to point those up."
By shifting into this mode of direct and meta-analytical address, the instructor focused Vuong's attention on the central rhetorical problem underlying the synthesis assignment: "How to mediate and make sense of different and conflicting voices from different sources of information" (Greene,
p. 86, this volume). Consequently, the student was made aware that conflict
is worth something to the instructor (and should therefore be worth something to him, as well). The exchange was valuable, in other words, in that
it guided Vuong to reconsider points of conflict as points of interest. As
the instructor explained, "Those are good insights. And they're good problems, because they're problems that are in all of this. . . ."

Vuong's ability to manipulate the contradictions he perceived was compromised by his lack of clear purpose in writing, although he came close
to identifying that purpose when he articulated a problem underlying
Hirsch's argument for cultural literacy. In response to his call for a unified
cultural literacy curriculum, Vuong suggested the problem must be historically contextualized: "[Cultural literacy] can't happen because we can't
just drop our present situation and go look for the future. . . . what happens
in the present affects the future." Sensing that the writer was on the verge
of real authorship, the instructor shifted once more into a directive mode,
urging Vuong to see the big picture that he was sketching aloud—indeed,
urging him to see the connection between the dialogue they were having
in the conference and the dialogue that could be happening in the paper.

I: Is there a way that you can back away from that and sort of give us
     a larger view? In other words, set out Rodriguez's ideas in a way
     that comes from you? You know, so just as you were sitting here
     talking to me in a very economical way, and sort of in a large—using
     large brush strokes, you told me what Rodriguez's position was and
     you told me what the problems were in terms of his internal
     consistency. That was all very clear to me when you told me that.
     Could you do that in your paper, with only occasionally dipping
     into the exact text?

R: Right now, I don't think so. I'm going to give quotations, support
     with evidence, then a broad view of what the author is saying.

I: Are you going to do that at some point? Are you going to move
     from the level of detail to a place where you tell your reader what
     all this means, how you see all this?

R: Yeah, that would probably be in the argumentative—the last part
     of my paper.

I: But you do want to communicate to your reader, even in the sections
     on the various authors—you want to communicate what you think

your reader needs to know, so that they can understand your
argument later, right?

R: Yeah.

Vuong's "yeah" suggests to me an acquiescing to the instructor's final
comment rather than a sign that he felt comfortable integrating his ideas
throughout the paper. Indeed, the final version of his paper indicated that
he stuck to his original plan, giving quotations that support his analysis of
each author, but keeping his analyses of their ideas separate and separating
those ideas from his own, which are reserved, as he said they would be,
for the final section of the paper.

If Vuong was able to productively interact with his sources during the
conference, why was he unable to assume the role of author in his paper?
Perhaps he had not yet grasped the practical implications of the dialogue
he had begun to observe. Vuong had begun to grapple with authoritative
discourses on a conscious and deliberate level, and he also understood
that his job was to foreground rather than resolve the conflicts he perceived
within and among the texts. This is a significant step toward authorship,
but it is not the same as understanding the cultural literacy conversation
as a dialogue he could join. Vuong still (mis)perceived that his rhetorical
task was to draw out the similarities and differences between the authors,
which suggests to me that he failed to grasp the conversation going on
among them; indeed, rather than seeing Rose, Rodriguez, and Hirsch in
discursive relationship with one another, he continued to see them giving
separate monologues on the same topic. In effect, then, Vuong remained
cowed by his sources not because he had nothing to say but because he
had no point of entry, and, thus, quite literally, nowhere in the paper to
express the reservations and corrections he proposed during the conference except in an appendixed way.

Further complicating Vuong's negotiation of authorship was the pressure on the part of his interpretive community to construct a tripartite,
neatly segmented final product. Greene suggested that Vuong might have
been resisting the role of author because he was unwilling to stand out
from his peers for his unorthodox ideas on the subject of bilingual education (Greene, p. 106, this volume). If this is the case, it is an ironic
testament to the efficacy of the workshop model, which seeks to transfer
authority in the classroom from instructor to peer writing groups. The
consensus among Vuong's classmates that the paper be structured around
the three authors was obviously strong enough to override the instructor's
suggestion that it be organized around a central idea, and this suggests
that concerns over conferencing undermining student authority may be
unfounded. The strength of the interpretive community is further illustrated in the second case example; however, whereas Jesus indicated a

great deal of anxiety over his departure from the consensus opinion, he also achieved what no other students in the class did: He assumed the role of author.

CASE #2: JESUS

Jesus' conference is different from Vuong's from the beginning. Whereas Vuong's comments were driven by a strong, if constricting, sense of organization, Jesus took an organic approach, indicating a sense of connection with his sources that grew out of his immersion in their ideas. Specifically, he noted that by going back to the texts over the weekend, he had found a way to clarify his own thoughts on the relationship between cultural diversity and literacy, his chosen topic.

> R: Yeah, what I did on the weekend was I sit and read Rose again. Because Rodriguez—I understand Rodriguez and Hirsch, but Rose is like, I don't get him. I don't know, he has a way of writing that—I don't get Rose. So anyway what I did was I read Rose again—the assignments that you did and all that. And now that I'm more focused on what I'm going to talk about—so I'm looking for something. I'm not . . . just reading.
>
> I: Yes.
>
> R: I'm looking for something.

Jesus' task conception and rhetorical relationship to Rose, Rodriguez, and Hirsch was defined in his description of his reading process: "I'm not . . . just reading. . . . I'm looking for something." By reading actively, as a participant in the construction of textual meaning, Jesus was already engaged in a dialogic exchange with his source authors. This helped him to see their texts in service to his own developing ideas about the relationship between cultural literacy and cultural diversity: "[M]aybe [Rose's] big idea is related to mine. Maybe what happens is that his big ideas is not specifically fit in mine, you know. But I try to relate it to look . . . you know to fix it with mine." At this point, the instructor was quick to assure Jesus that this was "exactly what one does in these papers," adopting the same directive tone with which he licensed Vuong to "point up" the "problems" in Rodriguez' argument.

The instructor was forced to assume this role in Jesus' conference much earlier than he did in Vuong's if only because where Vuong needed clarification, Jesus needed confirmation that he was on the right track. That Jesus had a much clearer grasp of the rhetorical task than his classmates was evidenced by his description of the paper's structure and how it differed from what he saw the other students doing. Jesus' description of the paper was couched in terms of its rhetorical purpose: to establish a "debate" among the three authors:

R: So, I use Hirsch trying to open the debate and then use Rose and Rodriguez to explain. And then at the end I explain what I think.

I: Great. Yeah, because Hirsch really does set the terms of the debate, in a way. Or at least he allows you a place to get at the argument. And then you can use Rose and Rodriguez as cases in point. Yeah, great.

R: That's the way I have—I didn't do it like—most of my group used like—they first talk about Hirsch. Then they—Hirsch like for a page and a half, all Hirsch—then they turn to Rose, all Rose. And then they turn all to Rodriguez. Because I think they should be—they're related one to the other. So what I'm doing is using—mixing—instead of using authors as divisions, ideas as divisions.

Like Vuong, Jesus seemed comfortable with the dialogic nature of the conference. He also seemed to use it consciously, as a tool, variously testing his task conception against the instructor's affirmations and asking pointed questions about the audience he potentially shared with Rodriguez, Hirsch, and Rose:

R: I have a question. Is it true that—I think that—not Rodriguez, but Hirsch and Rose—aren't they like writing to an audience of like educationalists?

I: Yeah, they are. And other people who would be interested in how education is set up and how it works in this country. So anybody who has a concern about educational institutions, they are writing to. Yeah, definitely, because it's a very hot area of debate these days, you know, the whole schools issue and money for schools and what's to be taught and how and all of that stuff.

Shaped by the writer's concerns about his own rhetorical objectives, the conference takes on a recursive quality. As Jesus' confidence grew, he stopped requiring the instructor's affirmation and began instead to detail the ways in which he would transform the debate on cultural diversity and literacy. Here, it is significant that Jesus was not only engaging in dialogue with his sources, but also revising the terms of the debate, literally rephrasing "cultural literacy" as "knowledge," and consequently opening the door to a more inclusive definition of the concept.

R: [In my paper] I was going to start talking about first cultural literacy, what it is and all that, what the three authors think that it must be and all that. Because Rose doesn't refer to it as cultural literacy, but as a knowledge. It's the same thing, just another word . . . Then I just want to see how can we achieve cultural literacy, you know, good cultural literacy in an environment of cultural diversity . . .

"It's the same thing, just another word. . . ." This is the language of an author, someone who understands that his job is not only to combine the ideas of others, but also to transform those ideas into a new and meaningful whole. Indeed, despite what Jesus said about the placement of his own ideas in the paper—"then at the end I explain what I think"—his finished essay was not a neatly segmented, tripartite essay, but rather, an idea-driven discussion integrating his own thoughts on the relationship between cultural literacy and diversity with those of Rose, Rodriguez, and Hirsch. Unlike Vuong, Jesus both targeted and explored the conflicts in his sources, using them as points of entry for his own opinions, which he wove throughout the essay. This was a bold move not only because it flew in the face of the class consensus about organizing the paper, but also because, as a native Spanish speaker, Jesus had a lot to contend with on a purely linguistic level. Coupled with his anxiety over striking out on his own was his anxiety over paraphrasing the ideas of native English speakers: "So when I do a paraphrase, I feel like I don't get [it]—[or] maybe I get it, but I'm not transmitting it as what he said." Then again, these are the universal concerns of authorship: Am I accurately representing my sources? Have I established a fair debate? Thus, ultimately, Jesus' success in assuming the role of author was indicated not only by the complexity of his finished paper but also by his lingering concern that it accurately expressed the ideas of those whose conversation he had joined.

CONCLUSIONS AND IMPLICATIONS

Greene identified the central problem of synthesis as "how to mediate and make sense of different and conflicting voices" from different sources of information (p. 86, this volume). In light of Jesus' success with the assignment, it is significant that he seemed comfortable interrogating his sources even before he began to draft the paper; this is indicated when he questioned the pragmatic implications of Hirsch's cultural literacy during the talk-aloud protocol: "Who will decide what changes are in minorities' best interests?" In raising the issue of applicability, Jesus entered into a dialogue with one of his sources even as he read the assignment for the first time. This does not necessarily imply that students who routinely question authority are closer to becoming authors of their own texts than those who assume a more passive relationship to their sources, but it does suggest that a

dialogic concept of meaning production may precede the ability to synthesize in the way required for this type of assignment. In contrast to Jesus,
who from the beginning actively interacted with the authoritative discourses
he was working with, Vuong seemed embarrassed by the conflicts he perceived in his source texts and both reticent and unclear about addressing
these conflicts in the paper. Clearly, he was also trapped by the tripartite
structure he was using to organize the paper because it created artificial
boundaries among the authors' thinking and between their thinking and
his own. Although Vuong began to reconceive his rhetorical task during
the course of his conference, he did not seem to grasp its practical implications for this paper. Lacking Jesus' conceptual advantage, he did well to
begin to negotiate the role of author, but he was not yet in a position to
assume that role.

Jesus may have begun with a more sophisticated concept of meaning
production, but it was not clear how he sustained faith in this approach in
the face of the consensus opinion among his peers that he was wrong.
Indeed, his pioneering spirit was especially remarkable given the strength of
this particular interpretive community (recall the influence of Vuong's
writing group, which apparently contributed to his decision to ignore the
instructor's advice about organizing the paper around his own ideas). Jesus'
authorship is immediately evident in the introduction of his paper, where
he took an unconventional stance on the concept of literacy.[7] Indeed,
despite some surface ambiguity, his opening assertion is remarkable for its
commanding tone: "To be able to read and write are merely skills rather than
effective thinking and analysis." He went on to align himself with an
unspecified group of "education-concerned people," who might consider
Hirsch's call for a unifying body of cultural knowledge problematic due to
the cultural plurality that "prevails in most of the regions of the United
States." In aligning himself with these particular (yet unspecified) teachers
and policy makers, Jesus claimed affiliation with a hypothetical group of
experts who value a democratic approach to the literacy debate; thus, he
adopted a posture of resistance to Hirsch by recourse to another official or
authoritative discourse. By adopting this posture of resistance, Jesus also
made clear that his identification with the ecumenical goals of the university
stopped precisely where his experience as a Latino student in a basic writing
classroom began. Claiming membership in an interpretive community
larger (and potentially stronger) than the workshop group authorized his
dissent from their consensus viewpoint. Perhaps, too, Jesus was able to resist

---

[7]Many beginning college writers enter the conversation by positing a commonplace
assumption about the issue they are writing about. When I have asked my students why they
do this, they explain that it is to orient their reader as well as establish credibility in the
person's eyes.

the consensus of his peer group because, unlike Vuong, he envisioned himself entering a personally significant conversation.

The synthesis assignment deliberately foregrounds the social and political factors that landed both Jesus and Vuong in the beginning writing course, yet only Jesus approached the assignment on a level of personal commitment. Jesus' response to the assignment began with an unspoken acknowledgment of his position within the university; ultimately, however (and unlike Vuong), he filtered the authoritative discourse of his sources through the lens of his own experience, reshaping their ideas according to what was from Jesus' perspective an internally persuasive discourse on the relationship between cultural literacy and diversity, a discourse that was tacitly based on his personal experiences. Whether Vuong intentionally assumed a posture of noncommitment because of peer pressure is unclear; however, by following the group's consensus about how to organize the paper, he limited himself to an oversimplified and perhaps personally insignificant response to the assignment. As I have already indicated, Vuong's failure to integrate his own ideas into the body of the paper suggested that he was stymied by his rigid organizational scheme. But why insist on this scheme in the first place, especially when the instructor suggested an alternative? Conceivably, Vuong did not discern the alternative in practical terms. Faced with the rhetorical challenge of a more complex (and messier) analysis, he opted for the tried-and-true strategy that got him through high school: the five-paragraph essay. In addition, Vuong's concept of academic conversation, at least as it applied to his writing, remained strictly metaphorical, his sense of the significance of his own personal contributions to that conversation purely theoretical.

Obviously, then, conferencing does not always work in the sense of guaranteeing that students will become authors of their own texts; Vuong's failure to assume the role of author is a case in point. However, as both Vuong's and Jesus' cases show, conferencing can help students become conscious of authorship as a concept and goal while guiding instructors to predict whether or not a student is ready and able to be pushed more aggressively in that direction. The implications of my thesis are multiple: Students like Jesus, who approach complex writing assignments already familiar with the dialogic terms of academic debate, may be in a position to use the conference to consciously and deliberately advance their rhetorical goals. By contrast, students like Vuong, who are just beginning to break away from constricting organizational models and develop an interrogative relationship with their sources, are in a position to learn the practical implications of authorship; instructors can help these students move closer to the goal of authorship by foregrounding it as both a combinatory and transformative activity. Ultimately, the goal of the dialogic writing conference is to foster a better understanding of the discursive production of texts. Students will be able to apply this concept to their own writing process only when they begin to appreciate the very real stake they have in the conversation and when the risk of remaining on the sidelines outweighs that of entering the fray.

WORKS CITED

Bakhtin, M. M. *The Dialogic Imagination: Four Essays.* Trans. Caryl Emerson and Michael Holquist. Ed. Michael Holquist. Austin: U of Texas P, 1981.

Bartholomae, David, and Anthony R. Petrosky. *Facts, Artifacts, and Counterfacts: Theory and Method for a Reading and Writing Course.* Portsmouth, NH: Boynton–Cook, 1986.

Bizzell, Patricia. *Academic Discourse and Critical Consciousness.* Pittsburgh: U of Pittsburgh P, 1992.

Bruffee, Kenneth A. "Collaborative Learning and the 'Conversation of Mankind.' " *College English* 46.7 (1984): 635–652.

Hirsch, E. D. *Cultural Literacy: What Every American Needs to Know.* Ed. Pat Mulcahy. New York: Random, 1988.

Ong, Walter J. *Orality and Literacy: The Technologizing of the Word.* New York: Routledge, 1988.

Rodriguez, Richard. *Hunger of Memory: The Education of Richard Rodriguez.* New York: Bantam, 1983.

Rose, Mike. *Lives on the Boundary: A Moving Account of the Struggles and Achievements of America's Educational Underclass.* New York: Penguin, 1990.

Trimbur, John. "Collaborative Learning and Teaching Writing." *Perspectives on Research and Scholarship in Composition.* Eds. Ben W. McClelland and Timothy R. Donovan. New York: MLA, 1985. 87–109.

Chapter 8

Teaching Talk About Writing: Student Conflict in Acquiring a New Discourse of Authorship Through Collaborative Planning[1]

Stuart Greene
University of Notre Dame

Erin Smith
University of Wisconsin–Madison

Ms. Smith:	Did you learn anything new from writing this paper? Did you experiment with something new as a writer? How did it go?
Eddie:	. . . making an argument, assuming that the readers will argue with.
TJ:	Yes, that I can now (hopefully) argue on a paper as well as doing it verbally. I experienced a weird transition in my paper by supporting an argument with specific evidence that seemed complicated to do—It was pretty tough, I admit but I managed to get into the flow of things.

Eddie and TJ are two beginning college writers who have just completed essays about family based on their own experiences and their analyses of two family sitcoms, one from the 1990s and one from the 1950s. In particular, the instructor, Ms. Smith (the second author of this chapter), asked her students to make an argument about families in their first-year writing class, a task that for them represented something new in their experiences as writers in school. Like the synthesis assignment in the literacy course discussed in the other chapters in this volume, this task about family re-

---

[1]A shorter version of this chapter was presented at the annual meeting of the National Council of Teachers of English in Orlando, Florida, November 1994.

quires that students read a number of texts, in this case family sitcoms and their own brief autobiographical essays focusing on family, and to advance their own points of view based on their reading and experiences. Specifically, students were asked to "Examine different conceptions of family in relation to a number of possible themes: parent–child relationships; family roles; family problems; financial security; and any other problem they might have felt was significant." Along with two other students, Eddie and TJ worked collaboratively for several weeks on plans and drafts for this and an earlier assignment that asked them to explore the relationship between their cultural backgrounds and identity as writers. In both, they struggled to understand and fulfill the demands of writing tasks that have challenged their prior notions of what it means to be an author. As their responses illustrate, both TJ and Eddie believed that, in this instance, they had begun to meet this challenge, moving through that "weird transition" from old writing conventions and on to newer, tougher conventions that seem "complicated to do."

In one sense, these responses simply represent two writers' descriptions of what they did in their papers. However, as important as what they did may be their ability to use a specific discourse of authorship in order to make these self-representations. The language they employed suggests a meta-awareness of not only what is at work, but how it is working.

The purpose of this chapter is to explore how the contexts of culture and schooling influence students' development as authors in a beginning writing class (cf. Leverenz, "Peer Response"). In this class, students collaborated with one another in composing essays that required them to integrate different and often conflicting points of view in developing their own rhetorical purposes. We use the construct of authorship to bring into focus the critical thinking skills students must learn as they sift through complex issues in reading and establish a sense of agency through adapting their knowledge in order to construct original arguments in their writing (Greene, "Making Sense"). We define *rhetorical* as the means and circumstances through which readers and writers represent and negotiate texts, tasks, and social contexts. A rhetorical perspective on literacy research and practice calls attention to the ways in which language use crystallizes relations between readers and writers. Such a perspective also brings into focus the extent to which the ways authors position themselves within a certain social space is contingent on (a) authority (e.g., a disciplinary community's conventions for inquiry, the institution of school, or a writer's expertise); (b) the purposes that bring writers together within a particular social forum; and (c) the topic of their discourse or task at hand (Greene & Ackerman 384; cf. Dyson 10).

To foster students' ability to think critically and independently, educators in composition studies have long touted the use of collaborative writing, making at least three assumptions about the role that collaborative writing can play in learning to write: (a) Students who write together understand that the purpose of writing is rhetorical, even though such understanding may be unconscious (Gere 641); (b) discourse provides the catalyst and support for learning by engendering conflict (e.g., Nystrand & Brandt); (c) conversation is the result of a "natural experience of co-operative, collaborative interaction through which people enact the essence of compromise" (e.g., Clark xvi); and that (d) students may be able to perform tasks together that would be too difficult to do individually (Vygotsky 188). At the same time, studies show that inexperienced writers may actually abandon their own intentions or plans when challenged by their peers (Leverenz 173–78), that they often focus on topic knowledge rather than on rhetorical concerns in writing (Flower, et al. "Making Thinking Visible"), and that students may settle for less demanding tasks of writing reports than the argumentative papers they set out to compose (cf. Nystrand & Brandt 220ff).[2]

It is one thing to create conditions of authorship by providing a supportive social context in which students write and share their writing. However, studies of collaborative writing reveal that it is quite another thing for students to enact the sort of strategies that will enable them to be authors in a mindful, principled way. The writing task is one factor that influences what students do. The context is another—in particular how students interpret what it means to collaborate and how they negotiate their roles as authors within a group. And, still further, how students negotiate these roles is shaped by what they feel it means to read, write, and talk in school.

Our research, based on 180 pages of transcripts of collaborative writing sessions, suggests that how students actually acquire this discourse is anything but natural. It is far more complicated than recent characterizations have shown. For example, we need to account for the ways in which writers use language to represent tasks, a language that is all too often based on a legacy of schooling that privileges recitation of received information, not the purposeful use of information in the service of particular rhetorical goals. It is relevant to our discussion of authorship that a legacy of remedial

---

[2]Nystrand and Brandt argue that "peer review works largely because it establishes reciprocity between writer and reader as a condition of discourse" (210). Moreover, they suggest that "The effectiveness of [peer review] lies largely in its efficacy in defining true troublesources—not discrepancies between the writer's text and some ideal text, but mismatches between what the writer actually has to say and what the reader actually needs and expects to find" (211). However, the case examples they present illustrate the extent to which both students' responses and revision choices can create problems for writers. For a review of the literature, see DiPardo and Freedman, "Peer Response Groups in the Writing Classroom."

education in the United States has often prevented beginning writing students from learning how to position themselves within an academic argument (e.g., Preus, chapter 4, this volume; Rose 167–204). Unfortunately, many beginning writers' experiences with writing have been restricted to exercises in grammar and punctuation so that these students have not had occasions to use writing as a way to explore their ideas and to develop arguments through reading and writing. Even when writers have been asked to concentrate on issues other than grammar and punctuation, they have infrequently been invited to talk about their writing with peers or, in many cases, with teachers. Thus, although perfectly able to converse about their papers and solve certain kinds of problems, it is unlikely that they have developed a meta-critical discourse that will enable them to enter academic conversations deliberately and strategically.

For instance, in spoken language, students are free to assert opinions without displaying evidence or to recount experiences without explaining what they mean. But in school, we reward students' ability to sustain a play of mind on ideas—teasing out contradictions and the ambiguities of statements (e.g., Rose 39–65). Therefore, when we admonish our students to be specific, we need to be aware that the conditions for specificity may not be present for them. An equally important point is that students may demonstrate a keen understanding of certain kinds of texts (e.g., film, the Internet) that they may not readily transfer to their reading of more traditional texts (e.g., Smagorinsky & Coppock 301–305).

Finally, writers may bring certain romantic notions about writing to the group, ideas that focus on the individual writer apart from any social or institutional practice and that may prove antithetical to the very goals of collaboration. As a consequence, writers may circumvent the sort of conflict that leads to the identification and resolution of problems within the context of the group by falling back on the idea that writing is a solitary process.

In short, writers already come to writing groups with a discourse about writing that not only embodies students' assumptions about what it means to read and write in school but that translates into activities that may or may not be appropriate to a task or context. The ways in which students construe a task are, in large part, dependent on prior learning experiences about what is appropriate and on what effects their actions are likely to have (Nelson 388). Therefore, we want to claim that acquiring a new discourse of authorship is marked by a complex interplay between new ways of speaking and the ways students are accustomed to talking (or not talking) about writing. This interplay is comprised of a dialectical relationship between the texts writers produce and the way they are able to talk about those texts.

To understand the nature of this dialectical relationship, it is useful to examine the transcripts of writers who in planning their essays are in the process of adapting a new discourse about writing arguments in an academic context. By closely observing four students' collaborative planning sessions three times a week for 15 weeks, we have located two places that foreground the ways in which learning a new discourse is marked by an ongoing process of negotiation that is at once cognitive and social (cf. Flower 36–84). First, this negotiation is evident in the role that conflict played in the development of authorship. Students' attempts to make sense of and use a new discourse of authorship often involved a struggle between beliefs they currently held about writing and those they were being asked to adopt—a struggle influenced by competing institutional, social, and cultural concerns. Second, this negotiation is evident in the shift these students made from their talk about arguments to their attempts to actually make arguments.

Before we actually explore how this negotiation is played out in these two areas, it is essential to see that some students bring fairly elaborate theories of authorship to the task of writing, as evidenced in the talk they used to describe the composing process. This is particularly true in the case of TJ, who we discuss at some length in the remainder of this chapter. Although the language he used to talk about writing is not necessarily representative of all the students in his class, the struggle he experienced in learning a new discourse does illustrate a problem that others did confront. In offering a picture of how students began to acquire a new discourse of authorship, we return to a key claim that we made earlier: Acquiring a new discourse of authorship is marked by a complex interplay between new ways of speaking and the ways students are accustomed to talking about writing.

THE TALK THAT STUDENTS BRING
TO A CONVERSATION ABOUT WRITING

Expand, exactly. I can pretty much expand what I have. Um, I also mention . . . I mean I'm not . . . I don't like to consider myself a writer, but if I write about it in this situation, I would more or less have a more clear idea of what I'll be doing. I'll have all my thoughts together, I could build, I could expand, I could change. Yet, I could still see as an overall picture how I want it through my eyes, and I can just play with that and just try and get down to the basic facts of reality of what I'm writing. Um, I think when I look at it, I can really change the way I am . . . And, um, there're a lot of positive and negative ways of how I grew up and I just want to talk about it. I feel that it needs to be talked about. I mean it's not just all bad, but yet it's not just all fantasy and happy land about everything. So you can just compare and contrast the positive and negative ways. So I pretty much got a start. I just got to start it, that's all.

As TJ explained his writing plans to his group members, the language he employed encodes a story about who writers are, what they do, and what it means to collaborate. Assuring his group that he did not "consider [himself] a writer," he nevertheless immediately invoked a discourse of authorship. Active and reflective, TJ's writer was someone who will expand, change, get down to the facts, just play, see an overall picture, talk, compare and contrast, and who will balance the positive and negatives. Moreover, this writer existed not in the present tense, there in the company of his collaborators, but at some time in the future—away from the group. The negotiation that occurs is not through the give-and-take between an author and his supporters but within an imagined set of possibilities. Here, TJ considered a number of possible options that he might pursue at some time in the future:

> I would more or less have a more clear idea of what I'll be doing. I'll have all my thoughts together, I could build, I could expand, I could change. Yet, I could still see as an overall picture how I want it through my eyes, and I can just play with that and just try and get down to the basic facts of reality of what I'm writing.

TJ's imaginary author is one who manipulates topic knowledge through the process of expansion. What motivated his sense of authorship was a faith that all a writer must do is write and somehow everything will fall into place. "If I write about it," he told his group, "then I'll have a more or less clear idea what I'm doing." Also implicit in this discourse is the idea that to declare one's intentions is equivalent to actually having done something: "So I pretty much got a start. I just got to start it, that's all." The contradiction inherent in these claims, like the distance that TJ placed between himself and this imaginary author, may actually reflect a very real gap in knowledge between the vocabulary of a writer and his activities.

TEACHING STUDENTS A NEW DISCOURSE OF AUTHORSHIP

A critical question is what happens when we teach beginning writers such as TJ a new discourse of authorship, in this case the language of collaborative planning. Linda Flower and her colleagues (e.g., Flower et al., *Making Thinking Visible,* esp. chap. 3) suggested that collaborative planning can be a useful approach to teaching writing, aimed at helping writers become more aware of their own thinking and planning processes. Within such an approach, students assume the role of writers or supporters. Supporters help writers identify the purpose of their essays (e.g., what the writers want readers to do or think about), discuss who they believe their readers are, explain the key point of their essay (i.e., the major claim), and analyze their use of different text conventions (e.g., the use of an example from a published authority). Specifically, collaborative planning provides social support that can help students move beyond topic knowledge, which they often feel more comfortable with in writing, into more rhetorical constructive planning; that is, using what they know to advance an argument that can influence what readers think and believe (Higgins, Flower, and Petraglia).

One way to think about the planning process is in terms of what Flower and her colleagues called the Planner's Blackboard (see Fig. 8.1), which identifies significant writing concerns (i.e., topic information, purpose and key point, audience, and text conventions) and the relationship between them (*Making Thinking Visible*). The Planner's Blackboard is a visual tool that can help writers keep in mind the relationship between plans to say something about a given topic and plans to do something in order to advance a rhetorical purpose. To foreground these rhetorical concerns, supporters encourage writers to address a number of key questions: "What more can you say about X? What do you see as your key point or purpose? How do you think your reader will react to what you say here? How do you plan to explain this point? and How does what you say here relate to or clarify what you say over here?"

The instructor of the course introduced this new discourse to students in the context of their writing an essay in which they explored their cultural heritage. In particular, the instructor asked students to "write on [their] sense of identity, cultural and otherwise, and its connection to the written word. How do you think your sense of identity intersects with your sense

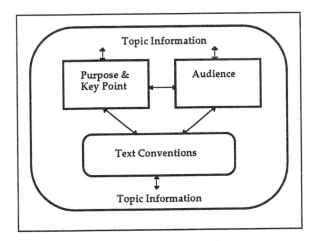

FIG. 8.1. Flower et al.'s (51) model of collaborative planning. Copyright © 1994 by the National Council of Teachers of English. Reprinted with permission.

of yourself as a writer (and reader)?" This assignment is similar to the literacy autobiography students in the literacy course wrote in that students writing about their cultural identity were encouraged to write about their experiences as writers in different settings (e.g., family, school, and community), although the primary emphasis was on culture. Such a task was the first of a number of writing assignments about popular culture and social issues (e.g., cultural identity) in a course designed to help beginning writers bridge the distance between life outside of school and life in school.

In giving this assignment, the instructor, Ms. Smith, sought to problematize the ways in which these students viewed writing in order to help them see that definitions of good and bad writing are constructed, not natural. Talking about writing as a construction enabled her to raise questions about both how writing had been defined and evaluated for them in the past as well as how it was now going to be defined and evaluated within an academic context. She believed that one important benefit of this approach was to help students see that writing is not an innate ability (an ability that they do not have), but rather is something that can be learned. Using collaborative planning became another way to foreground the idea that just as writing itself is not a natural process, neither is talk about writing.

She introduced this new discourse in two primary ways. First, she played the role of a supporter for another writer as her class observed and then discussed with them what they believed what was important to address in collaborative planning sessions. Although students were not always certain about what such terms as key point and text conventions mean, they recognized the legitimacy of challenging a writer and the potential value of conflict in coming to a solution to a rhetorical problem. One student, Arschelle, observed in class discussion that her instructor and the writer really were not arguing. Instead, she pointed out that:

> I mean, you were getting across to each other. He was taking your suggestions and actually thinking about what you were saying and applying it to his, uh, paper and [said] that "maybe that might be something I could do." And, also when you made suggestions that he may or may not thought was, uh . . . he thought about it.

Immediately following this kind of modeling and discussion, Ms. Smith's students worked with their own plans. In the class that followed this session, she brought her own plan for writing a paper on her cultural identity. She then asked students to play the role of supporters in order to give them an opportunity to try out some of the collaborative planning questions.

Students' early attempts to use this new discourse revealed a fundamental tension between familiar ways of talking about and conceptualizing writing and the new ways they were being taught. Learning a new discourse is not only marked by a complex interplay of competing voices, as we claimed earlier, but by conflict at both a cognitive and social level. These conflicts occur not only within individuals but among the members of the group. In fact, the language with which TJ and Arschelle discussed TJ's plans in the next excerpt reveals the ways in which old words and new words compete for attention in both the discussion and TJ's evolving draft. Here, the language that TJ was so accustomed to using to talk about writing—marked by such terms as *talk about, advantages and disadvantages, expand,* and *go into real depth*—competes both with TJ's desire to adopt new words—*key point* and *talk about how*—and Arschelle's attempts to use the language of collaborative planning, particularly in her insistence that TJ relate and connect his ideas about his cultural identity. We have italicized those familiar words and phrases that TJ used to talk about writing and that appear to guide his understanding of how he would pursue his goals as an author. We have also placed in italics those words that reflect his attempts to use the language of collaborative planning. However, the use of old and new discourses is not always distinct, which appears to be the case in his reference to *my points.*

TJ: Okay. What I just did, I basically broke it down to where I want to *talk in real depth about* more in my personality and childhood and, uh, one of the main factors that we wanted to discuss with my purpose was how a minority as myself, a Mexican American, was being brought up from more or less, like a ghetto area, a bad area . . .

A: m-huh.

TJ: . . . and family and surroundings around me really had an impact on how I grew up. So I mainly want *to talk about* how that affected me, how that changed me, and how that's bringing me to the way I am today.

A: So basically what you're focusing on is your upbringing, your raising . . .

TJ: More or less . . . and the experiences and all that I've gone through with my childhood and seen the way today is and like *I want to see the advantages and disadvantages there are* and, like you see, jobs, certain lifestyles have changed, my education, and then mainly on today, *how that really differs from the past.* I mean I can *go into real depth* about it, but my more or less key points that I want to really *hit these,* uh, now that I'm here I want to try to make a world of difference not only to my parents but to myself, that I can really make something of myself here.

A: m-huh.

TJ: Uh, there's so much in my past and my people that I've known
      and grown up with that gave up on life pretty quickly.

A: Uh-huh, that's what I was kind of talking about. . . . All of these
      negative things are around you and you kind of gotta separate
      yourself from them.

TJ: Exactly . . . Right. So, that's . . . I want to *talk about* that because
      I feel that it needs *to be talked about* because it's really happening.
      There tends to be more of a higher percentage of Mexican Ameri-
      cans really giving up on their lives. You know, dropping out of
      middle school, high school, trying to live off welfare, making babies
      left and right.

A: m-huh.

TJ: Trying to see if [something]'s gonna actually help pay for food
      expenses and rent. You know, that's too much.

A: I see a big similarity in . . .

TJ: Right, I mean . . . So, it's pretty, but I think with *my points*, with
      my key points that I have, that I have, that I can really . . .

N: *Expand* on them?

TJ: *Expand*, exactly . . .

A: So you're gonna relate all of that to what you feel about your
      cultural identity.

TJ: Pretty much.

A: Okay, 'cause I heard you talk about what went on and everything,
      so how are you going to connect that to what you feel about your
      cultural identity. Or what do you think your cultural identity is? I
      mean, just being Mexican American, or . . .

In this exchange between TJ and Arschelle, it is evident that both writers
were hard at work trying to use and make sense of the discourse of collaborative planning. As in the earlier example in which we discussed TJ's
representation of what it means to be an author ("I can just play with that
and just try to get it down to the basic facts of reality of what I'm writing"),
TJ again demonstrated that he approached writing with a well-developed
discourse that influenced his sense of how to organize the story he wanted
to tell about his cultural heritage (e.g., "I want to see the advantages and
disadvantages . . . I can go into real depth"). This discourse is not only
well-developed, but powerful—not just for TJ, but for Arschelle as well,
despite the fact that she more often employed terms from the new discourse
(e.g., "So you're gonna relate all that to what you feel about your cultural
identity?"). Its power is evident in the way it interferes with TJ's ability to

make use of the new discourse, which might in turn have enabled him to identify the overarching concept (or key point) that would draw together his different experiences. Its power for Arschelle is apparent not so much in her own use of this discourse but in the way that, quite often, she seemed persuaded by TJ.

At the same time, although TJ's familiar discourse about writing dominated his discussion, there were moments when he began to try out the discourse of collaborative planning. This is most apparent in his attempt to work with the new phrase "key point":

I mean I can *go into real depth* about it, but my more or less key points that I want to really *hit* [upon].

but I think with *my points*, with my key points that I have . . .

In some ways, by transforming the term *key point*, singular, into "my points" or "key points," plural, it seems as if TJ was simply mapping a new word onto an old practice. What appears to be lost in this transformation is the sense that a key point represents the activity of consolidating different ideas and organizing them with some overarching concept. Here, TJ made it interchangeable with any of several individual points that he wanted to make about his cultural identity, such as "certain lifestyles, jobs and education." However, if we consider what prompted him to introduce the term *key point* in the first place, we find that, on some level, TJ did recognize that it has something to do with consolidation. In both instances where TJ used "key point," it was in response to Arschelle's questions about focus and connections (e.g., "I see a big similarity in . . .").

Even though the responses themselves indicate that TJ associated *key point* more with the idea of a main point or a big point, his ability to invoke the term in an appropriate context suggested he was doing more than simply mimicking or misusing it. He was beginning to negotiate between the two discourses, attempting to determine what this new language meant in terms of what he already knew. Although he was aware that he needed to focus and make connections, he was not altogether sure how to do that. This was particularly evident in the cultural autobiography he wrote, which focused on the disadvantages of being a Mexican-American living in Texas, the conflicts that erupted in his family, the problems his father experienced as a non-native speaker of English in school, and the discipline he learned playing football. Each part of the essay contributes to our understanding of, to use TJ's words, "the important factors that took place to make me the person I am." Our point is that the talk TJ was accustomed to using, which embodies a theory of writing, and the discourse of collaborative planning represent two very different sorts of activities. What TJ had to learn was how to enact the very process he had come to recognize as necessary in writing academic essays: to consolidate his ideas in advancing a main point.

As important as the negotiation taking place between these conflicting discourses within the individual writer is the negotiation that occurs between supporter and writer. At several points during the previous exchange, Arschelle challenged TJ's seemingly romantic notions of authorship by insisting that he account for what he would do in the presence of the group. Perhaps more important, by introducing the language of collaborative planning into the discussion, she resisted TJ's old schema, introducing the possibility that there may be a conflict between old ways of thinking and doing and new ways. This sense of conflict seemed to motivate the negotiations that he began to undertake—that is, to effect a transformation of his understanding of what it means to be an author.

Thus far, we have characterized this negotiation as an attempt to make sense of competing discourses of authorship, which translate into different kinds of writing activities. Moreover, the kind of negotiations that we have focused on have centered on conflicts between different institutional constructions of what writing is or should be. However, we need to acknowledge the social and cultural factors involved both in how students construct a discourse about authorship and in their willingness to abandon those constructions.

TJ's notions of authorship provide evidence of how a writer's cultural and social background can determine his definition of certain text conventions. More than just comparing and contrasting, TJ talked about the need to account for advantages and disadvantages, positives and negatives. Although it seems as if these constructions relate to content-based concerns, the following excerpt about another writer's draft reveals that these phrases represent not just content, but text conventions. As TJ, Eddie, and Arschelle discussed Eddie's paper, TJ's concerns about representing positives and negatives in his own paper suddenly became a criterion for evaluating another writer's text—a set of conventions for writing.

Eddie: Key point is . . . key point is I feel I was born in wrong time, at the wrong place . . .

TJ: . . . at the wrong time?

Eddie: Yeah. So, I'm . . . two things. I talk about why I feel that way, about the way things . . . OK, why I feel that way. First, I talk about where I was born, OK, and how my life was over there, my native land. How I . . . we went, we escaped.

A: Well, I have a question. You said: "This is a dream. It must be a nightmare." Could you explain that?

Eddie: Um, I don't even know what I mean by that. I just write it . . . Um, what I was trying to say is that right now I feel like this periods of time, 1993, in United States, I feel like I'm, uh, living in a dream. Because I don't like to live in so . . . I don't like societies, I don't like . . .

A: I can understand that, coming from somewhere else.

TJ: Oh, I was just gonna say you're not liking the way this society is now, um, is it a lot . . . um, I'm sure it's different than from where you were, otherwise you wouldn't be thinking this.

Eddie: That's why I say I was born in wrong place and wrong time.

TJ: Are there any advantages or likes about this society here that you like other than back home? . . .

Eddie: There is nothing really, um . . .

TJ: Really?

Eddie: . . . um, I had everything I ever wanted, actually.

A: . . . What can you do to . . . I wouldn't say change your opinion about it, but what can you do to make it more of a better experience for you? I mean not that it's an experience cause you're probably gonna be here for the rest of your life, but I mean instead of just always looking at it like that because you can't change it, what can you do to just . . . ?

TJ: What do you think you can do about changing your way of life to make things better . . . ?

Eddie: There's nothings. I was just saying it is my destiny. It is my fate.

TJ: Ah!

A: Well you can't really . . .

[Eddie laughs.]

TJ: You're talking negative here. You gotta have a positive outlook on life. I mean, life's filled with the pain and agony and you name it. I mean I'm sure everybody at some time in their life's gonna go through it. But you just can't give up on yourself and see it one way and that's the only way it's gonna be. I feel there's always a chance to want to be somebody, to change an outlook on something that you wanted to put effort into it. If you look at it this way, from here on, um, . . .

A: What can you do to make . . . ?

Eddie: Something change . . .

A: We can't change everything . . .

Eddie: We can't change fact. We can't get around fact. Can we? We cannot change the facts?

TJ: True. No you can't. But you can change your way of life.

A: You can change the way *you* look at it.

This example provides us with another dimension of the negotiation or outright conflict that occurs within groups, thus challenging the notion that conversation is a "natural experience" of cooperation (Clark xvi). At various times during their discussion of these cultural identity papers, both TJ and Arschelle talked about their sense of themselves as people who have escaped from communities where people have essentially given up on life. In many ways, these escapes have depended on their ability to resist what they have characterized as self-defeating or negative talk and to instead find the good that comes out of the bad, to turn hard times into stories of success. This drive toward success had, for TJ, become so powerful that he had incorporated it into his talk about writing. Conflict arose within the realms of content and text conventions when Eddie insisted that he had nothing positive to say about his life in the United States.

In large part, this conflict plays itself out as one between the collaborative planning concept of key point and TJ's own requirement of positives and negatives. Eddie, attempting to use collaborative planning, came to the group with a key point, which is challenged because what it consolidates is an unacceptable value system or worldview. This challenge is first posed in the form of a question ("Are there any advantages or likes about this society here that you like other than back home?"), but later manifested itself in the supporters' shift in focus from the writer's draft to the writer himself. Clearly disturbed by Eddie's claim that life in the United States is "a nightmare," the talk quickly shifted from a discussion about Eddie's draft to one about what Eddie could do to improve his outlook on life. TJ, in particular, maintained that Eddie needed to "have a positive outlook," and told him, in no uncertain terms, that "you can't just give up on yourself." It is possible, if not probable, that to encourage Eddie in the development of this key point was to come dangerously close to that place from which TJ had only recently escaped (". . . one of the main factors that we wanted to discuss . . . was how a minority as myself, a Mexican American, was being brought up from more or less, like a ghetto area, a bad area . . ."). If our earlier excerpts suggested the way that the discourse of collaborative planning can get derailed by competing institutional discourses, this is a significant statement about how social and cultural concerns may motivate a student's resistance to adopting a different discourse of authorship.

To sum up, we argue that to simply expect students to acquire a new discourse in learning to perform complex academic tasks is to ignore the powerful institutional, cultural, and social concerns that may influence their decision to hold on to a familiar discourse. At the center of learning a new discourse of authorship is an ongoing process of negotiating old and new discourses and the sorts of literate acts that are associated with them. Moreover, conflict appears to play a key role in helping students acquire a new discourse, a fact that was evident in Arschelle's insistence that TJ focused his ideas and made connections. Unfortunately, many accounts of social interaction fail to acknowledge how writers negotiate conflict at various choice points during the process of composing (e.g., Bruffee, *Collaborative Learning*). What remains in our account of how students learn to use a new discourse of authorship in an academic context is the need to examine the relationship between the talk that evolves within the give and take of social interaction and the actual texts they produce.

FROM TALKING ABOUT ARGUMENTS TO MAKING ARGUMENTS: GETTING INTO THE FLOW OF THINGS

To characterize the weird transition that students make from using a discourse of authorship with which they are familiar to a new discourse, we return now to TJ's comments that appeared at the very outset of this chapter. In this assignment, the instructor asked students to "Examine different conceptions of family in relation to a number of possible themes: parent–child relationships; family roles; family problems; financial security; and any other problem they might have felt was significant." TJ explained to his teacher, in a writing conference that we audiotaped, his belief that he had constructed an argument about how families are represented in popular culture. Indeed, for him, it had been a difficult transition, as it had been for the other students in his writing group, but he was certain that he was now "getting into the flow of things." The sort of metacritical awareness he revealed in these comments and in a later response to his teacher's written comments suggest his increased ability to talk about his writing in terms of this new discourse. Still, we would claim that writers such as TJ may learn to adopt a new discourse, in this case the discourse of collaborative planning, before they are actually able to fully link this discourse to such literate acts as writing academic arguments. Thus, we would add one final feature to our characterization of students' attempts to negotiate competing discourses. Students' abilities to fulfill the promises of a new discourse hinge on their abilities to critically evaluate both what they know and what they need to know.

If students have difficulty learning new discourses, it may be because neither writing nor the discourse of authorship are monolithic. Instead, they reflect the changing tasks and contexts that students must negotiate in school. Therefore, when working with a model like that of collaborative planning, teachers must be alert to the ways in which it might be modified in order to better respond to what students already bring to the classroom as well as to the tasks at hand. In the context of this study, Ms. Smith sensed that perhaps because the term *key point,* as much as the concept, created some confusion for her students, she decided to replace it with the term *argument* for the next assignment. For the most part, her students did not associate a key point with an overarching claim; instead, they merged the notion of a key point with other concepts such as those that TJ seemed to have in mind when he talked about key points or "my main points."

Although the cultural identity assignment did, indirectly, call on students to make an argument about the relationship between culture and identity, by shifting the term to argument in the family assignment, Ms. Smith also helped to signal a change in the kind of paper they would be asked to write in the next two units. More to the point, she began to adapt the generic model of collaborative planning in order to help students think about how to use information from sources (print and nonprint) as evidence to advance their own arguments about the ways in which families are represented on television. Regardless of the theme her students chose, they were expected to place their examination in the framework of some central argument, one that "someone might reasonably debate" and that they could "support well with evidence from [the] source texts." One could imagine, for example, that a student might argue that television sitcoms seem to suggest that family problems can be solved by a little common sense. But on a closer examination, one finds that families on television are often able to solve problems because they have both time and money.

How TJ approached this task of writing an argument about family can throw some light on the difficult transition that other students also make from talking about arguments to actually making arguments. In the introduction to the argumentative essay he wrote, TJ addressed the source of family stability as it is represented in two different sitcoms. (See Appendix at the end of this chapter for the complete text of this essay.) Of particular interest is what this text reveals about the negotiation that was so central to TJ's attempts to learn a new discourse and to translate what he has learned into action (cf. Ackerman 184–87).

> Television sitcoms such as the Donna Reed Show and Thea both relate to one another in creating a good laugh about family life. However, the Stones, from the Donna Reed Show, find life easy to live because of their financial security. For having a lot of money both parents are able to spend time with their children. Furthermore, the use of money can help solve problems that the family might face. On the other hand, Thea's family is surrounded with problems in not having money which in turn leads to a difficult life to live.

Like the cultural identity paper we discussed earlier, it seems relatively clear that TJ brought the same powerful schema about writing to bear on the argument he began to construct here. He set up the paper by examining a contrast between two sitcoms, *The Donna Reed Show* and a show of the '90s, *Thea*. The Stones have financial stability, on the one hand, and on the other hand Thea's family has financial difficulties. Structuring his paper along the lines of compare and contrast, advantages and disadvantages, and negatives and positives, he used a familiar discourse. He called attention to the material and emotional benefits that financial security insures the Stones, although TJ pointed to the negatives that financial security can bring about as well. He also demonstrated in his written analysis of *Thea* that "low financial security" results in "hardships," "conflict," "pain," and "turmoil." To overcome these problems, TJ observed that Thea's family must "work together," a point that echoes the success story he detailed for his group in writing his cultural identity paper and at the end of his family paper. In the latter, he told us that, "It's knowing that we can count on each other for anything and cope with what we have regardless [of] our financial status."

TJ's argument, one that is more implicit than explicit, reflected his experience that families like his own or Thea's need money because it can bring about stability but if they do not have the necessary financial resources, families can and should draw on other strengths. Moreover, TJ suggested that people can actually learn things about responsibility and discipline that they may not have learned if they were in position to use money alone to solve their problems. As in the talk surrounding his cultural identity paper, where he described "the experiences and all that [he's] gone through with [his] childhood," he invoked an older, familiar discourse, one that enabled him to tell another success story: Out of hardship, we become stronger. And this is the very discourse he employed when he told Eddie in a collaborative planning session that he was "talking negative. . . . You gotta have a positive outlook on life. I mean, life's filled with . . . pain and agony and you name it. . . . But you can't just give up on yourself." Indeed, this may be the key point or argument that TJ made in his family paper, although the path from the claim that seems to inform this essay to the analysis and conclusions he made could be clearer. In fact, the comparison he drew between the two sitcoms obscures the major premise in large part because his analysis tended to center on the story or plot of the sitcoms, not the argument itself.

This problem can be illustrated by looking briefly at the topical structure of the five-page essay he wrote. After explaining the differences between *The Donna Reed Show* and *Thea* in terms of financial resources in his introduction, he began each subsequent paragraph of a five-page essay (double-spaced) with a detail about the sitcoms he discussed:

> The father's earnings as a doctor enables the mother to stay at home and spend a lot of time with the children. . . . After awhile the parents agree to let their daughter go to the dance, and in solving the problem they take her there themselves.

> . . . The sitcom show, "Thea," illustrates the life of a single mother raising four children on her own. . . . The siblings may work together in doing housework, but the absence of their mother all day and night creates conflicts and pain among the children. . . . My family has a resemblance of both the "Donna Reed Show" and "Thea" in various ways.

Not until he told other people's stories did TJ begin to address the importance of family support, regardless of "financial status" at the end of his essay.

Unless we look at the older, familiar discourse that TJ used, however, we may not see what is at work in his attempts to write an argument. Simply put, there is something else going on here. Whereas he appeared to understand that writing a comparison gave him license to write about anything related to his cultural identity (e.g., education, jobs, certain lifestyles), the family essay is far more focused. In fact, unlike the cultural identity paper he wrote, TJ had positioned himself to use the comparison in the service of an argument that he made.

The argument that TJ made may be more readily apparent in the talk that evolved in the context of the collaborative planning session we include here. TJ brought four different options to his group because he had not decided what he wanted to argue but soon agreed with his supporters that he should write about what factors can bring about family stability. What ensued was a form of negotiation that forced TJ to consider a number of possible alternatives. For instance, even though TJ suggested that money can provide a great deal, Eddie pointed out that such a position is open to question, thus affirming what he believed constitutes a "good argument." In turn, Eddie fueled the argument that TJ eventually made: "Money is not what matters. We still have family. Families are everything." But Arschelle challenged TJ to consider two rival claims that he had to reconcile. "Will you say . . . money does make a difference and then expand on that?" She wondered if he was saying that money does not make a difference, "it's just they're still a family."

TJ: But I assume that that would be a good argument, I think, is the financial.

A: Yeah. It would be.

TJ: Because, when you think about it, as long as the family has the money to put the food on the table, a roof over your head, clothing and still being able to have another parent be with their kids, I mean what more can you really ask for? As for Thea, they're really struggling. There's four children in the family . . .

Eddie: So the argument would be, you know, the way you [ ] audience might think, "Oh, that's not true."

A: Basically the same as yours.

Eddie: "Money is not what matters. We still have family. Families are everything, so you know . . ."

TJ: And some rely on money more than others. So you think that could be my argument?

A: That could be your argument.

Eddie: That's a good one, actually.

TJ: Really? Okay.

Eddie: Yeah. Because it's really about families. So you're talking about what really family means to you . . .

A: Will you say family, I mean, um, money does make a difference and then expand on that?

Eddie: And that's an argument. What TJ believes.

A: Or saying that money doesn't make a difference, it's just they're still a family.

Eddie: This way you're really talking about family values.

A: But they're not really struggling, struggling, but there is a difference.

TJ: All right. Well then I'll just go with that then.

E: Because a lot of people might say, you know "Money [ ] . . . we still got each other, we're still a family."

A: . . . about the father not being there or something like that.

TJ: Hm. About turning to for help?

A: Yeah. They only have one.

TJ: One parent.

A: Yeah. It's sort of like the opposite of mine. You know, you have two parents [ ] It's sort of like giving the same but you only have one.

TJ: Well, you know, I think I can blend the two together, sort of. When I think about how in the financial way, being able for the father to work or being the doctor that he is, he sometimes, most of the time at the house, like in that episode he was just there at the house all the time, but I'm sure there's other times he's . . .

A: That's not realistic, though.

TJ: Yeah, I know. But, then, the mother's not working, so that gives her the time to be with her kids. I could still bring that up to

> where the kids can still go to her and the father sometimes. As
> for the kids on the Thea show, they can only go to the mother
> regardless . . .

This kind of meta-talk underscores two key points about the transition
that TJ began to make from talking about argument to actually making
an argument. First, the language TJ used not only suggests that he had
begun to adopt a new discourse of authorship, but can articulate the
activities associated with that discourse. Thus it is one thing to talk about
argument as he did in several instances (e.g., "that would be a good argument"); it is quite another to sift through a number of options and plot
out a strategy for executing an argument. A second, related point is that
this new discourse seems to have reshaped his understanding of what it
means to be an author, one that is distinct from the image he constructed
when he talked about writing his cultural identity paper. Interestingly, in
this earlier context, TJ told his group that he was not a writer, creating a
story of an author who existed in the future and negotiated choices amid
an imagined set of possibilities apart from the give-and-take of collaboration. But the discourse of authorship he used here in describing his family
paper encodes a different story. The writer, TJ, existed in the here-and-now
and the negotiation that occurred was in the company of his supporters,
not within the mind of a writer isolated from the group. Moreover, in
developing his argument, he explained in the present tense how he thought
he could "blend together" the different ideas that Arschelle introduced to
the discussion.

This shift from future tense to the present provides a useful index for
understanding TJ's broadened sense of authorship, as does his ability to
evaluate both what he knew and needed to know when he responded in
writing to the written comments his teacher provided after he completed
his final draft. He told her that:

> I was trying to concentrate on [writing an argument] than anything else—
> making a statement and have other people disagree with me (which they
> did). I know now that I need to support my argument with more examples
> and evidence to make my paper better. Also I have to get rid of the stuff
> that doesn't directly relate to my argument.

Still, inasmuch as he had begun to use this new discourse, in actually
writing his essay he revealed the extent to which he continued to negotiate
the old and new discourse as well as the different activities that each entails.
This brings us back to the kind of dialectical interplay that we discussed
earlier. Students' attempts to use a new discourse begins to result in different writing activities, which in turn develop as students become better
able to apply the discourse metacritically to their writing.

CONCLUSION

Through close observation of students planning together in real time, we have been able to bring into focus the conflicts and decision-making points that are often left unaccounted for in studies of social interaction. Our analyses of collaborative planning, limited to a single writing group, leave us with an increased understanding that learning a new discourse is a dynamic process, one that is not only marked by growth but by conflict as well. This may be evident, but such a conclusion is not in the least bit trivial. Learning a new discourse not only positions our students in new ways, but our data reveal that when we ask our students to adopt the discourse of collaborative planning, we may be asking them to give up a discourse that in many ways is essential to their ability to maintain a sense of who they are. This was certainly the case with TJ, whose discourse of authorship provided him with the means to tell and retell a life-affirming story in a new and relatively alien environment. Given the rhythm of student learning depicted in our study, we are in a better position to see the logic that motivates students' choices in writing, knowing when it might be possible to intervene as teachers.

This intervention can take the form of students' self-analysis, focusing on the extent to which collaborative planning is helping writers develop their work and the strategies that group members can use in order to make their sessions more effective. We have seen that the instructor had modeled collaborative planning in two ways at the beginning of the term, and after 6 weeks, she transcribed collaborative planning sessions from each of the four groups in her class, so that students could see how well things were going. Specifically, she asked them to answer the following questions by referring to actual portions of the transcriptions she gave them and told them that they would be expected to give an oral presentation to the class based on their analyses:

- What did you get out of the session on this particular day? What did you learn as a "writer" or "supporter"?
- Is there a portion (or portions) of the transcript that illustrates what you think is working well in your collaborative planning session? If so, mark the portion (or portions) with a *. If you think there is a portion of the transcript that illustrates what you think is working well, can you explain *why* you think this way?
- Is there a portion (or portions) of the transcript that illustrates what you think is not working well in your collaborative planning session? If so, mark the portion (or portions) with a **. If you think there is a portion of the transcript that illustrates what you think is not working well, can you explain *why* you think this way?

- What could you and the other members of your group do to make collaborative planning more helpful to you as a writer?
- What could you do as a *supporter* to provide more help to the writers in your group?
- What could you do as a *writer* to help your group help you develop your ideas (e.g., your key point or purpose)?

This approach, one that invites students to be researchers, enabled students to consider the ways in which they assumed different roles (i.e., writers and supporters) to see whether they were able to sustain these roles and to examine the specific kinds of talk that might be of value to themselves and others in class. In addition, students' oral presentations of what they learned from their analyses gave students an opportunity to teach one another about how to make the most of their planning sessions. Thus, students became involved in the evaluation of what worked and what did not work in their sessions.

From our students' perspective, the analyses and presentations helped them see that group work is a serious, purposeful activity. The language they construct gives them a way to talk about what is working and perhaps not, to articulate their positions and to find ways to solve the rhetorical problems they identify in their writing. At the same time, we conclude with what we believe is an important caveat. Teaching students collaborative planning needs to go hand-in-hand with a more radical restructuring of the writing classroom, where students are encouraged to use what they know in purposeful ways, not to simply recite what they learn. If assignments ask students to reproduce information found in what they read, then students may not see any need to tailor this information for readers or for their own rhetorical purposes. But if students are expected to integrate their interpretations of information in advancing their own rhetorical purposes, as the students were in writing about their understanding of family, then they may see the need to transform given information in ways that are supported by collaborative planning. This is particularly true when students like TJ see alternative positions in an argument, but recognize with the help of supporters that they need to consolidate these points, using information as a way to influence what others think. In an excerpt from a collaborative planning session that we referred to earlier, TJ considered the information he gathered and concluded, at least implicitly, that the two points he could make needed to take the form of a "key point."

TJ: Well, you know, I think I can blend the two together, sort of. When I think about how in the financial way, being able for the father to work or being the doctor that he is, he sometimes, most of the time at the house, like in that episode he was just there at the house all the time, but I'm sure there's other times he's . . .

A: That's not realistic, though.

TJ: Yeah, I know. But, then, the mother's not working, so that gives her the time to be with her kids. I could still bring that up to where the kids can still go to her and the father sometimes. As for the kids on the Thea show, they can only go to the mother regardless . . .

The talk about writing that collaborative planning facilitates is talk about how to author texts that become part of the process of making knowledge within a given community, not simply the process of transmitting the extant knowledge of that community.

APPENDIX

TJ'S FAMILY PAPER
(unedited)

A Financial Argument between
the Donna Reed Show and Thea

Television sitcoms such as the *Donna Reed Show* and *Thea* both relate to one another in creating a good laugh about family life. However, the Stones, from the *Donna Reed Show*, find life easy to live because of their financial security. For having a lot of money both parents are able to spend time with their children. Furthermore, the use of money can help solve problems that the family might face. On the other hand, Thea's family is surrounded with problems in not having money, which in turn leads to a difficult life to lead.

The father's earnings as a doctor enables the mother to stay home and spend a lot of time with the children. They can discuss problems or whatever else might be bothering them. For example, in the *Donna Reed Show*, the daughter has been invited to a college dance and goes to her parents, which happen to be around and asks for their permission to go. It's fortunate for the daughter to have both parents there, because the mother disagreed and the father didn't mind letting her go. This shows that having two parents, one can benefit from one more than the other in observing different opinions or advices given.

After awhile the parents agree to let their daughter go to the dance, and in solving the problem they take her there themselves. In one night they all pack up their things and travel to college, but not to stay in just any place, a luxurious hotel to be exact. One can see that so long as one has money and is very wealthy, one can get whatever he/she wants. Having material benefits can lead to emotional benefits; for instance, having a lot of clothes, an enormous house to live in, abundance of toys, etc., can somewhat change the children's perspective about life with the existence of being wealthy. That to have good financial security, one can manipulate the use of it in solving problems being faced. Even though the mother has some control over the family as the aggressor, there is still not enough discipline enforced on the children. When told to do something, they do not do it; but, so long as money is brought up, the kids are willing to do anything that is asked of them. With this in mind, the parent's behavior with money reflects their children negatively. However, one can find life easy to live in the Stone family because of their financial security, the accessablity in solving problems with money, and having enough time to spend with their children.

The sitcom show, *Thea*, illustrates the life of a single mother raising four children on her own. The focus of attention is revolved around their low financial security and shows the hardships they all go through. Without the presence of a father, Thea picks up the slack in working two jobs day in and day out. In realizing their situation, the children from age six to eighteen, do all the housework while their mother is at work. The daughter makes dinner and occasionally makes breakfast for her brothers, the oldest of the family, Jarvis, takes care of his brothers and sister and plays the role of the man of the house, and the two youngest brothers take turns doing the dishes and other choirs together.

The siblings may work together in doing housework, but the absence of their mother all day and night creates conflicts and pain among the children. Wondering who has the most control, not being able to do whatever they want, and not getting the support from their mother creates turmoil and sometimes hatred with each other. It's hard enough not having a father around to help financially and with the control, but knowing that the mother isn't hardly there at the house, the children have no one else to turn to for advice, help, and most of all love. In a particular scene, Thea comes home late one night after her second job and is confronted by her children about their problems. Thea tells them not to worry and that she would find time to work out the problems with them and still maintain a job to put food on the table. Unfortunately, Thea's family doesn't have the wealthy life style like the Stone family, but she manages to support her children at any cost. The backbone of this family relys on having a father to help support the children financially, Thea finding time with her children, and most of all the children need to work together as a whole to overcome problems with each other. Furthermore, they have to sacrifise the things they want, and concentrate on the things they need.

My family has a resemblance of both the *Donna Reed Show* and *Thea* in various ways. I have an older sister that is three years older than me and when she was still in her teens, she was able to do things and go places all the time. I think the father of the Stone family said it best when he mentioned that as long as you are female, you can do whatever you want and get away with anything anytime. That was basically how it was in our family, my mother was always on my sister's side and my father and I always agreed on terms. Both my parents worked; my mother worked in the morning till the afternoon, which was great for us since we had school at the same time. My father had similar hours too, except sometimes he would come home late depending on how much he was needed at the office. This enabled my sister and I to spend time with our parents at night. If we didn't need our parents for something, it was good to know that they were there just in case. We weren't a wealthy family and my sister and I didn't always get what we wanted, but we were satisfied with what we had. At times we would go around the neighborhood and cut grass to make extra some extra money, and sometimes do it because our parents needed the extra money for rent and utilities. Although I have two parents and my sister and I are able to spend time with them, doesn't necessarily mean we have a happy life. It's knowing that we can count on each other for anything and cope with what we have regardless of our financial status. My family resembles both the *Donna Reed Show* and *Thea* in various aspects. For example, like the *Donna Reed Show* we have two parents and they are able to spend time with me and my sister. On the other hand, like Thea's family we do not have extra money to spend, we have a low income, and my sister and I support our parents by doing the housework while they're gone.

WORKS CITED

Ackerman, John. "Translating Context Into Action." *Reading to Write: Exploring a Cognitive and Social Process.* Ed. Linda Flower, Victoria Stein, John Ackerman, Margaret Kantz, Kathy McCormick, and Wayne Peck. New York: Oxford UP, 1990. 173–193.

Bruffee, Kenneth. *Collaborative Learning: Higher Education, Interdependence, and the Authority of Knowledge.* Baltimore: Johns Hopkins UP, 1993.

Clark, Gregory. *Dialogue, Dialectic, and Conversation: A Social Perspective on the Function of Writing.* Carbondale: Southern Illinois UP, 1990.

DiPardo, Anne, and Sarah W. Freedman. "Peer Response Groups in the Writing Classroom: Theoretic Foundations and New Directions." *Review of Educational Research* 58 (1988): 119–149.

Dyson, Anne Haas. *Social Worlds of Children Learning to Write in an Urban Primary School.* New York: Teachers College Press, 1993.

Flower, Linda. *The Construction of Negotiated Meaning*. Carbondale: Southern Illinois UP, 1994.

Flower, Linda, David L. Wallace, Linda Norris, and Rebecca E. Burnett, Eds. *Making Thinking Visible*. Urbana, IL: NCTE, 1993.

Gere, Anne Ruggles. *Writing Groups: History, Theory, and Implications*. Carbondale: Southern Illinois UP, 1987.

Greene, Stuart. " 'Making Sense of My Own Ideas': Problems of Authorship in a Beginning Writing Classroom." *Written Communication* 12 (1995): 186–218.

Greene, Stuart, and John M. Ackerman. "Expanding the Constructivist Metaphor: A Rhetorical Perspective on Literacy Research and Practice." *Review of Educational Research* 65 (1996): 383–420.

Greene, Stuart, and Erin Smith. "Teaching talk about writing: Student conflict in acquiring a new discourse of authorship through collaborative planning." Annual Meeting of National Council of Teachers of English, Orlando, FL. Nov., 1994.

Higgins, Lorraine, Linda Flower, and Joseph Petraglia. "Planning text together. The role of critical reflection in student collaboration." *Written Communication* 9 (1992): 48–84.

Leverenz, Carrie Shively. "Peer response in the multicultural composition classroom: Dissensus-A dream (deferred)." *Journal of Advanced Composition* 14 (1992): 167–186.

Nelson, Jennie. "Reading Classrooms as Texts." *College Composition and Communication* 46 (1995): 411–429.

Nystrand, Martin, and Deborah Brandt. "Response to Writing as a Context for Learning to Write." *Writing and Response: Theory, Practice, and Research*. Ed. Chris Anson. Urbana, IL: NCTE, 1989.

Rose, Mike. *Lives on the Boundary*. New York: Oxford UP, 1989.

Smagorinsky, Peter, and John Coppock. "Cultural Tools and the Classroom Context." *Written Communication* 11 (1994): 283–310.

Vygotsky, Lev S. *Thought and language*. Trans. A. Kozulin. Cambridge, MA: MIT Press, 1986.

Chapter 9

The Study of Error*

David Bartholomae
University of Pittsburgh

It is curious, I think, that with all the current interest in "Basic Writing," little attention has been paid to the most basic question: What is it? What is "basic writing," that is, if the term is to refer to a phenomenon, an activity, something a writer does or has done, rather than to a course of instruction? We know that across the country students take tests of one sort or another and are placed in courses that bear the title, "Basic Writing." But all we know is that there are students taking courses. We know little about their performance as writers, beyond the bald fact that they fail to do what other, conventionally successful, writers do. We don't, then, have an adequate description of the variety of writing we call "basic."

On the other hand, we have considerable knowledge of what Basic Writing courses are like around the country, the texts that are used, the approaches taken. For some time now, "specialists" have been devising and refining the technology of basic or developmental instruction. But these technicians are tinkering with pedagogies based on what? At best on models of how successful writers write. At worst, on old text-book models that disregard what writers actually do or how they could be said to learn, and break writing conveniently into constituent skills like "word power," "sentence power," and "paragraph power." Neither pedagogy is built on the

---

*This chapter was originally printed in *Composition and Communication 31*, 1980. Copyright © 1980 by the National Council of Teachers of English. Reprinted with permission.

results of any systematic inquiry into what basic writers do when they write or into the way writing skills develop for beginning adult writers. Such basic research has barely begun. Mina Shaughnessy argued the case this way:

> Those pedagogies that served the profession for years seem no longer appropriate to large numbers of students, and their inappropriateness lies largely in the fact that many of our students . . . are adult beginners and depend as students did not depend in the past upon the classroom and the teacher for the acquisition of the skill of writing.

If the profession is going to accept responsibility for teaching this kind of student, she concludes, "We are committed to research of a very ambitious sort"[1]

Where might such research begin, and how might it proceed? We must begin by studying basic writing itself—the phenomenon, not the course of instruction. If we begin here, we will recognize at once that "basic" does not mean simple or childlike. These are beginning writers, to be sure, but they are not writers who need to learn to use language. They are writers who need to learn to command a particular variety of language—the language of a written, academic discourse—and a particular variety of language use—writing itself. The writing of a basic writer can be shown to be an approximation of conventional written discourse; it is a peculiar and idiosyncratic version of a highly conventional type, but the relation between the approximate and the conventional forms is not the same as the relation between the writing, say, of a 7th grader and the writing of a college freshman.

Basic writing, I want to argue, is a variety of writing, not writing with fewer parts or more rudimentary constituents. It is not evidence of arrested cognitive development, arrested language development, or unruly or unpredictable language use. The writer of this sentence, for example, could not be said to be writing an "immature" sentence, in any sense of the term, if we grant her credit for the sentence she intended to write:

> The time of my life when I learned something, and which resulted in a change in which I look upon life things. This would be the period of my life when I graduated from Elementary school to High school.

When we have used conventional T-unit analysis, and included in our tabulations figures on words/clause, words/T-unit and clauses/T-unit that were drawn from "intended T-units" as well as actual T-units, we have found that basic writers do not, in general, write "immature" sentences.

---

[1]Mina Shaughnessy, "Some Needed Research on Writing," *CCC*, 28 (December, 1977), 317, 388.

They are not, that is, 13th graders writing 7th grade sentences. In fact, they often attempt syntax whose surface is more complex than that of more successful freshman writers. They get into trouble by getting in over their heads, not only attempting to do more than they can, but imagining as their target a syntax that is *more* complex than convention requires. The failed sentences, then, could be taken as stages of learning rather than the failure to learn, but also as evidence that these writers are using writing as an occasion to learn.

It is possible to extend the concept of "intentional structures" to the analysis of complete essays in order to determine the "grammar" that governs the idiosyncratic discourse of writers imagining the language and conventions of academic discourse in unconventional ways. This method of analysis is certainly available to English teachers, since it requires a form of close reading, paying attention to the language of a text in order to determine not only what a writer says, but how he locates and articulates meaning. When a basic writer violates our expectations, however, there is a tendency to dismiss the text as non-writing, as meaningless or imperfect writing. We have not read as we have been trained to read, with a particular interest in the way an individual style confronts and violates convention. We have read, rather, as policemen, examiners, gate-keepers. The teacher who is unable to make sense out of a seemingly bizarre piece of student writing is often the same teacher who can give an elaborate explanation of the "meaning" of a story by Donald Barthelme or a poem by e. e. cummings. If we learn to treat the language of basic writing *as* language and assume, as we do when writers violate our expectations in more conventional ways, that the unconventional features in the writing are evidence of intention and that they are, therefore, meaningful, then we can chart systematic choices, individual strategies, and characteristic processes of thought. One can read Mina Shaughnessy's *Errors and Expectations* as the record of just such a close reading.[2]

There is a style, then, to the apparently bizarre and incoherent writing of a basic writer because it is, finally, evidence of an individual using language to make and transcribe meaning. This is one of the axioms of error analysis, whether it be applied to reading (as in "miscue analysis"), writing, or second-language learning. An error (and I would include errors beyond those in the decoding or encoding of sentences) can only be understood as evidence of intention. They are the only evidence we have of an individual's idiosyncratic way of using the language and articulating meaning, of imposing a style on common material. A writer's activity is linguistic and rhetorical activity; it can be different but never random. The

---

[2]Mina Shaughnessy, *Errors and Expectations: A Guide for the Teacher of Basic Writing* (New York: Oxford University Press, 1977).

task for both teacher and researcher, then, is to discover the grammar of *that* coherence, of the "idiosyncratic dialect" that belongs to a particular writer at a particular moment in the history of his attempts to imagine and reproduce the standard idiom of academic discourse.[3]

All writing, of course, could be said to only approximate conventional discourse; our writing is never either completely predictable or completely idiosyncratic. We speak our own language as well as the language of the tribe and, in doing so, make concessions to both ourselves and our culture. The distance between text and conventional expectation may be a sign of failure and it may be a sign of genius, depending on the level of control and intent we are willing to assign to the writer, and depending on the insight we acquire from seeing convention so transformed. For a basic writer the distance between text and convention is greater than it is for the run-of-the-mill freshmen writer. It may be, however, that the more talented the freshman writer becomes, the more able she is to increase again the distance between text and convention. We are drawn to conclude that basic writers lack control, although it may be more precise to say that they lack choice and option, the power to make decisions about the idiosyncracy of their writing, Their writing is not, however, truly uncontrolled. About the actual distance from text to convention for the basic writer, we know very little. We know that it will take a long time to traverse—generally the greater the distance the greater the time and energy requires to close the gap. We know almost nothing about the actual sequence of development—the natural sequence of learning—that moves a writer from basic writing to competent writing to good writing. The point, however, is that "basic writing" is something our students *do* or *produce*; it is not a kind of writing we teach to backward or unprepared students. We should not spend our time imagining simple or "basic" writing tasks, but studying the errors that emerge when beginning writers are faced with complex tasks.

The mode of analysis that seems most promising for the research we need on the writer's sequence of learning is error analysis. Error analysis provides the basic writing teacher with both a technique for analyzing errors in the production of discourse, a technique developed by linguists to study second language learning, and a theory of error, or, perhaps more properly, a perspective on error, where errors are seen as (1) necessary stages of individual development and (2) data that provide insight into the idiosyncratic strategies of a particular language user at a particular point in his acquisition of a target language. Enough has been written lately about error analysis that I'll only give a brief summary of its perspec-

---

[3]The term "idiosyncratic dialect" is taken from S. P. Corder, "Idiosyncratic Dialects and Error Analysis," in Jack C. Richards, ed., *Error Analysis: Perspectives on Second Language Acquisition* (London: Longman, 1974), pp. 158–171.

tive on second language or second dialect acquisition.[4] I want to go on to look closely at error analysis as a method, in order to point out its strengths and limits as a procedure for textual analysis.

George Steiner has argued that all acts of interpretation are acts of translation and are, therefore, subject to the constraints governing the passage from one language to another.[5] All our utterances are approximations, attempts to use the language of, say, Frank Kermode or the language, perhaps, of our other, smarter, wittier self. In this sense, the analogy that links developmental composition instruction with second language learning can be a useful one—useful that is, if the mode of learning (whatever the "second" language) is writing rather than speaking. (This distinction, I might add, is not generally made in the literature on error analysis, where writing and speech are taken as equivalent phenomena.) Error analysis begins with the recognition that errors, or the points where the actual text varies from a hypothetical "standard" text, will be either random or systematic. If they are systematic in the writing of an individual writer, then they are evidence of some idiosyncratic rule system—an idiosyncratic grammar or rhetoric, an "interlanguage" or "approximative system."[6] If the errors are systematic across all basic writers, then they would be evidence of generalized stages in the acquisition of fluent writing for beginning adult writers. This distinction between individual and general systems is an important one for both teaching and research. It is not one that Shaughnessy makes. We don't know whether the categories of error in *Errors and Expectations* hold across a group, and, if so, with what frequency and across a group of what size.

Shaughnessy did find, however, predictable patterns in the errors in the essays she studied. She demonstrated that even the most apparently incoherent writing, if we are sensitive to its intentional structure, is evidence of systematic, coherent, rule-governed behavior. Basic writers, she demonstrated, are not performing mechanically or randomly but making choices and forming strategies as they struggle to deal with the varied demands of a task, a language, and a rhetoric. The "systems" such writing exhibits provide evidence that basic writers *are* competent, mature language users.

---

[4]Barry M. Kroll and John C. Schafer, "Error Analysis and the Teaching of Composition," *CCC,* 29 (October, 1978), 243–248. See also my review of *Errors and Expectations* in Donald McQuade, ed., *Linguistics, Stylistics and The Teaching of Composition* (Akron, Ohio: L & S Books, 1979), pp. 209–220.

[5]George Steiner, *After Babel: Aspects of Language and Translation* (New York: Oxford University Press, 1975).

[6]For the term "interlanguage," see L. Selinker, "Interlanguage," in Richards, ed., *Error Analysis*, pp. 31–55. For "approximate system," see William Nemser, "Approximate Systems of Foreign Language Learners," in Richards, ed., *Error Analysis*, pp. 55–64. These are more appropriate terms than "idiosyncratic dialect" for the study of error in written composition.

Their attempts at producing written language are not hit and miss, nor are they evidence of simple translation of speech into print. The approximate systems they produce are evidence that they can conceive of and manipulate written language as a structured, systematic code. They are "intermediate" systems in that they mark stages on route to mastery (or, more properly, on route to conventional fluency) of written, academic discourse.

This also, however, requires some qualification. They *may* be evidence of some transitional stage. They may also, to use Selinker's term, be evidence of "stabilized variability," where a writer is stuck or searching rather than moving on toward more complete approximation of the target language.[7] A writer will stick with some intermediate system if he is convinced that the language he uses "works," or if he is unable to see errors *as* errors and form alternate hypotheses in response.

Error analysis begins with a theory of writing, a theory of language production and language development, that allows us to see errors as evidence of choice or strategy among a range of possible choices or strategies. They provide evidence of an individual style of using the language and making it work; they are not a simple record of what a writer failed to do because of incompetence or indifference. Errors, then, are stylistic features, information about *this* writer and *this* language; they are not necessarily "noise" in the system, accidents of composing, or malfunctions in the language process. Consequently, we cannot identify errors without identifying them in context, and the context is not the text, but the activity of composing that presented the erroneous form as a possible solution to the problem of making a meaningful statement. Shaughnessy's taxonomy of error, for example, identifies errors according to their source, not their type. A single type of error could be attributed to a variety of causes. Donald Freeman's research, for example, has shown that, "subject-verb agreement . . . is a host of errors, not one." One of his students analyzed a "large sample of real world sentences and concluded that there are at

---

[7]The term "stabilized variability" is quoted in Andrew D. Cohen and Margaret Robbins, "Toward Assessing Interlanguage Performance: The Relationship Between Selected Errors, Learner's Characteristics and Learner's Explanations," *Language Learning*, 26 (June, 1976), p. 59. Selinker uses the term "fossilization" to refer to single errors than recur across time, so that the interlanguage form is not evidence of a transitional stage. (See Selinker, "Interlanguage.") M. P. Jain distinguishes between "systematic," "asystematic" and "nonsystematic" errors. (See "Error Analysis: Source, Cause and Significance" in Richards, ed., *Error Analysis*, pp. 189–215.) Unsystematic errors are mistakes, "slips of the tongue." Systematic errors "seem to establish that in certain areas of language use the learner possesses construction rules." Asystematic errors lead one to the "inescapable conclusion" that "the learner's capacity to generalize must improve, for progress in learning a language is made by adopting generalizations and stretching them to match the facts of the language."

least eight different kinds, most of which have very little to do with one another."[8]

Error analysis allows us to place error in the context of composing and to interpret and classify systematic errors. The key concept is the concept of an "interlanguage" or an "intermediate system," an idiosyncratic grammar and rhetoric that is a writer's approximation of the standard idiom. Errors, while they can be given more precise classification, fall into three main categories: errors that are evidence of an intermediate system; errors that could truly be said to be accidents, or slips of the pen as a writer's mind rushes ahead faster than his hand; and, finally, errors of language transfer, or, more commonly, dialect interference, where in the attempt to produce the target language, the writer intrudes forms from the "first" or "native" language rather than inventing some intermediate form. For writers, this intrusion most often comes from a spoken dialect. The error analyst is primarily concerned, however, with errors that are evidence of some intermediate system. This kind of error occurs because the writer *is* an active, competent language user who uses his knowledge that language is rule-governed, and who uses his ability to predict and form analogies, to construct hypotheses that can make an irregular or unfamiliar language more manageable. The problem comes when the rule is incorrect or, more properly, when it is idiosyncratic, belonging only to the language of this writer. There is evidence of an idiosyncratic system, for example, when a student adds inflectional endings to infinitives, as in this sentence, "There was plenty the boy had to *learned* about birds." It also seems to be evident in a sentence like this: "This assignment calls on *choosing* one of my papers and making a last draft out of it." These errors can be further sub-divided into those that are in flux and mark a fully transitional stage, and those that, for one reason or another, become frozen and recur across time.

Kroll and Schafer, in a recent *CCC* article, argue that the value of error analysis for the composition teacher is the perspective it offers on the learner, since it allows us to see errors "as clues to inner processes, as windows into the mind."[9] If we investigate the pattern of error in the performance of an individual writer, we can better understand the nature of those errors and the way they "fit" in an individual writer's program for writing. As a consequence, rather than impose an inappropriate or even misleading syllabus on a learner, we can plan instruction to assist a writer's internal syllabus. If, for example, a writer puts standard inflections on irregular verbs or on verbs that are used in verbals (as in "I used to

---

[8]Donald C. Freeman, "Linguistics and Error Analysis: On Agency," in Donald McQuade, ed., *Linguistics, Stylistics and The Teaching of Composition* (Akron, Ohio: L & S Books, 1979), pp. 143–44.

[9]Kroll and Schafer, "Error Analysis and the Teaching of Composition."

runned"), drill on verb endings will only reinforce the rule that, because the writer is overgeneralizing, is the source of the error in the first place. By charting and analyzing a writer's errors, we can begin in our instruction with what a writer *does* rather than with what he fails to do. It makes no sense, for example, to impose lessons on the sentence on a student whose problems with syntax can be understood in more precise terms. It makes no sense to teach spelling to an individual who has trouble principally with words that contain vowel clusters. Error analysis, then, is a method of diagnosis.

Error analysis can assist instruction at another level. By having students share in the process of investigating and interpreting the patterns of error in their writing, we can help them begin to see those errors as evidence of hypotheses or strategies they have formed and, as a consequence, put them in a position to change, experiment, imagine other strategies. Study-ing their own writing puts students in a position to see themselves as language users, rather than as victims of a language that uses them.

This, then, is the perspective and the technique of error analysis. To interpret a student paper without this frame of reference is to misread, as for example when a teacher sees an incorrect verb form and concludes that the student doesn't understand the rules for indicating tense or num-ber. I want, now, to examine error analysis as a procedure for the study of errors in written composition. It presents two problems. The first can be traced to the fact that error analysis was developed for studying errors in spoken performance.[10] It can be transferred to writing only to the degree that writing is like speech, and there are significant points of difference. It is generally acknowledged, for example, that written discourse is not just speech written down on paper. Adult written discourse has a grammar and rhetoric that is different from speech. And clearly the activity of pro-ducing language is different for a writer than it is for a speaker.

The "second language" a basic writer must learn to master is formal, written discourse, a discourse whose lexicon, grammar, and rhetoric are

---

[10]In the late 60's and early 70's, linguists began to study second language acquisition by systematically studying the actual performance of individual learners. What they studied, however, was the language a learner would speak. In the literature of error analysis, the reception and production of language is generally defined as the learner's ability to hear, learn, imitate, and independently produce *sounds*. Errors, then, are phonological substitutions, alterations, additions, and subtractions. Similarly, errors diagnosed as rooted in the mode of production (rather than, for example, in an idiosyncratic grammar or interference from the first language) are errors caused by the difficulty a learner has hearing or making foreign sounds. When we are studying written composition, we are studying a different mode of production, where a learner must see, remember, and produce marks on a page. There may be some similarity between the grammar-based errors in the two modes, speech and writing (it would be interesting to know to what degree this is true), but there should be marked differences in the nature and frequency of performance-based errors.

learned not through speaking and listening but through reading and writing. The process of acquisition is visual not aural. Furthermore, basic writers do not necessarily produce writing by translating speech into print (the way children learning to write would); that is, they must draw on a memory for graphemes rather than phonemes. This is a different order of memory and production from that used in speech and gives rise to errors unique to writing.

Writing also, however, presents "interference" of a type never found in speech. Errors in writing may be caused by interference from the act of writing itself, from the difficulty of moving a pen across the page quickly enough to keep up with the words in the writer's mind, or from the difficulty of recalling and producing the conventions that are necessary for producing print rather than speech, conventions of spelling, orthography, punctuation, capitalization and so on. This is not, however, just a way of saying that writers make spelling errors and speakers do not. As Shaughnessy pointed out, errors of syntax can be traced to the gyrations of a writer trying to avoid a word that her sentence has led her to, but that she knows she cannot spell.

The second problem in applying error analysis to the composition classroom arises from special properties in the taxonomy of errors we chart in student writing. Listing varieties of errors is not like listing varieties of rocks or butterflies. What a reader finds depends to a large degree on her assumptions about the writer's intention. Any systematic attempt to chart a learner's errors is clouded by the difficulty of assigning intention through textual analysis. The analyst begins, then, by interpreting a text, not by describing features on a page. And interpretation is less than a precise science.

Let me turn to an example. This is part of a paper that a student, John, wrote in response to an assignment that asked him to go back to some papers he had written on significant moments in his life in order to write a paper that considered the general question of the way people change:

> This assignment call on chosing one of my incident making a last draft out of it. I found this very differcult because I like them all but you said I had to pick one so the Second incident was decide. Because this one had the most important insight to my life that I indeed learn from. This insight explain why adulthood mean that much as it dose to me because I think it alway influence me to change and my outlook on certain thing like my point-of-view I have one day and it might change the next week on the same issue. So in these frew words I going to write about the incident now. My exprience took place in my high school and the reason was out side of school but I will show you the connection. The situation took place cause of the type of school I went too. Let me tell you about the situation first of all what happen was that I got suspense from school. For thing that I fell was

out of my control sometime, but it taught me alot about respondability of a growing man. The school suspense me for being late ten time. I had accummate ten dementic and had to bring my mother to school to talk to a conselor and Prinpicable of the school what when on at the meet took me out mentally period.

One could imagine a variety of responses to this. The first would be to form the wholesale conclusion that John can't write and to send him off to a workbook. Once he had learned how to write correct sentences, then he could go on to the business of actually writing. Let me call this the "old style" response to error. A second response, which I'll call the "investigative approach," would be to chart the patterns of error in this particular text. Of the approximately 40 errors in the first 200 words, the majority fall under four fairly specific categories: verb endings, noun plurals, syntax, and spelling. The value to pedagogy is obvious. One is no longer teaching a student to "write" but to deal with a limited number of very specific kinds of errors, each of which would suggest its own appropriate response. Furthermore, it is possible to refine the categories and to speculate on and organize them according to cause. The verb errors almost all involve "s" or "ed" endings, which could indicate dialect interference or a failure to learn the rules for indicating tense and number. It is possible to be even more precise. The passage contains 41 verbs; only 17 of them are used incorrectly. With the exception of four spelling errors, the errors are all errors of inflection and, furthermore, these errors come only with regular verbs. There are no errors with irregular verbs. This would suggest, then, that when John draws on memory for a verb form, he gets it right; but when John applies a rule to determine the ending, he gets it wrong.

The errors of syntax could be divided into those that might be called punctuation errors (or errors that indicate a difficulty perceiving the boundaries of the sentence), such as

> Let me tell you about the situation first of all what happen was that I got suspense from school. For thing that I fell was out of my control sometime, but it taught me alot about respondability of a growing man.

and errors of syntax that would fall under Shaughnessy's category of consolidation errors,

> This insight explain why adulthood mean that much as it dose to me because I think it alway influence me to change and my outlook on certain thing like my point-of-view I have one day and it might change the next week on the same issue.

One would also want to note the difference between consistent errors, the substitution of "situation" for "situation" or "suspense" for "suspended," and unstable ones, as, for example, when John writes "cause" in one place and "because" in another. In one case John could be said to have fixed on a rule; in the other he is searching for one. One would also want to distinguish between what might seem to be "accidental" errors, like substituting "frew" for "few" or "when" for "went," errors that might best be addressed by teaching a student to edit, and those whose causes are deeper and require time and experience, or some specific instructional strategy.

I'm not sure, however, that this analysis provides an accurate representation of John's writing. Consider what happens when John reads this paper out loud. I've been taping students reading their own papers, and I've developed a system of notation, like that used in miscue analysis,[11] that will allow me to record the points of variation between the writing that is on the page and the writing that is spoken, or, to use the terminology of miscue analysis, between the expected response (ER) and the observed response (OR). What I've found is that students will often, or in predictable instances, substitute correct forms for the incorrect forms on the page, even though they are generally unaware that such a substitution was made. This observation suggests the limits of conventional error analysis for the study of error in written composition.

I asked John to read his paper out loud, and to stop and correct or note any mistakes he found. Let me try to reproduce the transcript of that reading. I will underline any substitution or correction and offer some comments in parentheses. The reader might first go back and review the original. Here is what John read:

> This assignment calls on *choosing* one of my incident making a last draft out of it. I found this very difficult because I like them all but you said I *had* to pick one so the Second incident was decide*d on.* Because (John goes back and rereads, connecting up the subordinate clause.) So the second incident was decided on because this one had the most important insight to my life that I indeed learn*ed* from. This insight explains why adulthood *meant* that much as it dose to me because I think it always influenc*es* me to change and my outlook on certain thing*s* like my point-of-view I have one day and it might change the next week on the same issue. (John goes back and rereads, beginning with "like my point of view," and he is puzzled but he makes no additional changes.) So in these *few* words *I'm* going to write about the incident now. My exp*e*rience took place *be*cause of the type of school I went to (John had written "too.") Let me tell you about the situation (John

---

[11]See Y. M. Goodman and C. L Burke, *Reading Miscue Inventory: Procedure for Diagnosis and Evaluation* (New York: Macmillan, 1972).

comes to a full stop.) first of all what happen*ed* was that I got *suspended* from school (no full stop) for thing*s* that I *felt* was out of my control sometime, but it taught me a lot about *responsibility* of a growing man. The school *suspended* me for being late ten time*s*. I had *accumulated* (for "accumate") ten *demerits* (for "dementic") and had to bring my mother to school to talk to a counselor and *the Principal* of the school (full stop) what *went* on at the meet*ing* took me out mentally (full stop) period (with brio).

I have chosen an extreme case to make my point, but what one sees here is the writer correcting almost every error as he reads the paper, even though he is not able to recognize that there *are* errors or that he has corrected them. The only errors John spotted (where he stopped, noted an error and corrected it) were the misspellings of "situation" and "Principal," and the substitution of "chosing" for "choosing." Even when he was asked to reread sentences to see if he could notice any difference between what he was saying and the words on the page, he could not. He could not, for example, see the error in "frew" or "dementic" or any of the other verb errors, and yet he spoke the correct form of every verb (with the exception of "was" after he had changed "thing" to "things" in "for thing*s* that I *felt* was out of my control") and he corrected every plural. His phrasing as he read produced correct syntax, except in the case of the consolidation error, which he puzzled over but did not correct. It's important to note, however, that John did not read that confused syntax as if no confusion were there. He sensed the difference between the phrasing called for by the meaning of the sentence and that which existed on the page. He did not read as though meaning didn't matter or as though the "meaning" coded on the page was complete. His problem cannot be simply a syntax problem, since the jumble is bound up with his struggle to articulate this particular meaning. And it is not simply a "thinking" problem—John doesn't write this way because he thinks this way—since he perceives that the statement as it is written is other than that which he intended.

When I asked John why the paper (which went on for two more pages) was written all as one paragraph, he replied, "It was all one idea. I didn't want to have to start all over again. I had a good idea and I didn't want to give it up." John doesn't need to be "taught" the paragraph, at least not as the paragraph is traditionally taught. His prose is orderly and proceeds through blocks of discourse. He tells the story of his experience at the school and concludes that through his experience he realized that he must accept responsibility for his tardiness, even though the tardiness was not his fault but the fault of the Philadelphia subway system. He concludes that with this realization he learned "the responsibility of a growing man." Furthermore John knows that the print code carries certain conventions for ordering and presenting discourse. His translation of the notion that "a paragraph develops a single idea" is peculiar but not illogical.

It could also be argued that John does not need to be "taught" to produce correct verb forms, or, again, at least not as such things are conventionally taught. Fifteen weeks of drill on verb endings might raise his test scores but they would not change the way he writes. He *knows* how to produce correct endings. He demonstrated that when he read, since he was reading in terms of his grammatical competence. His problem is a problem of performance, or fluency, not of competence. There is certainly no evidence that the verb errors are due to interference from his spoken language. And if the errors could be traced to some intermediate system, the system exists only in John's performance as a writer. It does not operate when he reads or, for that matter, when he speaks, if his oral reconstruction of his own text can be taken as a record of John "speaking" the idiom of academic discourse.[12]

John's case also highlights the tremendous difficulty such a student has with editing, where a failure to correct a paper is not evidence of laziness or inattention or a failure to know correct forms, but evidence of the tremendous difficulty such a student has objectifying language and seeing it as black and white marks on the page, where things can be wrong even though the meaning seems right.[13] One of the hardest errors for John to spot, after all my coaching, was the substitution of "frew" for "few," certainly not an error that calls into question John's competence as a writer. I can call this a "performance" error, but that term doesn't suggest the constraints on performance in writing. This is an important area for further study. Surely one constraint is the difficulty of moving the hand fast enough

---

[12]Bruder and Hayden noticed a similar phenomenon. They assigned a group of students exercises in writing formal and informal dialogues. One student's informal dialogue contained the following:

What going on?
It been a long time . . .
I about through . . .
I be glad . . .

When the student read the dialogue aloud, however, these were spoken as

What's going on?
It's been a long time . . .
I'm about through . . .
I'll be glad . . .

See Mary Newton Bruder and Luddy Hayden, "Teaching Composition: A Report on a Bidialectal Approach," *Language Learning*, 23 (June, 1973), 1–15.

[13]See Patricia Laurence, "Error's Endless Train: Why Students Don't Perceive Errors," *Journal of Basic Writing*, 1 (Spring, 1975), 23–43, for a different explanation of this phenomenon.

to translate meaning into print. The burden imposed on their patience and short term memory by the slow, awkward handwriting of many inexperienced writers is a very real one. But I think the constraints extend beyond the difficulty of forming words quickly with pen or pencil.

One of the most interesting results of the comparison of the spoken and written versions of John's text is his inability to *see* the difference between "frew" and "few" or "dementic" and "demerit." What this suggests is that John reads and writes from the "top down" rather than the "bottom up," to use a distinction made by cognitive psychologists in their study of reading.[14] John is not operating through the lower level process of translating orthographic information into sounds and sounds into meaning when he reads. And conversely, he is not working from meaning to sound to word when he is writing. He is, rather, retrieving lexical items directly, through a "higher level" process that by-passes the "lower level" operation of phonetic translation. When I put *frew* and *few* on the blackboard, John read them both as "few." The lexical item "few" is represented for John by either orthographic array. He is not, then, reading or writing phonetically, which is a sign, from one perspective, of a high level of fluency, since the activity is automatic and not mediated by the more primitive operation of translating speech into print or print into speech. When John was writing, he did not produce "frew" or "dementic" by searching for sound/letter correspondences. He drew directly upon his memory for the look and shape of those words; he was working from the top down rather than the bottom up. He went to stored print forms and did not take the slower route of translating speech into writing.

John, then, has reached a stage of fluency in writing where he directly and consistently retrieves print forms, like "dementic," that are meaningful to him, even though they are idiosyncratic. I'm not sure what all the implications of this might be, but we surely must see John's problem in a

---

[14]See, for example, J. R. Frederiksen, "Component Skills in Reading" in R. R. Snow, P. A. Federico, and W. E. Montague, eds., *Aptitude, Learning, and Instruction* (Hillsdale, N.J.: Erlbaum, 1979); D. E. Rumelhart, "Toward an Interactive Model of Reading," in S. Dornic, ed., *Attention and Performance VI* (Hillsdale, N.J.: Erlbaum, 1977); and Joseph H. Denks and Gregory O. Hill, "Interactive Models of Lexical Assessment during Oral Reading," paper presented at Conference on Interactive Processes in Reading, Learning Research and Development Center, University of Pittsburgh, September 1979.

Patrick Hartwell argued that "apparent dialect interference in writing reveals partial or imperfect mastery of a neural coding system that underlies both reading and writing" in a paper, " 'Dialect Interference' in Writing: A Critical View," presented at CCCC, April 1979. This paper is available through ERIC. He predicts, in this paper, that "basic writing students, when asked to read their writing in a formal situation, . . . will make fewer errors in their reading than in their writing." I read Professor Hartwell's paper after this essay was completed, so I was unable to acknowledge his study as completely as I would have desired.

new light, since his problem can, in a sense, be attributed to his skill. To ask John to slow down his writing and sound out words would be disastrous. Perhaps the most we can do is to teach John the slowed down form of reading he will need in order to edit.

John's paper also calls into question our ability to identify accidental errors. I suspect that when John substitutes a word like "when" for "went," this is an accidental error, a slip of the pen. Since John spoke "went" when he read, I cannot conclude that he substituted "when" for "went" because he pronounces both as "wen." This, then, is not an error of dialect interference but an accidental error, the same order of error as the omission of "the" before "Principal." Both were errors John corrected while reading (even though he didn't identify them as errors).

What is surprising is that, with all the difficulty John had identifying errors, he immediately saw that he had written "chosing" rather than "choosing." While textual analysis would have led to the conclusion that he was applying a tense rule to a participial construction, or over-generalizing from a known rule, the ease with which it was identified would lead one to conclude that it was, in fact, a mistake, and not evidence of an approximative system. What would have been diagnosed as a deep error now appears to be only an accidental error, a "mistake" (or perhaps a spelling error).

In summary, this analysis of John's reading produces a healthy respect for the tremendous complexity of transcription, for the process of recording meaning in print as opposed to the process of generating meaning. It also points out the difficulty of charting a learner's "interlanguage" or "intermediate system," since we are working not only with a writer moving between a first and a second language, but a writer whose performance is subject to the interference of transcription, of producing meaning through the print code. We need, in general, to refine our understanding of performance-based errors, and we need to refine our teaching to take into account the high percentage of error in written composition that is rooted in the difficulty of performance rather than in problems of general linguistic competence.

Let me pause for a moment to put what I've said in the context of work in error analysis. Such analysis is textual analysis. It requires the reader to make assumptions about intention on the basis of information in the text. The writer's errors provide the most important information since they provide insight into the idiosyncratic systems the writer has developed. The regular but unconventional features in the writing will reveal the rules and strategies operating for the basic writer.

The basic procedure for such analysis could be outlined this way. First the reader must identify the idiosyncratic construction; he must determine what is an error. This is often difficult, as in the case of fragments, which are conventionally used for effect. Here is an example of a sentence whose syntax could clearly be said to be idiosyncratic:

> In high school you learn alot for example Kindergarten which I took in high school.[15]

The reader, then, must reconstruct that sentence based upon the most reasonable interpretation of the intention in the original, and this must be done *before* the error can be classified, since it will be classified according to its cause.[16] Here is Shaughnessy's reconstruction of the example given above: "In high school you learn a lot. For example, I took up the study of Kindergarten in high school." For any idiosyncratic sentence, however, there are often a variety of possible reconstructions, depending on the reader's sense of the larger meaning of which this individual sentence is only a part, but also depending upon the reader's ability to predict how this writer puts sentences together, that is, on an understanding of this individual style. The text is being interpreted, not described. I've had graduate students who have reconstructed the following sentence, for example, in a variety of ways:

> Why do we have womens liberation and their fighting for Equal Rights ect. to be recognized not as a lady but as an Individual.

It could be read, "Why do we have women's liberation and why are they fighting for Equal Rights? In order that women may be recognized not as ladies but as individuals." And, "Why do we have women's liberation and their fight for equal rights, to be recognized not as a lady but as an individual?" There is an extensive literature on the question of interpretation and intention in prose, too extensive for the easy assumption that all a reader has to do is identify what the writer would have written if he wanted to "get it right the first time." The great genius of Shaughnessy's study, in fact, is the remarkable wisdom and sympathy of her interpretations of student texts.

Error analysis, then, involves more than just making lists of the errors in a student essay and looking for patterns to emerge. It begins with the double perspective of text and reconstructed text and seeks to explain the difference between the two on the basis of whatever can be inferred about the meaning of the text and the process of creating it. The reader/researcher brings to bear his general knowledge of how basic writers write,

---

[15]This example is taken from Shaughnessy, *Errors and Expectations,* p. 52.
[16]Corder refers to "reconstructed sentences" in "Idiosyncratic Dialects and Error Analysis."

but also whatever is known about the linguistic and rhetorical constraints that govern an individual act of writing. In Shaughnessy's analysis of the "kindergarten" sentence, this discussion is contained in the section on "consolidation errors" in the chapter on "Syntax."[17] The key point, however, is that any such analysis must draw upon extra-textual information as well as close, stylistic analysis.

This paper has illustrated two methods for gathering information about how a text was created. A teacher can interview the student and ask him to explain his error. John wrote this sentence in another paper for my course:

> I would to write about my experience helping 1600 childrens have a happy christmas.

The missing word (I would *like* to write about . . .) he supplied when reading the sentence aloud. It is an accidental error and can be addressed by teaching editing. It is the same kind of error as his earlier substitution of "when" for "went." John used the phrase, "1600 childrens," throughout his paper, however. The conventional interpretation would have it that this is evidence of dialect interference. And yet, when John read the paper out loud, he consistently read "1600 children," even though he said he did not see any difference between the word he spoke and the word that was on the page. When I asked him to explain why he put an "s" on the end of "children," he replied, "Because there were 1600 of them." John had a rule for forming plurals that he used when he wrote but not when he spoke. Writing, as he rightly recognized, has its own peculiar rules and constraints. It is different from speech. The error is not due to interference from his spoken language but to his conception of the "code" of written discourse.

The other method for gathering information is having students read aloud their own writing, and having them provide an oral reconstruction of their written text. What I've presented in my analysis of John's essay is a method for recording the discrepancies between the written and spoken versions of a single text. The record of a writer reading provides a version of the "intended" text that can supplement the teacher's or researcher's own reconstruction and aid in the interpretation of errors, whether they be accidental, interlingual, or due to dialect interference. I had to read John's paper very differently once I had heard him read it.

More importantly, however, this method of analysis can provide access to an additional type of error. This is the error that can be attributed to

---

[17]Shaughnessy, *Errors and Expectations,* pp. 51–72.

the physical and conceptual demands of writing rather than speaking; it can be traced to the requirements of manipulating a pen and the requirements of manipulating the print code.[18]

In general, when writers read, and read in order to spot and correct errors, their responses will fall among the following categories:

1. overt corrections—errors a reader sees, acknowledges, and corrects;
2. spoken corrections—errors the writer does not acknowledge but corrects in reading;
3. no recognition—errors that are read as written;
4. overcorrection—correct forms made incorrect, or incorrect forms substituted for incorrect forms;
5. acknowledged error—errors a reader senses but cannot correct;
6. reader miscue—a conventional miscue, not linked to error in the text;
7. nonsense—In this case, the reader reads a non-sentence or a nonsense sentence as though it were correct and meaningful. No error or confusion is acknowledged. This applies to errors of syntax only.

Corrections, whether acknowledged or unacknowledged, would indicate performance-based errors. The other responses (with the exception of "reader miscues") would indicate deeper errors, errors that, when charted, would provide evidence of some idiosyncratic grammar or rhetoric.

John "miscues" by completing or correcting the text that he has written. When reading researchers have readers read out loud, they have them read someone else's writing, of course, and they are primarily concerned with the "quality" of the miscues.[19] All fluent readers will miscue; that is, they will not repeat verbatim the words on the page. Since fluent readers are reading for meaning, they are actively predicting what will come and processing large chunks of graphic information at a time. They do not read individual words, and they miscue because they speak what they expect to see rather than what is actually on the page. One indication of a reader's proficiency, then, is that the miscues don't destroy the "sense" of the passage. Poor readers will produce miscues that jumble the meaning of a passage, as in

---

[18]For a discussion of the role of the "print code" in writer's errors, see Patrick Hartwell, " 'Dialect Interference' in Writing: A Critical View."

[19]See Kenneth S. Goodman, "Miscues: Windows on the Reading Process," in Kenneth S. Goodman, ed., *Miscue Analysis: Applications to Reading Instruction* (Urbana, Illinois: ERIC, 1977), pp. 3–14.

Text: Her wings were folded quietly at her sides.
Reader: Her wings were floated quickly at her sides.

or they will correct miscues that do not affect meaning in any significant way.[20]

The situation is different when a reader reads his own text, since this reader already knows what the passage means and attention is drawn, then, to the representation of that meaning. Reading also frees a writer from the constraints of transcription, which for many basic writers is an awkward, laborious process, putting excessive demands on both patience and short-term memory. John, like any reader, read what he expected to see, but with a low percentage of meaning-related miscues, since the meaning, for him, was set, and with a high percentage of code-related miscues, where a correct form was substituted for an incorrect form.

The value of studying students' oral reconstruction of their written texts is threefold. The first is as a diagnostic tool. I've illustrated in my analysis of John's paper how such a diagnosis might take place.

It is also a means of instruction. By having John read aloud and, at the same time, look for discrepancies between what he spoke and what was on the page, I was teaching him a form of reading. The most dramatic change in John's performance over the term was in the number of errors he could spot and correct while re-reading. This far exceeded the number of errors he was able to eliminate from his first drafts. I could teach John an editing procedure better than I could teach him to be correct at the point of transcription.

The third consequence of this form of analysis, or of conventional error analysis, has yet to be demonstrated, but the suggestions for research are clear. It seems evident that we can chart stages of growth in individual basic writers. The pressing question is whether we can chart a sequence of "natural" development for the class of writers we call basic writers. If all non-fluent adult writers proceed through a "natural" learning sequence, and if we can identify that sequence through some large, longitudinal study, then we will begin to understand what a basic writing course or text or syllabus might look like. There are studies of adult second language learners that suggest that there is a general, natural sequence of acquisition for adults learning a second language, one that is determined by the psychology of language production and language

---

[20]This example was taken from Yetta M. Goodman, "Miscue Analysis for In-Service Reading Teachers," in K. S. Goodman, ed., *Miscue Analysis,* p. 55.

acquisition.[21] Before we can adapt these methods to a study of basic writers, however, we need to better understand the additional constraints of learning to transcribe and manipulate the "code" of written discourse. John's case illustrates where we might begin and what we must know.[22]

---

[21]Nathalie Bailey, Carolyn Madden, and Stephen D. Krashen, "Is There a 'Natural Sequence' in Adult Second Language Learning?" *Language Learning,* 24 (June, 1974), 235–243.

[22]This paper was originally presented at CCCC, April 1979. The research for this study was funded by a research grant from the National Council of Teachers of English.

Afterword:
A Nation of Authors

Deborah Brandt
University of Wisconsin–Madison

Teaching Academic Literacy begins with the premise that multiple ways of reading and writing animate American society, including, of course, its classrooms. A pluralistic notion of literacy is a realistic fit for a diverse and dynamic culture where competing forms of interpretation and expression breathe purpose into the First Amendment. Recognizing literacy as pluralistic also simply acknowledges that in the late 20th century, American students' contact with reading, writing, and print comes from a dizzying array of sources, secular and religious, popular and academic, local and distant, old and new. Beginning with the earliest years of life, print is now present at nearly every public event imaginable. As Katherine Weese suggests in her first chapter, such eclectic conditions of literacy acquisition need to be consciously considered by students and teachers. Becoming literate today requires becoming aware of the contingency of one's own literacy, how one way of reading or writing differs from other ways. Teaching literacy today requires helping students to navigate an increasingly wider set of interpretive styles, materials, and skills involving reading and writing. It also requires helping students learn ways of reading and writing that are responsive to rapid social and institutional change.

Teaching Academic Literacy makes us confront the full significance of multiple literacies by asking what it means to learn, teach, and research in these conditions. The teacher–scholars represented in this volume have designed an introductory writing program that is sensitive to the cultural changes affecting higher education everywhere. This is a course that stresses

195

the interconnections between writing and reading, the interconnections between texts and their contexts, and the interconnections between writers and their responsible roles in the world. While students learn how to approach academic writing through active interpretation and dedication to projects, they ideally acquire skills of perspective, stance, responsibility, and authority that will allow them to participate in other contexts, academic or otherwise. Teachers and administrators at other institutions find in this volume no lock-step formula for how to conduct first-year writing courses. However, readers do find a blueprint for productive collaborations between program administrators and their teachers based in shared inquiry and bottom-up problem solving. We find in this collection, then, both curricular materials that highlight the new historical conditions in which students are developing as literate citizens and also, more importantly, habits of teaching and administering courses that use locally produced knowledge to understand students and further institutional reform. Whereas some may regard teacher research as a luxury unaffordable in overcrowded classrooms and overworked schedules, this book presents teacher-driven, program-based research as a sound investment of time and resources. In fact, this book itself speaks to the payoff by providing instructive portraits of classroom life, familiar to anyone who has taught first-year composition yet objectified enough to pose important questions about our assumptions, procedures, and goals as teachers.

What I hear over and over again in these probing and inquisitive chapters are teachers trying to figure out how classrooms can be reconceived to greet the new historical conditions in which writing is being taught and learned. That task, as this research suggests, is as difficult as it is desirable. What are the new conditions to which these teacher–researchers are responding? What makes them such a challenge?

If college composition courses traditionally were designed to show students how to write, with a focus on appropriate forms and procedures, the course described in this volume invites students first to learn to be writers. Right off the bat they take on and must take seriously the role of academic authorship. This is an astonishing shift in status, especially for so-called remedial or basic writing students from whom the fancier privileges of critical reading, debate, and original scholarship are so often withheld. Beginning with the literacy autobiography, however, students in these classes are invited to see themselves as writers in the making, as their past encounters with reading and writing and the institutions that sponsor them are revisited and assessed for their contributions, positive and negative, to a writer's identity. Then these stories are shared and compared. This is when the multiple ideological and material avenues to literacy come tangibly to the surface and when forms of academic literacy begin to appear in surprising places. When they work right, literacy autobiographies can serve as an intellectual guide for the rest of a term, an inventory of raw materials from which new knowledge and new chapters of the autobiography will be made.

Several teachers represented in this volume follow up on the impulse of the literacy autobiography by building on genres and source materials that are part of the deep background of many students' life experiences— talk, film, journals, electronic bulletin boards to name a few. As Dell Hymes observed, "Every form of human speech has gained the right to contribute on equal footing to what is known of human languages" (60). Students' out-of-school discourse enters the classroom not as a feel-good celebration of difference nor a temporarily tolerated crutch but as a compatible resource for academic knowledge-making and author-making.

All of the teachers in this volume also make sure students experience an environment supportive of writing, as ample time and space are given to the work of it—planning, organizing, drafting, revising, editing. Students feel their work being read as any author's text might be read. They are encouraged to articulate their hard-won insights into the complexities of written representation. Ideally in draft groups or conferences, students do not learn to iron out their differences with others so much as they learn how to put sufficient starch into them.

This emphasis on learning how to be writers derives from the process orientation of composition pedagogy, which began 30 years ago with attention paid to the work habits of well-known, mostly literary writers. This orientation has evolved into a pretty consistent and serious attempt to make the role of the ordinary writer a center of attention in both writing pedagogy and research. But I also want to think that this concern with becoming writers is a response to new developments in the wider history of literacy itself, as writing has begun to overtake reading as the more fundamental literate skill. Increasingly, writing activates reading, whether, mundanely, as a way to access information on a computer or, in the composition course described here, as a sponsoring occasion for engaging with scholarly arguments. Increasingly, Americans will need to read from prior positions as writers. Their economic and political rights will depend on it. So much power and activity reside now in print and its derivatives that writing in many circumstances is the only way to talk back, the only effective way to lay claim to one's interests. The role of the writer has never really been mass distributed in society before. College composition classes are important places for working out the social, political, and practical tensions surrounding this new development.

Such a heavy focus on the role of writer in writing theory and research also means that teachers now are able to bring to the classroom highly developed understandings about the nature of authorship, particularly academic authorship, at the end of the 20th century. Stuart Greene, the architect of the course described in this volume, has spent a decade looking closely at the authoring processes of academic writers at all levels and in different fields. Using think-aloud protocols, retrospective interviews, close observations, and powerful theories of how human beings make meaning, the research of Greene and others charts the staggeringly complex busyness of composing—the way choices are made, sources are exploited, knowledge is fused, difference is negotiated, traditions are invoked, authority is marshalled—the ways, in short, that written representations come about. Above all, these portraits suggest, academic writers must know how to affiliate their language with the powers of academic fields, being cognizant of disciplinary norms and expectations while being creative and assertive with the potentials that institutions make available for challenging existing thought. This is one of the great insights from research on academic authorship, yet, as we see in this volume, it poses one of the greatest dilemmas in the undergraduate writing classroom: What are the differences between an institution's authority, which students need to absorb and invoke, and its authoritarianism, which, although an indispensable ingredient of authority, seems, paradoxically, to undermine authorship? How does a curriculum save the one and throw off the other? How do teachers and students walk this thin line together? (For useful investigations of these issues, see Goldblatt.)

We see in this volume how tricky the line is, how subtle these differences can appear to inexperienced college writers and what radical transformations in teacher–student relationships will have to come about if schools really want to develop the fearlessness and independence that authorship in this culture apparently requires. The task is not easy and the potential for confusions and blunders is great. Whereas as teachers we may draw on language theories and models of authorship to develop rich and inventive assignments for students, our plans go off course because these theories and models are rarely calculated for the skewing effects of authoritarian pressures—the coercion, passivity, the limited control and social inconsequence that define school writing for most students. What is still poorly understood (although I think the detectives in this volume are beginning to move in on it) is exactly how the independent thought that teachers look for develops in learning writers. Is it a matter of building up enough knowledge about one's subjects? Is it a matter of technical power and skill, knowing how to manipulate the resources of texts to make them do what we want them to do? Or is it a more basic matter of social and political opportunity—having conditions right for the will of authorship to emerge? We need clearer pictures of writing development that address the interrelationships of these matters, from both within and without the classroom context. Also, when we identify problems, we must resist seeing them as residing solely within the inexperienced writer or even within the conditions and social relations of the individual writing classroom. When so many students in so many classrooms, for instance, keep doing the same disappointing things—sticking with summary when interpretation is called for, subordinating their thoughts to powerful others, diluting dissension for the sake of a tidy thesis or a happy ending—we have to appreciate that authoritarian legacies exist far beyond the minds of student.

The history of literacy puts the college classroom in a paradoxical position. Successful over the last century in spreading a serviceably advanced reading ability throughout much of the population, the nation's colleges and universities have been one of the major engines propelling the development of a symbol-driven information economy. Mass education, including higher education, has been pretty good at creating readers, at least of certain kinds. But as the information economy in turn makes tighter claims on the populace—demanding more people in more spheres able to render thought in writing—there are serious questions about whether schools can respond adequately to the very conditions they have helped to create. Schools have never before been required to produce a nation of authors; they were not configured for that purpose. That is why I see *Teaching Academic Literacy* as an experiment in timely institutional change.

If changes conducive to authorship are to be brought about, they will be through the means enacted by teachers like the cadre represented in this volume. Most fundamentally, this means that the diversity of experience, position, and worldview that students bring to the classroom are not ignored, suppressed, or simply honored and left alone. Rather, pluralism is recognized as the rhetorical if not the epistemological condition in which all Americans must learn to think, talk, and write. In a nation of authors, my differences from you give shape to the possibility of your authorship, and yours mine. On top of that, this volume suggests, institutional change will happen when teachers and students together investigate their own enterprise, when the inner workings of assignments, genres, drafts, and teacher–student relationships are opened up for explicit investigation and challenge. The teachers in this volume are self-conscious in the best sense— aware that the words they use, the assignments they devise, the technologies they introduce all matter. And to be good teachers, they need to know how they matter. The most radical promise for institutional change that I found in these chapters was the desire to produce knowledge whose immediate contributions pour back into the local life of a writing program, where teachers (and, I hope, more often students) begin to author more of the conditions in which they work and study together.

WORKS CITED

Hymes, Dell. *Ethnography, Linguistics, Narrative Inequality: Toward an Understanding of Voice.* London: Taylor and Francis, 1996.

Goldblatt, Eli. *'Round My Way: Authority and Double-Consciousness in Three Urban High School Writers.* Pittsburgh: University of Pittsburgh Press, 1994.

Appendix A:
Major Assignments in the
UW-Madison Literacy Course

FORMAL ESSAY #1: LITERACY AUTOBIOGRAPHY

A first draft is due on —. You will begin working in your peer groups at this time, so please bring an original and four copies: one for each group member, and one for me.

The aim of this assignment is to explore in some depth the origins of some of the theories that you hold about reading, writing, and language, and your own learning processes. Try to give an account of significant factors that have contributed to your development as a reader and writer. As you give the account, answer these questions: in your experience, what does it mean to be literate? What is language (reading, writing) used for—what is its purpose in your experience? How did you formulate these attitudes toward literacy? How might your experience help all of us in the class understand what literacy means?

The form your essay takes is up to you, but as it evolves, it needs to have a deliberate plan. In other words, it should not be a random accumulation of unrelated facts about your background as a reader and writer. Try to weave these facts into a coherent account of your literacy history. Try to create an *argument* about why you hold the attitudes you hold, and how you came to hold them. At first, of course, it's okay just to generate ideas without worrying too much about organizing them. But you will need to structure the essay as it evolves.

Consider the following issues to help you get started. Use these questions as guidelines for the kind of information you might want to include, but do not organize your essay around the questions in the order they are presented here. Instead, come up with an organization plan that makes sense for the point you are making in your essay.

- The levels of education and literacy that your family (both current and preceding generations) has achieved; the role that reading and writing play in your family life.
- Your earliest recollection of writing. What was it? Where did it take place? Why did it take place?
- Any memories of writing in school. Talk about whatever you can recall—assignments, instructors, responses to your writing by the teacher, your own responses to being asked to write
- Memories of writing out of school: letters, journals, diaries, etc., writing contests, creative writing, writing you did for extracurricular activities or religious or social organizations you were involved in. Did writing ever play a role in the development or maintenance of friendships?
- People who were important to your development as a writer
- Institutions (educational, religious, social, etc.) that were important
- Barriers to your development as a writer
- Significant memories of successes and failures
- The role of reading and writing in the development of your identity
- Observations about any college writing you have been asked to do so far
- Any other information that you think is pertinent

You will revise and expand this essay over the next few weeks. When you have produced a final draft, all the essays will be collected and distributed to the class. Everyone will be required to read them all. This "book" of essays that you as a class produce will become one of the textbooks that we consider later in the course, and we will use the arguments you make about literacy and its development when we consider professional writers' books on the same subject matter.

FORMAL ESSAY #2: A CONVERSATION
ABOUT LITERACY

The readings we've been doing throughout the semester have provided us with a number of different perspectives on literacy: what it means, what is involved in becoming a part of a literate community, what being literate can provide us as individuals. As we've discussed the readings, you have also been contributing your own ideas and assessing the strengths and weaknesses of the positions the authors have taken in the various readings. You have also begun to come to some conclusions about how to organize, structure, and support an argument.

Mike Rose, in his book *Lives on the Boundary*, addresses a crucial factor in discussions of literacy—the notion of contributing to an ongoing conversation. In order to enter the conversation, you need to have something to say, an argument to make about the issue. But you also need to demonstrate your awareness of what others have been saying as you voice your own opinions, ideas, and arguments. Understanding what others have said on the topic of literacy allows you to place your ideas in the context of an ongoing conversation. It can help you begin to develop your own thinking, and it can provide you with some possible strategies for shaping your own argument. It also allows you to take issue with what others have said, pointing out the limitations in their thinking and gaps in their arguments. Thus as you synthesize these different points of view, you can use what you know of other writers' arguments in order to get people to think about the topic in new and interesting ways.

In writing your essay, I would like you to discuss an issue (something open to dispute) related to literacy that arises in the readings, our discussions, or your own experience. Then you need to demonstrate how the readings are relevant to your issue. As you write the paper, putting the authors' ideas together and showing how they interrelate with each other and with your own ideas, you need to demonstrate you understand what the authors are saying about literacy. However, you need to go beyond merely summarizing their ideas to thinking critically about their ideas (and you've been doing this in class discussion all along). So your paper needs to *make an argument* that takes a position on the literacy issue you pick.

- You are looking for what is interesting not just to you or me but to those who have a vested interest in this issue. What is still in dispute? What ideas need to be emphasized more than they already are? What do people need to know? Why?

- Feel free to play ideas off one another in formulating your own ideas, keeping in mind that the argument you set up should probably be based more on conflict than on agreement. It may help you to consider the following questions as you begin to plan and draft your essay: Is there a clear problem or issue (something in dispute) that motivates your essay? Is it held in focus throughout the paper? Does the essay help clarify the issue? Does it go beyond the sources you have read to make an original claim?

FORMAL ESSAY #3: THE INTERVIEW–FIELD PROJECT

In order for you to get a realistic view of the kinds of writing teachers in other disciplines assign, what they value, and what they expect, I would like each of you to explore the nature of academic writing in a field that interests you—perhaps one you want to major in. You will interview a professor (or professors) in your chosen discipline about the kind of writing he or she assigns, about the role writing plays in the course, and about what that teacher expects in student writing. You will also need to obtain from the teacher an example of student writing that illustrates what he or she considers to be a good piece of writing. The purpose of this assignment is to help us all understand what is expected in different disciplines in terms of writing. You'll find many conventions of writing cut across disciplines, while some are unique to specific types of writing. You'll gain a better sense of what types of writing are common in the college setting. We'll share the results of your interviews in the last class meetings.

Some examples of questions you might ask:

- What is your goal in assigning writing in your course?
- What do you want students to learn from completing a given writing assignment?
- What are the most important goals of a student writer?
- What characterizes good student writing in your academic field?
- Who is the student's audience?
- What role do you play as you evaluate a student's paper?
- What do you expect in terms of format, documentation, and style?
- How are these expectations about format and style related to your purpose of giving a writing assignment?

As you write up the results of your interview, you should not only recount the information that the professor gives you, but you should *analyze* and *evaluate* that information. How does this professor's approach relate to the ideas about education, effective instruction, the role of writing, etc., that we have been considering all semester? How does writing relate to learning in his or her courses? What kind of learning does the professor promote, and does he or she set standards that encourage the kinds of learning we have been discussing? Why or why not? Ultimately, your paper should create an *argument* about what you have learned from studying writing conventions in the discipline you choose.

Appendix B: Prewriting Exercises and Writing Assignments to Aid Students in Composing the Formal Papers

FIRST ASSIGNMENT ON *HUNGER OF MEMORY*

Read pp. 1–40. You will notice as you read that Rodriguez tells many strong and vivid stories about his experiences growing up that helped to shape his understanding of his education and how he became a writer. You will also notice many places where he stops and comments on his experience, looking back on his past with a critical or interpretive eye. In your journal, write down the page numbers of two such passages where he stops telling the story in order to analyze the meaning of the events or to explore their implications for his own development as a person. Then *summarize* what he says in each of these two sections. Finally, give your reactions to his ideas about literacy. Are there words or images or writing strategies he uses that you think help make his point vivid for you? Do you agree with his ideas or not? Is his experience in any way like your own? Be prepared to share your responses with your group. (Note: the language and strategies for this assignment are drawn from similar assignments devised by David Bartholomae and Anthony Petrosky as printed in *Facts, Artifacts and Counterfacts*. See especially "Reading Assignment D," 63–64.)

SECOND ASSIGNMENT ON *HUNGER OF MEMORY*

Read 41–73.

Today you'll need to bring a first draft of a response paper to *Hunger*. This paper is more formal than your journal entries and will have to be typed and handed in with your autobiographies in October. It should be 1–2 typed pages. Answer *one* of the following sets of questions:

a) Rodriguez focuses on the separation of his private self and his public self, and the role language plays in this separation. He writes that growing up speaking Spanish created both feelings of separateness (from the English-speaking world) and feelings of intimacy (with his family). In what ways have you seen language help define an individual as belonging to a group or serve to exclude membership from a group? You don't necessarily need to consider bilingualism, although you may if it's relevant to your experience.

b) Rodriguez also maintains that becoming educated fundamentally separated him from his parents, who had much less schooling. Do you think that education inevitably causes (or hastens) a separation from one's past? In what ways have you seen this happen?

c) Compare Rodriguez's experiences in becoming literate either to Eudora Welty's or to Judy's in Lorri Neilsen's book. How are their experiences and views on literacy alike? How are they different? How does the *context* of each author (that is, the specific situation in which she acquired and used her literacy) help account for some of these differences?

THIRD ASSIGNMENT ON *HUNGER OF MEMORY*

Last week we discussed the ways an author's specific uses of organization and language (diction, figurative language, richness of detail) can help convey that author's larger purpose or meaning. This handout explains this concept further.

Keep in mind that every word in the works we read is a *deliberate choice* made by the writer. A writer has any number of options available, and he or she chooses one set of strategies or options over other possibilities to create a specific effect.

On the level of structure: For example, as we saw in class, Eudora Welty views childhood memories as made up of moments, not a steady stream, but a pulse that beats and stops, beats and stops (p. 9). Therefore, her organizational strategy is to recount these moments in an essay that doesn't necessarily connect them all in one steady flow, but which describes the isolated moments that constitute her memory of her learning. If her theory of how children remember learning were a different one, she would have needed to choose a different type of organization for her essay.

On the level of language: Here are several examples from *Hunger of Memory* that illustrate how Rodriguez makes careful choices in the language that he uses to help convey his meaning:

1) He writes "There are those in White America who would *anoint* me to play out for them some drama of ancestral reconciliation" (top of p. 5). Now, he could have just written "who would *ask* me to. . . .", but instead he chose the word "anoint." Why? What does this word convey that "ask" doesn't? If you look up anoint, you'll see it means "to rub oil or ointment on; to put oil on in a ceremony of consecration" (*Webster's New World Dictionary*). Thus the word anoint gives the sentence a very formal, ceremonial, even religious tone, perhaps because Rodriguez feels that the White Americans who would want him to explore his connection with his past view this as some kind of holy sacrament that he ought to play out. Rodriguez clearly disagrees with this sense of mission.

2) He ends the following paragraph with the statement, "This is my story. An American story." His emphasis here falls on the "Americanness" of his story, and by concluding the paragraph on this note, he is able to stress that he does not think his mission is to uncover or recover ties to his Mexican past; he considers himself not a Mexican-American but an American.

3) Later in *Hunger* (p. 16), he includes a one-word paragraph in parentheses: "(Ricardo.)" This mention of his Spanish name occurs in the context of a discussion of the feelings of closeness that the Spanish language brings him. It emphasizes the difference between his home identity, where he is "Ricardo," and his public identity, where, as we have learned earlier, he is "Richard."

Produce your own written analysis of the structure of the "Aria" section of *Hunger of Memory*. Try to figure out why Rodriguez makes the choices he does in putting together this account of his childhood. Note that he ends with a description of his grandmother's appearance in her casket. Why do you think he does so?

ASSIGNMENT ON EUDORA WELTY'S "LISTENING"

This assignment is designed to help you understand how a writer uses language of a certain quality to evoke a particular feeling in the reader or a picture in the reader's mind. You should use this knowledge in your own writing as well, by making deliberate choices about the quality of your language. Your choices will vary, depending upon what kind of paper you're writing, and upon what specific impression you want to create for the reader. For this journal entry, take these two steps:

1) As you read Welty's piece, in your journal try to describe her language itself. That is, what kinds of words does she use frequently? (list some of them in your journal). What feeling do these words create for you? What adjectives would you use to describe her language? What mental picture do you have of the house she grew up in?

2) Think about the house you grew up in, and decide whether or not this type of language is appropriate for your own experiences. Decide what impression you'd like the reader to have of the atmosphere in your house. Then write a paragraph describing this atmosphere in your house, taking care to choose words that help convey this impression. Be prepared to explain to your group members *why* you chose the style you chose.

ASSIGNMENT FOR HIRSCH'S *CULTURAL LITERACY*

Read the first part of *Cultural Literacy*, the Preface and pages 1–18 of "Literacy and Cultural Literacy." Write a 1–2 page summary of what Hirsch says. Focus on the key points of his argument. Your summary should identify what he considers the problem in the American educational system, the solutions that some thinkers have tried, and Hirsch's own solution for cultural literacy. What strategies does he use to support his position?

For the next class, complete your summary of the rest of the reading, pp. 18–32, considering the same issues as above.

ASSIGNMENT FOR READING ROSE'S
LIVES ON THE BOUNDARY

Read Chapter One, "Our Schools and Our Children," and Chapter Eight, "Crossing Boundaries," from Mike Rose's *Lives on the Boundary*. Write down what the main issues or problems are that Rose identifies in attaining a "literate" culture. What are his key points about academic literacy? What solutions does he suggest? How would you compare his ideas about literacy to E.D. Hirsch's? Try to focus only on how they are alike or different, not on whose ideas you like more. So instead of evaluating their positions, try to describe them in relation to one another.

Some tips on writing the summary: Since the reading is relatively long, it would take too much time to write down everything Rose says. The key is to extract his points without losing the main sense of the argument, even if you do not fit every detail into your summary. So when he uses lengthy case histories to make a point, you don't need to re-tell the case histories; rather, just sum up the conclusion he draws from his evidence.

Also, when you are writing a summary, it is helpful to provide readers with guides that will help them follow the shape of the argument you are summarizing. So it might be wise to start with the author's controlling idea, purpose in writing, and goal. What is Rose saying, who is he saying it to, and why? Then go back and fill in the key sub-points and details of how he supports this main idea. As you do this, try to see how Rose organizes or structures his own argument.

An example: If you were summarizing Hirsch's chapter, you might have said that he used the preface to identify the problem with the American education system, to explain the educational theory it's based on, and to show the shortcomings of that theory. Then in the next section, Hirsch goes on to. . . . After he has described the problem in more detail, the subsequent three sections of the argument spell out possible solutions. The first of these three is based on the idea that. . . . The second. . . . . Finally, Hirsch's third recommendation involves. . . . . Hirsch concludes by focusing on universal communication in an argument that. . . . .

These kinds of guides to the author's organization can guide the reader through your own piece. They clearly signal the different parts of the argument. Try this strategy when you summarize Rose. This means you'll have to figure out the purpose and point of the whole piece, then go back and incorporate the sub-points into your summary. We will probably find when we compare our summaries in class that different people have em-phasized different points. We will discuss these differences in our class meeting to illuminate why people create different summaries.

FINAL ASSIGNMENT ON *SONG OF SOLOMON*

Read chapters 10–15. Answer questions A and B:

A) I asked you last time to think about Milkman's identity. Lorri Neilsen maintains in her book *Literacy and Living* that in part literacy is learning to be at home in the world, being attuned to the people and events that surround you. As you read about Milkman's journey, think about it in terms of how he is fulfilling Nielsen's definition of what it means to be literate. How "literate" is he when he gets to the South? What does he gradually learn, about himself and the ways of the South, and how does this knowledge help him function in this world? How does his identity change as a result? Write down page numbers of passages that helped you arrive at your answers, so you can refer to these passages quickly in class.

B) E.D. Hirsch defined what he believed constituted "cultural literacy." Morrison, of course, does not use this term in her novel, but in a way *Song of Solomon* might be considered Milkman's education in cultural literacy. What might the term "cultural literacy" mean for Milkman and for Morrison? How would Morrison's definition differ from Hirsch's? Draw on specific passages from the last part of the novel to support your ideas about what constitutes cultural literacy in *Song of Solomon.*

WORKSHEETS FOR SYNTHESIS PAPER

These two worksheets on the following pages can be used to help students begin writing the synthesis paper. The first asks them to review the positions of all the authors studied in the course; the second asks them to focus on three authors.

Positions On Literacy: Worksheet to be completed as you plan your synthesis paper

	Definition of literacy	Issues author addresses	Ideas similar to . . .	Does not consider . . .
SMITH				
WELTY				
NEILSEN				
RODRIGUEZ				
MORRISON				
HIRSCH				
ROSE				

Second worksheet on comparing authors' views of literacy:

	ROSE	HIRSCH	3RD author of your choice.
Definition of literacy			
what's left out			
issues; what's at stake			
Assumptions (explicit)			
assumptions (implicit)			
Points you agree with			
Points you disagree with			

Appendix C:
Suggested Readings

Bartholomae, David. "Inventing the University." *When A Writer Can't Write.* Ed. Mike Rose. New York: Guilford Press, 1985. 134–165.

Garnes, Sara, et al. *Writing Lives: Exploring Literacy and Community.* New York: St. Martin's Press, 1997. (An anthology of readings compiled by and edited by teachers in the Ohio State University Composition Program.)

Heath, Shirley Brice. *Ways With Words: Language, Life and Work in Communities and Classrooms.* Cambridge, England: Cambridge UP, 1983.

Hirsch, E. D. *Cultural Literacy: What Every American Should Know.* Boston: Houghton Mifflin, 1987.

Morrison, Toni. *Song of Solomon.* New York: Signet, 1977.

Neilsen, Lorri. *Literacy and Living: The Literate Lives of Three Adults.* Portsmouth, NH: Heinemann, 1989.

Nelson, Jennie, Christine Haas and Stuart Greene, eds. *Educated in the USA: Readings on the Problem and Promise of Education.* Dubuque, Iowa: Kendall Hunt Publishing Company, 1996.

Rodriguez, Richard. *Hunger of Memory.* New York: Bantam, 1983.

Rose, Mike. *Lives on the Boundary.* New York: Penguin, 1990.

Simonson, Rick, and Scott Walker, eds. *Multi-Cultural Literacy: The Opening of the American Mind.* Saint Paul, MN: Graywolf Press. [Contains essays by Carlos Fuentes, Michelle Cliff, Gloria Anzaldua, and Ishmael Reed, among others.]

Welty, Eudora. "Listening." *One Writer's Beginnings.* Cambridge, MA: Harvard University Press, 1984. 1–39.

Wright, Richard. *Black Boy.* 1945. New York: Harper, 1969.

This is by no means an exhaustive list; it merely represents the readings instructors have found valuable in teaching Forms of Academic Literacy. Instructors typically use four or five of these sources.

Author Index

Subject Index